Life

ELEMENTARY

TEACHER'S BOOK

Mike Sayer

Life Elementary Teacher's Book

Mike Sayer

Publisher: Jason Mann

Publishing Consultant: Karen Spiller

Development Editor: Clare Shaw

Strategic Marketing Manager: Michelle Cresswell

Project Editor: Amy Borthwick

Production Controller: Elaine Willis

National Geographic Liaison: Anna Kistin

Art Director: Natasa Arsenidou

Cover design: Vasiliki Christoforidou

Text design: Vasiliki Christoforidou

Compositor: QBS Learning

Audio: Prolingua Productions

ISBN: 978-1-133-31609-1

National Geographic Learning

Cheriton House, North Way, Andover, Hampshire, SP10 5BE United Kingdom

Cengage Learning is a leading provider of customised learning solutions with office locations around the globe, including Singapore, the United Kingdom, Australia, Mexico, Brazil and Japan. Locate our local office at **international.cengage.com/region**

Cengage Learning products are represented in Canada by Nelson Education Ltd.

Visit National Geographic Learning at **ngl.cengage.com**
Visit our corporate website at **www.cengage.com**

CREDITS

Although every effort has been made to contact copyright holders before publication, this has not always been possible. If notified, the publisher will undertake to rectify any errors or omissions at the earliest opportunity.

Photos
The publisher would like to thank the following sources for permission to reproduce their copyright protected photographs.
Cover: Simon Wong/Getty Images
Inside: 12tl (Helen and Morna Mulgray), 12ml (camille and Kennerly Kitt), 12bl (Steve Holland/AP/Press Association Images), 13 (Kzenon/Alamy), 15 (Reinier Gerritsen), 16bl (Shutterstock), 16br (Shutterstock).
Illustrations by Stephen Dew pp 140, 141, 152, 153, 156, 173; Julian Mosedale pp 147, 150, 151

Printed in Greece by Bakis
1 2 3 4 5 6 7 8 9 10 – 17 16 15 14 13

Contents

Contents

Listening	Reading	Critical thinking	Speaking	Writing
a photographer talking about a climber an interview with an explorer people at a conference	an article about a family of explorers an article about world population	the writer's purpose	asking questions friends and family facts about countries	text type: a personal description writing skill: *and, but*
someone talking about a family's plastic possessions an interview with Andy Torbet	an article about four apartments in Seoul an article about a global product	close reading	your objects and possessions a room in your home where things are from	a description of a room in your home text type: adverts writing skill: describing objects with adjectives
someone talking about a 24-hour restaurant in Norway an interview with a student living in London an interview with Beverley Goodman	an article about no-car zones an article about languages spoken around the world	relevance	your life exchanging information about a photographer favourite numbers and their relevance	text type: a description of a place writing skill: capital letters
three people talking about their free-time activities an interview with Norbert Rosing	an article about identical twins an article about a nature photographer an article about extreme sports an advert for volunteer work	fact or opinion	likes and dislikes daily life your abilities	text type: short emails writing skill: reference words
someone talking about a noodle chef in Chinatown people describing famous dishes from their countries a conversation at a market	an article about food markets around the world an article about the Svalbard Global Seed Vault	summarising	famous dishes from different countries planning a special meal buying food at a market summarising an article	text type: instructions writing skill: punctuation
someone talking about a street musician an interview with two people at a museum people asking for money in different situations	an article about currency an article about treasure an article about the history of money	relevance	someone's past life important years in your life a survey about money	a description of someone's life text type: thank you messages writing skill: formal and informal expressions

Contents

Contents

Listening	Reading	Critical thinking	Speaking	Writing
someone talking about the Mayflower a programme about journeys in history a programme about animal migration	an article about a flight from the past an article about space travel	fact or opinion	a journey you made your opinion a general knowledge quiz	a general knowledge quiz text type: a travel blog writing skill: *so*, *because*
someone describing the Dinagyang festival a conversation about masks at a festival	an article about a fashion photographer an article about tattoos a text about emoticons	close reading	people's appearance what people are wearing	text type: texts and online messages writing skill: textspeak
someone talking about an outdoor cinema two people at a film festival an interview with Adrian Seymour two people discussing a Broadway show	an article about the *All roads film festival* an article about a wildlife filmmaker an article about nature in art	the writer's preferences	deciding which films to see your future plans explaining preferences	text type: reviews and comments writing skill: giving your opinion with sense verbs
someone talking about the human brain an interview with someone about technology a news report about a memory champion someone phoning his office	a survey about outdated technology jigsaw reading about memory an article about new inventions	the main argument and supporting information	experience with technology something you have learned	the main argument text type: a telephone message writing skill: imperatives
someone talking about their holiday a podcast from a travel programme two friends discussing a trip to South America	a quiz from a travel magazine a tourist information leaflet a travel article	arguments for and against	advice for a tourist rules what's important in a hotel	a description of a tourist destination text type: a feedback form writing skill: closed and open questions
a documentary about a photographer an interview about film director James Cameron and the Mariana Trench	maps showing climate change an article about unexplored places on Earth an article about a new planet an article about Earth Day	structuring an argument	your future places on Earth life on another planet	text type: a poster writing skill: important words and information

Introduction

National Geographic

National Geographic was founded in 1888 and defines its mission as 'to inspire people to care about the planet'. The *National Geographic Society* is one of the world's largest non-profit scientific and educational organisations. It reaches more than 325 million people in more than 30 languages through its magazines, books, TV channels, interactive media, maps, films and music. Proceeds from these activities have funded more than 9,000 scientific, conservation and educational projects around the world. *LIFE* is published in partnership with *National Geographic*, using *National Geographic*'s content and values to 'inspire people to learn English'.

National Geographic topics

The topics are paramount and are the starting point for the lessons. These topics have been selected for their intrinsic interest and ability to fascinate students – and teachers. Once the material has been gathered from the *National Geographic* archives, the language objectives have been matched to the content and then organised into a tried and tested syllabus. The richness of the listening and reading texts and video means that students are so engaged in learning about the content, and expressing their own opinions, that language learning has to take place in order for students to satisfy their curiosity and then react personally to what they have learnt. This element of transfer from the topics to students' own realities and experiences converts the input into a vehicle for language practice and production which fits the recognised frameworks for language learning and can be mapped to the CEFR scales. (Full mapping documents are available separately.)

People and places

LIFE takes students around the globe, investigating the origins of ancient civilisations, showing the drama of natural forces at work and exploring some of the world's most beautiful places. These uplifting tales of adventure and discovery are told through eyewitness accounts and first-class reportage, with superb photos, maps and videos. For example, Unit 9 of the Elementary level introduces the work of wildlife filmmaker Adrian Seymour, and then students can watch a film made by him in the accompanying DVD.

Science and technology

Students learn about significant scientific discoveries and breakthroughs, both historic and current. These stories are related by journalists or told by the scientists and explorers themselves through interviews or first person accounts. Students see the impact of the discoveries on our lifestyles and cultures. Because the material comes from a huge archive that has been developed and designed to appeal to the millions of individuals who make up *National Geographic*'s audience, it reflects the broadest possible range of topics. For example, Unit 10 of the Elementary level compares the human brain to modern technology and tells us how we can train our minds to memorise things.

History

History can be a dry topic, especially if it's overloaded with facts and dates. However, the *National Geographic* treatment of historical events brings them to life and there is often a human dimension and universal themes that keep the events relevant to students and to our time. History – or the re-telling of historical events – can also be influenced by a culture or nation's perception of the events. *National Geographic*'s non-judgemental and culture-neutral accounts allow students to look behind the superficial events and gain a deeper understanding of our ancestors. For example, Unit 6 of the Elementary level takes an alternative view of history by looking at how the images and designs on money from the past can provide a historical record of key people and places.

Animals

The animal kingdom is exceptionally generative in terms of interesting topics. *LIFE* provides astonishing photos that give a unique insight into the hidden lives of known and lesser-known animals, offering rare glimpses of mammals, birds, bugs and reptiles in their daily struggle for survival. It also informs and surprises with accounts of animals now extinct, species still evolving and endangered species which are literally fighting for their existence. For example, Unit 7 of the Elementary level follows the amazing migrations of some of the world's most beautiful and exotic animals.

Environment

It isn't always possible to find clarity in texts on the environment and climate change, or trust that they are true and not driven by a political agenda. *National Geographic*'s objective journalism, supported by easy-to-understand visuals, presents the issues in an accessible way. The articles are written by experts in their fields. It's often true that those who have the deepest understanding of issues are also able to express the ideas in the simplest way. High-quality thinking and expertise are not synonymous with complicated concepts expressed through complicated language – usually quite the reverse is true. For example, Unit 12 of the Elementary level takes a fresh look at the Earth and the way in which its climate is changing, as well as considering the planet's relationship to the rest of the universe.

National Geographic photography

We live in a world where images are used more than ever to reinforce, and at times replace, the spoken and written word. To present discourse without them is both unrealistic and unhelpful. Our memories work in pictures, our experiences and the things we learn about the world are stored using them. Raising awareness of this can help students to remember language more easily. All too often photos in books are cosmetic and without impact. *National Geographic* has great photography and powerful images at its core, so it seems natural that photographs in *LIFE* should serve as the starting point for each unit. The photographs in each spread are also integral to the written and recorded content and every opportunity has been taken to use photographs to stimulate learning.

There are photographs which:

- tell a story by themselves
- support understanding of a text and make it memorable
- provoke debate
- stimulate critical thinking by asking you to examine detail OR think about what is NOT shown OR by questioning the photographer's motives
- mean little without a caption or accompanying explanation
- raise questions about the ethics of journalism and photojournalism
- are accompanied by a memorable quotation
- help to remember a lexical set
- help to learn functional language (e.g. how something works)
- lend themselves to practice of a specific grammar point (e.g. significant historical events)

As a first exercise when handing out the new book to your students, why not ask them to flick through the book, select their favourite photograph, and then explain to the class what it is they like about it. You will find specific suggestions in the teacher's notes for using the photographs featured within each unit, but two important things to note are:

- pictures of people or animals capture a moment, so ask students to speculate on the events that led up to this moment and those that followed it
- pictures of places aim to capture their essence, so feed students the vocabulary they need to describe the details that together convey this (the light, the colours, the landscape, the buildings)

National Geographic video

At the back of the Student's Book is a DVD with twelve different *National Geographic* videos on a whole range of subjects. Each video is connected with the topic of a corresponding unit and can be used in conjunction with the video lesson pages in the unit. Typically, a video lesson is divided into three parts:

Before you watch

This section leads students in to the topic of the video and engages them in a pre-watching task.

While you watch

These exercises provide detailed comprehension of the video itself, both in terms of what a student sees and what they hear.

After you watch

This section allows students to respond to the video as a whole and take part in a productive speaking task using language and contexts from the video.

The videos are designed to form part of your lessons. However, if you don't have time in class to watch

them all, you can ask students to watch the videos and complete many of the exercises on the page in the Student's Book. This can form a useful part of their self-study. Students can also watch the videos again after seeing them in class. This is useful for review and students can focus on parts of the audio that particularly interest them.

For further variation with the videos, here are some more ideas you can use and develop:

- Play the video with the sound down. Students predict what the narrator or people are saying. Then play with the sound up and compare.
- Play the sound only with no video. Students predict where the video takes place and what is happening on the screen. Then play with the screen on and compare.
- Show the first part of the video, pause it, and then ask students what they think happens next.
- Give students a copy of the audioscript for the video and ask them to imagine they are the director. What will they need to film and show on the screen? Afterwards, they present their 'screen play' and finally watch the original.
- Write a short text on the same topic as the one in the video. However, don't include the same amount of information and leave some facts out. Students read the text and then watch the video. They make notes on any new information and rewrite the text so it includes the new details.
- With monolingual groups, choose part of the video with someone talking. Ask students to listen and write down what they say. Then, in groups, ask them to create subtitles in their own language for that part of the video. Each group present their subtitles and the class compares how similar they are.

National Geographic and critical thinking

There is a graded critical thinking syllabus in *LIFE* that starts with the Elementary level and runs through all the later levels. The critical thinking activities appear in the c spreads in each unit. The syllabus covers areas such as reading between the lines, differentiating between opinion and fact, evaluating the reliability of source material, assessing the relevance of information, identifying the techniques used by an author to persuade the reader, weighing up evidence, etc. These activities require students to engage with the reading texts at a deeper level and to show real understanding – not just reading comprehension. This training – in evaluating texts, assessing the validity and strength of arguments and developing an awareness of authorial techniques – is clearly a valuable skill for those students learning English for academic purposes (EAP), where reflective learning is essential. However, it is also very much part of the *National Geographic* spirit which encourages people to question assumptions and develop their own well-informed and reasoned opinions. In this sense it adds another dimension to the experience of learning English through *National Geographic* material.

LIFE methodology

Treatment of grammar

Target grammar is presented through texts in the first two spreads of each unit. These texts are authentic reading and listening texts, adapted for level as necessary, which use the target language in natural and appropriate linguistic contexts. Such texts not only aid comprehension, but present good models for the learner's own language production through a variety of 'voices' and genres. The main input alternates between reading and listening on these first two spreads. Where a presentation is a listening text, written examples of the grammar structures are given on the page, for example in content comprehension tasks, so that visual support is also provided.

The primary focus is on the topic content before the learner's attention is drawn to the target grammar structures. Learners are first directed to *notice* this language by various means, such as using highlighting within the text, extracting sample sentences or having learners locate examples themselves.

A variety of task formats are used to lead learners to *analyse* the form, meaning and use of the grammar structures, as appropriate. Such an approach can be highly motivational by actively engaging learners in the lesson and allowing them to share and discuss their interpretation of the new language. After this stage, clear paradigms or examples of form and use are given on the page in a simple *summary* box. This supports the learners and is a 'check point' for the teacher and learners alike as it summarises the information learners will have arrived at through completing the discovery tasks. A cross-reference is provided to more detailed information and additional exercises at the back of the book. These are suitable for use both in class and for self-study, according to the needs of the learners.

The grammar *practice* tasks within the unit are linked to the presentation text and topic and are thus content-rich in the same way. They move from more supported exercises through to more challenging tasks. Depending on the level, they have a differing emphasis on form and use. The practice tasks give learners an opportunity to *personalise* the structures and practise them in the context of their own experiences and situations. This *anchors* the new language in existing frameworks and leads to a clearer understanding of the usage of this new or revised language. Equally, the practice exercises incorporate a real reason to use the target structure whether by devices such as quizzes, games, etc. or by genuine exchange of information between students.

A final task on each spread allows the learners to create their own output and is structured so that learners have the opportunity to use the target grammar as well as other target language, for example vocabulary, in a meaningful context. This final task has a variety of formats such as discussions, personal narratives, task-based activities (ranking, etc.) and the emphasis from the learner's perspective is on *content and fluency* rather than grammatical accuracy.

Aside from the two main grammar input spreads, the target grammar is also recycled in the subsequent spreads of each unit and beyond.

Treatment of vocabulary

LIFE teaches vocabulary in a range of different ways. This eclectic approach takes account of recent research, but doesn't abandon tried and tested methods. There is further practice of all of this vocabulary input (apart from words occurring in glossaries) in the Workbook.

1 Lexical sets

Some of the benefits generally associated with teaching words in lexical sets are:

- learning words in a set requires less effort
- retrieving related words from memory is easier
- seeing how knowledge can be organised can be helpful to learners
- it mirrors how such information is stored in the brain
- the meaning of words can be made clearer by comparing and contrasting them to similar words in the set

Each unit usually has two or more lexical sets. The lexical sets also cover commonly-confused words. There is evidence to suggest that once students have learnt one or more of the words that belong to a group of commonly-confused words (e.g. *job* and *work*), it is useful to compare and contrast these words directly to clarify the differences (or similarities) in meaning. *LIFE* focuses on these groups of words as and when they come up.

2 Word focus

The *Word focus* sections take high-frequency words and give examples of the different meanings they can have according to the contexts in which they appear and the different words they collocate with. At higher levels there is increased exposure to idioms and colloquial usage. The Workbook expands the range of phrases and expressions generated by these key words and provides further practice.

3 Wordbuilding

The independent wordbuilding syllabus offers students another opportunity to expand their vocabulary. The *Wordbuilding* boxes in the units focus on areas such as prefixes, suffixes, collocations, parts of speech (e.g. noun→adjective), compound nouns, phrasal verbs, and highlight examples from the reading or listening texts. The box gives a brief explanation and some examples. There is an activity for further practice and a reference to an activity in the Workbook which introduces more words that belong to the same morphological area.

4 Glossaries

Where certain words are important to the meaning of a text, but are above the level of the student, they are glossed. Students aren't expected to learn these words, but the short and simple definitions prevent them from being a barrier to understanding.

Learning skills

There is a comprehensive learning skills syllabus in the Workbook. This covers traditional learning skills, such as recording new vocabulary, using a dictionary, remembering new vocabulary, planning study time, assessing your own progress, etc.

Assessment

Students and teachers can assess progress in the following ways:

- Each unit in the Student's Book finishes with a one-page review where students do the exercises and complete a number of 'can-do' statements linked to the objectives of the unit.

- There are photocopiable tests in the Teacher's Book.

- There is a *Check!* section at the end of each unit in the Workbook for students to check what they have learnt (general knowledge as well as language).

- There are IELTs practice tests at the end of the Workbooks. These have been graded to the level of the course, but follow the format of the test. These allow students to benchmark their progress against the course objectives, whilst becoming familiar with a global test format.

Components

- Student's Book + DVD
- Workbook + audio
- Teacher's Book and class audio

Overview of a Student's Book unit

Opener: a one-page introduction to the unit that gets students interested in the topic

a and b: double-page lessons that teach grammar and vocabulary through reading and listening texts

c: a double-page lesson that focuses on reading comprehension

d: a one-page lesson that teaches a speaking skill and functional/situational language

e: a one-page lesson that teaches a writing skill and the features of a text type

f: a double-page lesson of video comprehension exercises

Review: a one-page lesson of practice activities and 'can-do' check statements

Lesson type a

Grammar and vocabulary

This double-page spread is a grammar and vocabulary lesson: Lesson 4a *100% identical*.

The main target grammar is presented through texts in the first two spreads of each unit. These texts are authentic or realistic reading and listening texts, adapted for level as necessary, which use the target language in natural and appropriate linguistic contexts. Such texts not only aid comprehension, but present good models for the learner's own language production through a variety of 'voices' and genres. The main input alternates between reading and listening on these first two spreads.

The primary focus is on the topic content before the learner's attention is drawn to the target grammar structures.

---

reading **same or different** • vocabulary **free-time activities** • grammar *like/love + -ing* • pronunciation /ŋ/ • speaking **likes and dislikes**

4a 100% identical?

100% IDENTICAL?

Identical twins have the same eyes and the same hair, but do they do the same things? What do they do in their free time?

The Mulgray Twins

Morna and Helen Mulgray are seventy-three-years old. They love books and they write books together. They live in the same house and they like the same free-time activities. They like gardening, and at the weekend, they go walking together.

The Kitt Twins

Camille and Kennerly Kitt are musicians and actors. They both play the same musical instrument, the harp. They don't have much free time, but they do Tae Kwon Do and they like swimming, together, of course.

The Bryan Twins

Mike and Bob love playing tennis. They are professional players and they play tennis all over the world. In their free time, they watch films and play computer games. But they don't do everything together. On their day off, Bob likes going to the gym, but Mike doesn't. He likes meeting friends at the beach.

identical (adj) /aɪˈdentɪkl/ exactly the same
twins (n pl) /twɪnz/ two children born on the
   same day from the same mother
day off (n) /ˈdeɪjɒf/ free day from work

Reading

1 Discuss these questions.

  1 Do you know any twins? Do they do the same job? Do they have the same hobbies and interests?

  2 Do you have any brothers or sisters? Do you spend your free time together?

2 Read the article about identical twins. Is it about their work, their free time or both?

3 Read the article again and complete the table with information about the twins.

	The Mulgray Twins	The Kitt Twins	The Bryan Twins
Job?	*writers*		
Free-time activity?			*Bob goes to the gym.*
Who with?			

46

Unit 4 **Free time**

Vocabulary **free-time activities**

4 Match the verbs with the nouns to make free-time activities. Then check your answers in the article.

1	go	computer games
2	play	films
3	do	friends
4	play	the gym
5	watch	walking
6	play	Tae Kwon Do
7	go to	a musical instrument
8	meet	tennis

> **WORDBUILDING verb + noun collocations**

We use certain verbs with certain nouns. These are called collocations. For example: *play golf, do yoga, go cycling, go running, watch TV, play computer games, play music, go camping, play football, read a magazine*

For further information and practice, see page 35 of the Workbook.

5 Complete the questionnaire with five free-time activities of your choice.

Example:
In your free time, do you go fishing?

In your free time, do you ...

- _____ ? ☐
- _____ ? ☐
- _____ ? ☐
- _____ ? ☐
- _____ ? ☐

6 Work in pairs. Interview your partner with your questionnaire.

Do you go fishing?

Yes, I do. / No, I don't.

Grammar *like/love + -ing*

7 Look at the underlined words in these sentences from the article in Exercise 2. Which two sentences have a) *like/love + noun*? b) *like/love + verb + -ing*?

1 They <u>love</u> <u>books</u>.
2 They <u>like</u> the same <u>free-time activities</u>.
3 Mike and Bob <u>love</u> <u>playing</u> tennis.
4 Bob <u>likes</u> <u>going</u> to the gym.

> **LIKE/LOVE + -ING**

I like/love swimming.
He likes singing.
I don't like clubbing.
She doesn't like dancing.
Do you like shopping?
Does he like shopping?

For further information and practice, see page 160.

8 Pronunciation /ŋ/

🔊 **1.28** Listen and repeat these verbs in the *-ing* form.

playing	listening	singing	watching
going	doing	dancing	shopping

Speaking

9 Write three sentences (two true and one false) about your free-time activities, interests or hobbies. Use *love, like* or *don't like*.

Example:
I love playing the guitar. (true)
I don't like going out for dinner. (false)
I like watching football. (true)

10 Work in pairs. Read your three sentences to your partner. He/She guesses which one is false.

11 Ask you partner more questions about his/her likes and dislikes. Ask about these topics:

- books and films
- music
- sport
- food and shopping
- computer games

What's your favourite book?

What kinds of music do you like?

Why do you like tennis?

Does your family also like computer games?

Lesson type c

Reading

This page is the first page of a double-page reading lesson. The reading text is always on the right-hand page, and the activities on the left.

> The mini contents section at the beginning of every lesson sets clear targets.

> Critical thinking activities require students to engage with the reading texts at a deeper level, and require them to show real understanding – not just reading comprehension. This training – in evaluating texts, assessing the validity and strength of arguments and developing an awareness of authorial techniques – is clearly a valuable skill for those students learning English for academic purposes (EAP) where reflective learning is essential. Moreover, it is also very much part of the *National Geographic* spirit which encourages people to question assumptions, and develop their own well-informed and reasoned opinions.

> The *Word focus* sections take high-frequency words and give examples of the different meanings they can have according to the contexts in which they appear and the different words they collocate with.

---

reading **food for the future** • word focus **of** • pronunciation **linking of** • critical thinking **summarising** • speaking **summarising the article**

5c The seed vault

Reading

1 Do you ever grow plants from seeds? Do you ever grow your own food? Why? / Why not?

2 Read the article on page 63. Is it about growing, storing or buying seeds?

3 Read the article again. Answer the questions.

1 Why don't plants sometimes grow?
2 Who needs new seeds?
3 Do seeds grow in the vault?
4 Which country has the biggest seed vault in the world?
5 Is the seed vault at the North Pole or in Norway?
6 Is the seed vault above or below the ground?
7 How many varieties of seed are in the vault at the moment?
8 How many seeds can you put in the vault?

Word focus *of*

4 Look at the underlined phrases in these sentences from the article. Notice the position of *of*. Then write *of* in the sentences (1–6).

A lot of countries need different types of seeds. The vault is on the island of Spitsbergen.

1 A lot people in China eat rice for breakfast.
2 The United States America is famous for burgers.
3 I'd like a bottle water, please.
4 A friend mine is vegetarian.
5 I eat my main meal in the middle the day.
6 There are many varieties potato.

5 Pronunciation **linking of**

🔊 **1.38** Listen to the completed sentences in Exercise 4. Notice the link between *of* and the word before each time. Listen again and repeat.

A lot_of people in China eat rice for breakfast.

Critical thinking **summarising**

6 Match these summary sentences with the paragraphs (1–5) in the article.

a A seed vault is a place for different types of seeds.
b There are many different seeds from all over the world in the vault.
c Most of the Svalbard Global Seed Vault is under the ground.
d The seed vault is important for humans.
e It's important to have new seeds.

Speaking

7 Work in pairs. Cover the article on the next page. Summarise the main points of the article. Use all these phrases.

store different types of seed
Svalbard Global Seed Vault   cold place
one hundred and thirty metres
island of Spitsbergen   three large areas
half a million varieties   thousands of years

62

Lesson type d

Real life

This page is the one-page functional lesson from Unit 8.

8d The photos of Reinier Gerritsen

Real life **talking about pictures and photos**

1 Do you like looking at paintings and photos? Who is your favourite artist or photographer?

2 Look at the photo. Discuss the questions.

1 Where are these people? How do they feel?
2 Do you think it is an interesting photograph? Why? / Why not?

3 🔊 2.12 The photo is by Reinier Gerritsen. Listen to someone talking about him and his photography. Answer the questions.

1 Why does the person like his photos?
2 Where are the people in this photo?
3 The speaker talks about the people in the photo. Who does she talk about first, second, third, fourth and fifth?

4 🔊 2.12 Listen again and match the sentence beginnings (1–10) with the endings (a–j).

1	His photos are	a people in their everyday life.
2	They often show	b very interesting.
3	This one is	c the man and woman are talking.
4	On the right	
5	The woman in the middle	d is watching her.
6	In front of her the woman with blonde	e a bit sad.
7	Then the other blonde woman on the left	f is reading her book.
8	She looks	g I don't normally look at people very closely.
9	Look at the other woman	h hair is listening to music.
10	I like it because	i at the back.
		j on the New York subway.

> **TALKING ABOUT PICTURES AND PHOTOS**
>
> **Introduce the photo**
> This photo shows …, I can see …
>
> **Location**
> On the left/right, in the middle, at the front/back
>
> **The people (appearance and actions)**
> She looks sad. He is reading.
>
> **Your opinion**
> I think …, I like it because …

5 Pronunciation silent letters

🔊 2.13 Listen to these words from the Listening. Which letter is silent? Then listen again and repeat.

interesting	sometimes	everyday
listening	blonde	closely

6 Work in pairs. Look at another photo by Reinier Gerritsen on page 156.

7 Choose a picture or photo you like. Show it to your partner and talk about it.

TALK ABOUT ▶ PEOPLE'S APPEARANCE ▶ CLOTHES ▶ TATTOOS ▶ PICTURES AND PHOTOS
WRITE ▶ TEXTS AND ONLINE MESSAGES

The d lessons have clear 'Real life' functional aims.

The pronunciation syllabus covers sounds and spelling; connected speech; stress and intonation.

Lesson type e

Writing

This page is the one-page writing lesson from Unit 4.

A different writing skill is presented and practised in every e lesson.

Every e lesson has a specific text type.

Every writing lesson includes a model.

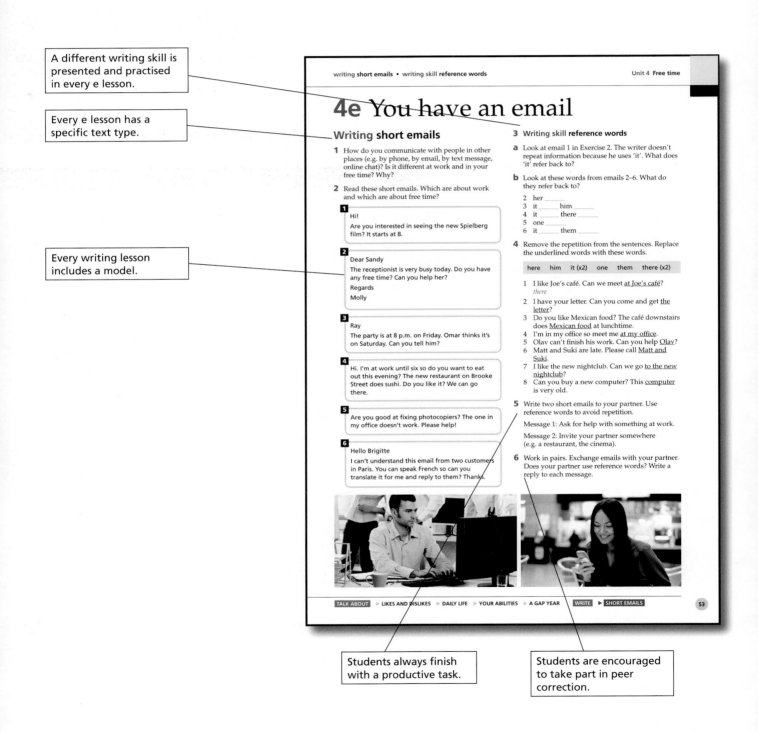

writing **short emails** • writing skill **reference words**   Unit 4 **Free time**

4e You have an email

Writing short emails

1 How do you communicate with people in other places (e.g. by phone, by email, by text message, online chat)? Is it different at work and in your free time? Why?

2 Read these short emails. Which are about work and which are about free time?

1
Hi!
Are you interested in seeing the new Spielberg film? It starts at 8.

2
Dear Sandy
The receptionist is very busy today. Do you have any free time? Can you help her?
Regards
Molly

3
Ray
The party is at 8 p.m. on Friday. Omar thinks it's on Saturday. Can you tell him?

4
Hi. I'm at work until six so do you want to eat out this evening? The new restaurant on Brooke Street does sushi. Do you like it? We can go there.

5
Are you good at fixing photocopiers? The one in my office doesn't work. Please help!

6
Hello Brigitte
I can't understand this email from two customers in Paris. You can speak French so can you translate it for me and reply to them? Thanks.

3 Writing skill **reference words**

a Look at email 1 in Exercise 2. The writer doesn't repeat information because he uses 'it'. What does 'it' refer back to?

b Look at these words from emails 2–6. What do they refer back to?

2 her _____
3 it _____ him _____
4 it _____ there _____
5 one _____
6 it _____ them _____

4 Remove the repetition from the sentences. Replace the underlined words with these words.

| here   him   it (x2)   one   them   there (x2) |

1 I like Joe's café. Can we meet <u>at Joe's café</u>?
   there
2 I have your letter. Can you come and get <u>the letter</u>?
3 Do you like Mexican food? The café downstairs does <u>Mexican food</u> at lunchtime.
4 I'm in my office so meet me <u>at my office</u>.
5 Olav can't finish his work. Can you help <u>Olav</u>?
6 Matt and Suki are late. Please call <u>Matt and Suki</u>.
7 I like the new nightclub. Can we go <u>to the new nightclub</u>?
8 Can you buy a new computer? This <u>computer</u> is very old.

5 Write two short emails to your partner. Use reference words to avoid repetition.

Message 1: Ask for help with something at work.

Message 2: Invite your partner somewhere (e.g. a restaurant, the cinema).

6 Work in pairs. Exchange emails with your partner. Does your partner use reference words? Write a reply to each message.

TALK ABOUT ▶ LIKES AND DISLIKES ▶ DAILY LIFE ▶ YOUR ABILITIES ▶ A GAP YEAR WRITE ▶ SHORT EMAILS   53

Students always finish with a productive task.

Students are encouraged to take part in peer correction.

Unit 1 People

Lead-in

Getting to know you 1 (the ball game)

Bring a ball, bean bag or other light object (which is easy to throw and catch) into the class.

Ask students to stand up and stand in a circle. Say, *Hi! My name's (Mike). What's your name?* and throw the ball to a student. The student says, *Hi! My name's (…?). What's your name?* and throws the ball to another student. (Students will soon understand what to do after a little trial and error!) Continue until all the students have had a chance to introduce themselves.

Then say, *My name's (Mike) and her name's (Clara).* Throw the ball to (Clara). This student must say, *My name's (Clara) and his name's (Ivan).* Then she throws the ball to (Ivan). Continue until all the students have had a go. To do this part of the game, they must remember other students' names.

There are many variations on this game (including remembering all the students' names in a chain, remembering the nationality of each student, etc.). The main thing is that at the start of the course, you and all the class know and remember everybody's name.

Getting to know you 2

With a new class, ask students to write their name on a name card. It is a good idea to bring into class a set of A5-size pieces of card or sturdy paper for this purpose. Students fold the card and write their names. Then they place the names on the desk in front of them. Tell students to ask each other's names. Get students to use name cards until you know each other well enough not to need them.

1 Ask students to look at the photo. Ask the questions.

> ANSWERS
> He's in Majlis al Jinn Cave, Oman
> His surname is Alvarez.

Background notes

Depending on where your students are from, you may need to point out that, in English-speaking countries, the first name (here, *Stephen*) comes before the surname or family name (here, *Alvarez*). Sometimes people have a middle name (e.g. Stephen John Alvarez) but it is often omitted or reduced to an initial (e.g. Stephen J. Avarez).

The **Majlis al Jinn Cave** is the ninth largest cave chamber in the world. It has a volume of 4 million cubic metres and is in a remote area of the Selma Plateau in the Sultanate of Oman in the Middle East.

2 💿 [1.1] Play the recording. Students listen and match the questions with the answers.

> ANSWERS
> 1 c   2 a   3 b   4 d

Audioscript 💿 [1.1]

I = interviewer, R = Richard Turner

I: What's your name?

R: Richard Turner.

I: Where are you from?

R: The UK, but I'm an explorer for *National Geographic* so I travel all over the world.

I: I really like this photo.

R: Yes, it's in Oman.

I: And the photographer, what's his name?

R: Stephen Alvarez.

I: Where's he from?

R: He's from the USA.

Extra activity

To practise pronunciation before doing Exercise 3, play the recording again and ask students to listen and repeat the key questions and answers. Once they have repeated the phrases from the recording, go round the class, nominating individuals to ask and answer the questions as in Exercise 2, e.g. 'What's your name?' 'Stephen Alvarez', etc.

3 Organise this activity in one of a variety of ways. Students could ask and answer with a partner first, then change partners to ask and answer the third person questions, *What's his / her name?*, etc. Alternatively, they could ask and answer in groups of four before changing groups, or students could mingle, walk round the class, and ask a number of people.

Extra activity

Students interview each other to find out names and nationalities, but must then do a task. For example, tell them to ask the questions and then order themselves according to the alphabetical order of their first names or surnames (so Adam would sit in the first seat to the right of the class, and Zoe would end up sitting in a seat to the far left). Or, in a class of mixed nationalities, tell them to sit next to a person from the country that is closest to their own country.

Teaching notes: teaching elementary students

Teachers at Elementary level need to think in terms of visuals and mimes. It is a good idea to build up a set of flashcards or pictures, or use slide presentation software or interactive whiteboard software to show visuals. You don't need to speak to explain words or to set up activities. Mime words or use a picture. Act out or model an activity so that students can see what you want them to do. Grade your language and limit your talking time. It's also important to make lessons varied at beginner level. Plan lessons that incorporate a bit of listening, a bit of reading, some basic language, some writing, and some speaking. Activities should be short and you should try to vary interaction, too, so mix up the pairs and have groupwork and mingles.

It is important to keep recycling language from one lesson to the next, so try to include warmers or short communicative activities at the start or end of lessons to allow students to reuse and recycle language they've acquired.

And, finally, establish good practice. Encourage a classroom situation where only English is spoken, and introduce students gradually to the idea of speaking in pairs and groups.

1a Explorers

Lead-in

Introducing the theme: explorers

Write *explorers* on the board and ask students to give you the names of some famous explorers that they know (e.g. Christopher Columbus, Captain Cook, Neil Armstrong, Scott of the Antarctic, etc.).

Once you have three or four names, ask students in pairs to think of three facts about one of the explorers that they can tell the class.

Listening

1 Ask students to look at the photos and say where the explorers are from. Ask: *What do explorers do?* (They visit unusual places or find new places.)

> **ANSWERS**
>
> The flags on the coats show that they are from Canada and Britain.

2 💿 [1.2] Play the recording. Students listen and decide if the sentences are true or false.

> **ANSWERS**
>
> 1 T
> 2 F (Wales, in Great Britain)
> 3 T
> 4 T
> 5 F (explorer)
> 6 F (She's from Canada)
> 7 F (He's thirty-six and she's thirty-five)

Audioscript 💿 [1.2]

I = interviewer, M = Mike Burney

I: Hello. What's your name?

M: My name's Mike Burney.

I: Are you from Great Britain?

M: Yes, I'm from Wales, but I travel all the time.

I: And are you married?

M: Yes, I am. My wife's name is Sally. She isn't at home at the moment.

I: Why? What's her job?

M: She's also an explorer and we often travel together.

I: Is she from Wales too?

M: No, she isn't. She's from Canada.

I: Are you the same age?

M: No, we aren't. I'm thirty-six and Sally is thirty-five.

Extra activity

Ask students to write true answers for the false sentences.

Background notes

Wales is a country that is part of Great Britain. Great Britain describes the island that is comprised of Scotland to the north, England to the south, and Wales to the west.

Welsh people tend to see themselves as Welsh first and British second (and never call themselves English!)

Vocabulary personal information

3 Students complete the table with underlined words from Exercise 2. Do the first line as an example. Let students compare their answers in pairs before discussing as a class.

> **ANSWERS**
>
> | | | |
> |---|---|---|
> | First name | Mike | Sally |
> | Surname | Burney | |
> | Age | twenty-six | thirty-five |
> | Job / Occupation | explorer | photographer |
> | Country | USA | Wales |
> | Marital status | single | married |
> | Relationship | husband | wife |

4 Students add their own information to the table. In feedback, ask some questions and elicit answers (*What's your first name? How old are you? Where are you from? Are you married?*, etc.).

Grammar be (am / is / are)

5 💿 [1.2] Play the recording again. Students listen and circle the forms of *be*. Let them compare their answers in pairs before discussing as a class. In feedback, elicit answers and establish that there are three forms (*am, is* and *are*).

> **ANSWERS**
>
> I: Hello. What's your name?
> M: My name's Mike Burney.
> I: Are you from Great Britain?
> M: Yes, I'm from Wales but I travel all the time.
> I: And are you married?
> M: Yes, I am. My wife's name is Sally. She isn't at home at the moment.
> I: Why? What's her job?
> M: She's also an explorer and we often travel together.
> I: Is she from Wales too?
> M: No, she isn't. She's from Canada.
> I: Are you the same age?
> M: No, we aren't. I'm thirty-six and Sally is thirty-five.

6 Ask students to work in pairs to discuss the questions. In feedback, point out the way the different forms are pronounced (see Pronunciation notes below).

Look at the grammar box with the students and refer them to the information and practice on page 157.

Grammar notes

- We use *am* with the first person *I* (*I am*). This is often abbreviated to *I'm* in spoken English and informal written English. We add *not* to make the negative (*I'm not*) and invert with the subject to make the question (*Am I ... ?*). In short answers, we use *Yes, I am* (not *I'm*), and *No, I'm not*. Note that *I amn't* or *I'mn't* are not possible.

- We use *is* with the third person (*he, she, it is*). This is often abbreviated to *He's, She's* or *It's* in spoken English and informal written English. We add *n't* to make the negative (*He isn't*, etc.) and invert with the subject to make the question (*Is she ... ?* etc.). In short answers, we use *Yes, he is* or *Yes, it is*, etc. (not *Yes, he's* or *Yes, it's*), and *No, he isn't*. Note that *he's not* or *she's not* are possible but less common uses.

- We use *are* with the second and third person plural forms (*you, we, they are*). This is often abbreviated to *You're, We're* or *They're* in spoken English and informal written English. We add *n't* to make the negative (*We aren't*, etc.) and invert with the subject to make the question (*Are you ... ?* etc.). In short answers, we use *Yes, we are* or *Yes, they are*, etc. (not *Yes, we're* or *Yes, they're*), and *No, they aren't*. Note that *they're not* or *we're not* are possible but less common uses.

Pronunciation contracted forms

7a 💿 [1.3] Lead in by asking students to read through the contractions and think about how they are pronounced. Then play the recording. Students listen and tick the forms they hear.

ANSWERS			
1 'm	3 'm not	5 aren't	7 isn't
2 Are	4 's	6 're	8 Is

Audioscript 💿 [1.3]

1 I'm thirty-one.
2 Are you from England?
3 No, I'm not.
4 Her name's Helena.
5 We aren't from the USA.
6 We're from Canada.
7 No, he isn't.
8 Is he married?

7b 💿 [1.3] Play the recording again. Students listen and repeat. For further practice, ask students to practise reading out the conversation in Exercise 5 in pairs.

Pronunciation notes

The pronunciation of the contractions is quite difficult for elementary students. It involves getting their tongue round long vowels and diphthongs. Point out the diphthong in *I'm* /aɪm/, the /z/ sound in *he's* and *she's* /ʃiːz/, and the long vowel sound in *are* and *aren't* /ɑːnt/. Both *we're* /wɪə/ and *they're* /ðɛə/ have tricky diphthongs.

8 💿 [1.4] Lead in by checking the meaning of *customs official* (a person who looks at passports when you arrive in a country). Ask students to complete the conversation. Let students compare their answers in pairs. Then play the recording. Students listen and check.

ANSWERS			
1 Are	3 's	5 're	7 isn't
2 'm	4 're	6 Is	8 's

Audioscript 💿 [1.4]

C = customs officer, M = Mike Burney

C: Good afternoon. Are you in New Zealand for work or a holiday?
M: For work. I'm an explorer.
C: I see. What's your address in Auckland?
M: We're at 106a Eglinton Road.
C: We?
M: Yes, my wife and two children. They're with me.
C: Is your wife also an explorer?
M: Yes, she is, but she isn't in Auckland for work. She's on holiday.

Extra activity

Students could practise reading out the conversation in pairs, paying attention to the pronunciation of the forms of *be*. Alternatively, elicit and write up the official's questions on the board, then ask students to close their books and practise the conversation in pairs. One student asks questions. The other remembers answers.

Speaking

9 Organise the class into pairs. Tell them to work together to think about how to form questions to get the information. Then ask students to take turns to interview each other and to take brief notes.

10 Once students have finished their interviews, ask individuals to tell the class about their partner.

Teaching notes

Use the opportunity of this extended speaking activity to listen and note down errors with form and pronunciation. At the end, write four or five inaccurate sentences on the board and ask students to correct them as a class or in pairs.

It is a good idea to do an error feedback stage at the end of a fluency activity. It reminds students that being accurate is important and focuses on the kind of errors students regularly make.

Homework

Ask students to write a short blog to introduce themselves. Tell them to write about their name and their job, their country and their marital status.

1b A family in East Africa

Lead-in

Using words

Write two first names on the board (the name of your mother or father, and the name of your brother or sister). Tell students that they are important people to you. In pairs, students must think of questions to ask you to find out about the people. Give students one minute to think of questions (e.g. *How old is George? Is he your brother? What's his job? Is he single?*) *Students interview you to find out about the two family members.*

Reading

1 Ask students the questions and elicit answers.

2 Ask students to read the questions. Focus students on the questions by asking them how many names of people in the Leakey family they can find (six).

Students read the text and find answers to the questions. Let them compare their answers in pairs.

> ANSWERS
> 1 England
> 2 Yes, they are.
> 3 He's a farmer.
> 4 He's an explorer and a scientist.
> 5 No, she isn't.
> 6 Yes, he is.

3 Students read the text again and complete the family tree. Let them compare their answers in pairs.

> ANSWERS
> 1 Mary   3 Richard   5 Katy
> 2 Colin   4 Maeve   6 Samira

Extra activity

Tell students to close their books or cover the text and family tree. Then ask questions. For example, *Who's Phillip? Where does Samira work?* Find out how much students can remember.

Vocabulary family

4 Ask students to work in pairs to categorise the words. In feedback, you could draw your own family tree on the board in order to point out the different family relationships.

> ANSWERS
> M: father, uncle, nephew, step brother
> F: mother, aunt, niece, mother-in-law
> B: cousin, parent, grandparent

5 Students complete the phrases. Let them compare their answers in pairs. Read through the *Wordbuilding* box with

the class. Refer students to page 11 of the Workbook for further information and practice.

> ANSWERS
> 1 uncle, aunt   5 mother-in-law
> 2 niece, nephew   6 parent
> 3 cousin   7 grandparent
> 4 step brother

Extra activity

Ask students to add as many other family words as they can to the words in the categories in Exercise 4, e.g. *sister, grandfather, grandmother, great-grandfather, grandchildren, son, daughter, wife, husband, sister-in-law, step father,* etc.

Grammar notes

Note that English nouns do not have masculine or feminine endings, so words like *cousin* or *parent* do not differentiate according to sex.

Grammar possessive 's and possessive adjectives

6 Read through the grammar box with the class. Ask them to find examples in the text and let them compare their answers in pairs. Refer students to page 157 for further information and practice.

> ANSWERS
> Possessive 's in the article: Louise's mother, Richard's step brother, Louise's grandparents, Louise's sister
> Possessive adjectives in the article: her family, Her father, Their uncle and aunt

Grammar notes

We use *possessive 's* (or the *saxon genetive* as it is sometimes called) to show possession in English. You add 's to the end of the noun which has possession.

Note that the position of the apostrophe changes between singular and plural: *My sister's bedroom* (one sister) but *My sisters' bedroom* (two or more sisters).

's is pronounced /s/ after unvoiced sounds and /z/ after voiced sounds.

His and *her* are second person singular possessive adjectives. *His* (like *he*) refers to a male 'possessor'. *Her* (like *she*) refers to a female 'possessor'.

Note that *its* is used to show possession with animals, objects, countries, etc.

Possessive adjectives do not change their form if the noun they are showing possession of is plural. So, *their mother* and *their parents,* NOT *theirs parents.*

7 Students choose the correct word to complete the sentences. Let them compare their answers in pairs.

> ANSWERS
> 1 My   3 your   5 She   7 Our
> 2 I   4 you   6 His   8 Their

Pronunciation the same or different sounds?

8 🔊 [1.5] Play the recording. Students listen and decide whether the pronunciation is the same or different.

ANSWERS
1 ✓   2 ✗   3 ✓   4 ✗   5 ✓

Pronunciation notes

Both *their* and *there* are pronounced with a diphthong: /ðɛə/.

Note the long sound in *he's* /hiːz/ and the short vowel sound in *his* /hɪz/.

Note the long sound in *are* /ɑː/ and the triphthong in *our* /aʊə/.

9 Model the activity first by reading out the example. Then ask students in pairs to take turns producing sentences with possessive adjectives.

ANSWERS
2 Her sister's Claire.
3 Their cousins are Juliet and Jane.
4 His grandparents are dead.
5 Is your name Sylvain?
6 Helen is our niece.

Speaking

10 Divide the class into pairs to do the activity. Tell them to write five names and think about what to say about each person. Then tell them to take turns to tell their partner about the people.

1c The face of seven billion people

Reading

1 Lead in by asking students to look at the picture of the face on page 15. Ask, *What can you see? What does this show?*

Then discuss the question in the exercise as a class. In a class of mixed nationalities, ask for individual answers and find out who comes from the most populous country. (Note: it is a good idea to look up the populations of your students' countries before the lesson.)

2 Ask students how to say the numbers in the box. Then ask them to read the sentences and predict what numbers go with each sentence.

Students read the article and match the numbers to the information.

ANSWERS
1 85	4 21%	7 2.5 billion
2 1.2 billion	5 38%	8 5 billion
3 1 billion	6 51%	

Critical thinking the writer's purpose

3 Ask students to read the article again and choose the correct answer. Let them compare their answers in pairs. In feedback, ask students to say why they chose their answer (see notes below).

ANSWER
a

4 Organise the class into pairs first to think about and share what they find surprising. Then ask individuals to tell the class.

Vocabulary everyday verbs

5 Students find the verbs then complete the fact file. Do the first as an example. Let students compare their answers in pairs.

> ANSWERS
> FACT FILE: China
> 1.2 billion people **live** in China.
> 70% of the population **speak** the language of Mandarin Chinese.
> Over 1 billion Chinese people **have** a mobile phone.
> 65% of the population **work** in agriculture.
> 35% of the Chinese **use** the Internet.

Background notes

Standard Mandarin is the official language of mainland China. However, there are many regional Chinese languages, notably Cantonese, and other languages, such as Tibetan, Mongolian and Uyghur, are spoken among China's ethnic minorities.

The percentage of China's population in agriculture continues to shrink rapidly. Whilst official figures from the early 2000s show the figure as about 65%, it may well be down to 55% or less by now as a result of the rush to urbanisation.

Extra activity

Write the verbs from Exercise 5 on the board. Then use them to provide 'figures' for people in your house, e.g. *Three people live in my house – me, my husband, and my daughter. 100% of the population speak English. 33% – my husband – speak French. 66% have a mobile phone. My daughter is only three. Only 33% of the population work in the kitchen.*

Ask students in pairs to think of and share figures for their house.

Word focus *in*

6 Students look at the use of *in* in Exercise 5 and tick the correct rules. Do the first as an example. In feedback, elicit other examples of words students have seen used with *in*.

> ANSWERS
> We use *in* with:
> countries and cities (e.g. *in China*)
> areas of work or industry (e.g. *in agriculture*).
> Note that we do not use *in* to talk about what languages people speak, e.g. *I speak English but my friend speaks French*. But we can use *in* in other contexts, e.g. *the book was written in Chinese.*

Grammar notes

In is a preposition with a variety of uses.

Here, it is used to say that something is inside a place, container or substance (*in a bag, in soup, in China*), and it is used to say that something or someone is involved in a particular type of activity (*in a race, in agriculture*).

Extra activity

Elicit and build up on the board a list of other phrases using *in* that students already know (*in hospital, in the evening, in love, in the rain*, etc.).

Speaking

7 Divide the class into pairs. Ask students to decide who is A, and who is B, then tell them to find and read their information. Elicit the questions they need to ask their partner to find the missing information. Model and drill the questions if necessary. When students are ready, they take turns to ask and answer questions to find the missing information.

In feedback, ask the questions in open class and elicit the information.

ANSWERS		
	Spain	The USA
population	47 million	300 million
Spanish	100%	12%
a service industry (hotels, banks, etc.)	70%	55%
mobile phones	Everyone	Everyone
the internet	30 million	250 million

Extra activity

In a mixed nationality class, ask students to write figures in a third column of the table in Exercise 7 to show facts and figures for their own country. Students then ask and answer questions about their countries in pairs.

Homework

Students write a fact file for their own country, using the verbs in Exercise 5.

1d At a conference

Lead-in

Introducing the theme: meeting people for the first time

Bring in four good-sized pictures of famous people that your students should know (film stars, sports stars, etc.). Put them on the wall. If possible, put one picture on each wall of your classroom.

Walk up to one of the pictures and say *Hello*. Then have a brief imaginary conversation with the famous person, pausing slightly to pretend that you're listening to a question or an answer. For example (with Leo di Caprio): *Hi Leo … Oh, I'm fine, fine … I'm Mike … Oh, I'm a teacher. What's your job? Really? Wow! … Oh, from Britain. Where are you from? … Oh, OK. Goodbye!*

Model a similar conversation with another picture then ask students to stand up, go to a picture and have an imaginary one-sided conversation. They can, of course, say anything, so this is an opportunity for students to 'free-wheel' with the limited amount of English they have.

If you have a large class, bring in more pictures.

Speaking Pronunciation: spelling

1 [1.6] Play the recording. Students listen and repeat the letters.

Pronunciation notes

Note that many of the letters share the same vowel sounds:

/eɪ/ A, H, J, K

/iː/ B, C, D, E, G, P, T, V

/e/ F, L, M, N, S, X, Z

/aɪ/ I, Y

/əʊ/ O,

/uː/ Q, U, W

/ɑː/ R

Note that Z is pronounced /zed/ in British English, but /ziː/ in US English.

2 Students take turns to dictate names, countries and jobs. In feedback, ask some students to say and spell out their partners' names.

Extra activity

Spell out the names of famous film stars. Students listen until they guess who the film star is. Then they shout out the name. If they are wrong, they are out. If they are right, they get a point. Spell out a few names and find out who gets most points. For example, *J-U-D- Oh, Jude Law!*

Listening

3 [1.7] Students look at the photos. Ask: *Who are they? Where are they? What are they doing? What are they saying?* Elicit ideas and language.

Play the recording. Students listen and answer the questions. Let them compare their answers in pairs.

> **ANSWERS**
> 1 Conversation 1 = 2 people; Conversation 2 = 3 people
> 2 They are at a conference

Audioscript [1.7]

Conversation 1

R = Rita, **G** = Gary

R: Hello, can I help you?

G: Hi. Yes, I'm at this conference, but I'm early.

R: Yes, you are the first! That's OK. What's your name?

G: Gary.

R: Hi Gary. My name's Rita. I'm the conference manager.

G: Nice to meet you, Rita.

R: Nice to meet you too. What's your surname, Gary?

G: Laurens.

W: Laurens? Are you on my list? Err, can you spell that?

G: Sure. It's L-A-U-R-E-N-S.

R: OK. There are two people with that name at this conference.

G: Really?

W: Yes, but her surname is Lawrence. L-A-W-R-E-N-C-E.

Conversation 2

R = Rita, **V** = Valérie, **G** = Gary

R: Oh! Here's someone else. Hello. My name's Rita and I'm the conference manager.

V: Hi, I'm Valérie.

R: That's a beautiful French name. What's your surname Valérie?

V: Moreau. That's M-O-R-E-A-U.

R: M, M, M, Mason, Moore, Moreau! OK. Well you're the second person here Valérie so I'd like to introduce you to Gary. He's from England.

G: Nice to meet you Valérie.

V: Nice to meet you too.

G: Are you from France?

V: Actually no, I'm from an island in the Pacific Ocean.

G: New Caledonia?

V: That's right!

R: Err, I have to go. Nice talking to you.

G: Bye Rita. See you later.

V: Bye.

4 🔊 [1.7] Play the recording again. Students listen and choose the correct word.

ANSWERS

1 first	5 Moreau
2 is	6 New Caledonia
3 first	7 Valérie
4 Laurens	

Real life meeting people for the first time

5 Ask students to read through the expressions carefully. Then play recording 1.7 again. Students listen and tick the expressions they hear.

ANSWERS

Students should tick:

My name's …

I'm …

I'm from …

Nice to meet you.

Nice to meet you too.

I'd like to introduce you to …

He's from …

Nice talking to you.

See you later.

Bye.

Vocabulary notes

Note that we say *Nice to meet you* when we are introduced to someone for the first time, and *Nice meeting you* or *Nice talking to you* (using the *-ing* form) at the end of the conversation as we prepare to leave.

This is … and *I'd like to introduce you to …* are ways of introducing people. The second of these is very formal and is generally used in business situations.

Extra activity

Let students check their answers by looking at the audioscript on page 170. Then ask them in pairs to practise reading out the conversations.

6 Divide the class into groups of three to practise the conversation. Students choose their roles then prepare what to say, using phrases from Exercise 5. Depending on the level and ability of your class, you could ask them to script the conversation first, or improvise it.

1e Introduce yourself

Lead-in

Introducing the theme: introductions

Write *Gary* and *Valérie* on the board. Remind students that they were introduced to these people in 1d. Ask students to tell you what they remember (Gary's surname is Laurens, and he's from England; Valérie's surname is Moreau and she's from New Caledonia and speaks French).

Writing a personal description

1 Ask students to read the introductions and answer the questions. Let them compare their answers in pairs before discussing as a class.

ANSWER

They are at a conference.

2 Ask students to read the introductions again and tick the information.

ANSWERS

Students should tick all boxes in the table except for Valérie's job. The information they give is as follows:

	Gary	Valérie
First name	Gary	Valérie
Surname	Laurens	Moreau
Job	Science lecturer	–
Country / languages	UK / English	New Caledonia / French
Other information	lives in USA, married, two children	Speaks English and Spanish

Writing skill *and, but*

3a Ask students to look back at the texts and find and underline the words. Discuss the questions as a class.

ANSWERS

and is for extra information

but is for a difference

Grammar notes

And and *but* are conjunctions. We use *and* to join two sentences. We use *but* to join two sentences when there is a contrast between the sentences.

Note that we often use a comma before *but* when joining sentences.

3b Read the examples with the class and make sure they are clear about whether they are adding extra information or showing a difference.

Ask students to join the sentences. Let them compare their answers in pairs before discussing as a class.

ANSWERS

3 I'm British, but Hindi is my first language.
4 He's from Germany, but he's in Russia at the moment.
5 My friend is 30 and he's single.
6 I live in Spain, but I work in France.
7 She's a student and she's at Oxford University.
8 My family is in the countryside, but I'm in the city.

4 Students write their own introduction. Tell them to start by noting things to write about under the headings in the table in Exercise 2.

When students have some ideas, ask them to try to join sentences using *and* or *but*.

5 Students exchange their introductions with a partner. Monitor and note how well students correct each other.

6 Depending on your classroom, collect and put the introductions on walls, the noticeboard, the board, or on tables round the side of the class. Students walk round and read the introductions. In feedback, ask students what interesting information they read.

Extra activity

Ask students to write five short sentences about themselves in a list on a piece of paper. Tell them to exchange the lists with a partner, who must then add another clause with *and* or *but* to each of their partner's sentences. For example, Student A may have written *I'm Spanish.* Their partner might write … *and I'm from Valencia,* or might write … , *but I speak English.* Students return the pieces of paper and read what their partners have written.

Homework

Students could write an extended introduction for homework. Alternatively, they could write a profile of their favourite celebrity.

1f World party

Before you watch

1 Ask students to work in groups. Tell them to look at the title of the video and the photo, and answer the questions.

ANSWERS

1 in Bangkok
2 to celebrate Chinese New Year

2 Discuss the questions as a class.

While you watch

3 Ask students to number the questions in order while they watch the video.

ANSWERS

b, a, c

4 Go through the information box with students and pre-teach *foot / feet, mile.* Give students some time to read through the sentences. Play the video again for students to match the sentences with the numbers.

ANSWERS

1 e   2 a   3 f   4 g   5 d   6 b   7 c   8 h

5 Give students some time to read through the sentences. Play the whole of the video again for the students to watch and order the sentences.

6 Play the whole of the video again. Students watch and check their answers.

ANSWERS

| a | 1 | c | 8 | e | 3 | g | 4 | i | 7 |
| b | 2 | d | 5 | f | 10 | h | 6 | j | 9 |

After you watch

7 Divide the class into groups of four or five. Tell them to use the questions to prepare a party.

8 Ask one person from each group to tell the class about the party.

9 Ask students in pairs to prepare questions using the prompts. For example, *Do you have a job? Are you under 30?* Ask students to walk round the class and interview as many students as they can in five minutes. Tell students to sit down with their partner and compare their answers.

10 Go through the examples with students and ask them to write their report. You could also set this task as homework.

Videoscript

There are seven billion people in the world. But how big is seven billion? One, two, three, four … Don't count from one to seven billion! It takes two hundred years.

00.21   There are seven billion stars. But from Earth, you can see a thousand at night, not billions. Walk around the Earth 133 times and that's seven billion steps. People send seven billion texts every 30 hours in the USA. That's 65,000 texts every second.

01.00   And what about a party with seven billion people? Everyone can come. But where on Earth is there a place for a world party? Let's go and take a look.

01.15   Actually, a place for seven billion people isn't very big compared to the Earth. One person needs about three square feet. But it's a party. So everyone needs about six square feet.

So for everyone in the world, that's about 42 billion square feet or 1,500 square miles.

01.40   So, where is a good place for this party?

The Juneau Icefield in Alaska is the correct size, but it's a bit cold.

Or there's the state of Rhode Island. It's 1,500 square miles.

What about French Polynesia? Its islands are beautiful and they are about 1,500 square miles.

02.03   Oh, and for a photograph of seven billion people, with everyone next to each other, we need an area of 500 square miles.

Yes! Seven billion people in 500 square miles.

Los Angeles is 500 square miles. So we can take the photograph there.

Here comes the photographer in a helicopter. Smile!

UNIT 1 Review

Grammar

1 Students put the words in order to write questions.

ANSWERS
1 What 's your name?
2 Are you from England?
3 Where are you from?
4 Are you single or married?
5 Are you an explorer?

2 Students ask and answer the questions from Exercise 1.

3 Ask students to read and complete the conversation.

ANSWERS

| 1 's | 3 's | 5 are | 7 's | 9 isn't |
| 2 's | 4 Are | 6 aren't | 8 's | 10 's |

4 Ask students to read the sentences and choose the correct option.

ANSWERS
1 your   4 photographer's, my
2 His   5 Her, I'm
3 They

Vocabulary

5 Ask students to match the categories 1–6 from a form to the details a–f.

ANSWERS
1 f   2 c   3 a   4 e   5 b   6 d

6 Ask students to complete the sentences with verbs.

ANSWERS
1 have   2 speak   3 live   4 work

Real life

7 Ask students to read the parts of the conversation and number them in order.

ANSWERS
5, 2, 4, 1, 3

8 Students roleplay a conversation using the new details to adapt the conversation from Exercise 7.

Speaking

9 Students write sentences about themselves, including one false sentence.

10 Students work in pairs to read their sentences and guess their partner's false sentence.

Unit 2 Possessions

Lead-in

Introducing the theme: possessions

In front of the class, take five possessions out of your pocket or bag. These might be your watch, phone, pen, glasses, etc., or they could include one or two more personal or unusual items. Tell the class what they are and why they are important to you.

Ask students to take five possessions out of their pockets or bag. In pairs, students describe their possessions and say why they are important.

1 Ask students to look at the photo. Ask the questions. Elicit responses.

> **ANSWERS**
>
> There are seven people.
> The possessions are made of plastic.

2 🎧 [1.8] Check that the students know the words by asking them to find them in the picture. Then play the recording. Ask students to match numbers to words.

> **ANSWERS**
>
> 22 balls   50 shoes and boots   1 sofa   3 TVs

Audioscript 🎧 [1.8]

This photo is by Sarah Leen. It's about people and their possessions. The photo shows all the plastic objects in this family's house. There are seven people in the Stow family and they've got hundreds of possessions! I think there are 22 balls, 50 shoes and boots, a sofa, three TVs…

3 Divide the class into pairs to find the objects and their colours. In feedback, build up a list on the board.

> **ANSWERS**
>
> | | |
> |---|---|
> | balls | yellow, blue, red, orange; black and white |
> | boots | black, grey, white, blue, red, green |
> | a chair | black |
> | roller blades | white; black |
> | a sofa | red (or brown) |
> | shelves | white |
> | shoes | white, blue, black |
> | a toy car | red and yellow |
> | TVs | black, silver |

4 Students work in pairs to find objects. In feedback, ask students to tell you what they found, and write any new words on the board.

Extra task

Play *Kim's Game*. Ask students to look at the picture for one minute then close their books. Give everybody one minute to write down all the objects they can remember. At the end, find out which student has the longest list. Ask him or her to read out their list to check.

2a My possessions

Lead-in

Using words

Write three everyday objects on the board, e.g. *a pen, a mobile phone, a watch*.

Ask students in pairs to choose one of the words and to think of as many adjectives as they can to put in front of it, e.g. *a big, black, expensive pen*.

After a minute or so, ask pairs to tell you which adjectives they thought of.

Vocabulary everyday objects

1 Ask students to look at the picture of the website. Ask: *What's his name? What's his website address? What can you see in the pictures?* Discuss the question as a class and use the photos to check the meaning of the words.

> **ANSWERS**
>
> kayaker, climber, diver

Vocabulary notes

Kayakers propel their kayak (/ˈkaɪæk/) with a double-bladed oar, unlike canoeists, who propel their canoes with a single-bladed oar.

Background notes

Andy Torbet is a presenter on the BBC's TV series *Coast*, which looks at the geology, communities and outdoor activities on Britain's coastline. He is interested in extreme diving.

2 Ask students to look at the photos of the objects from the rucksack. Ask them to work in pairs to match the words to the objects. In feedback, elicit the words and drill them for pronunciation.

> **ANSWERS**
>
> | | | | |
> |---|---|---|---|
> | 1 first-aid kit | 5 boots | 9 gloves |
> | 2 compass | 6 mobile phone | 10 torch |
> | 3 camera | 7 hat | 11 map |
> | 4 pens | 8 knife | |

Pronunciation notes

Point out the difficult pronunciation of some of the words: *compass* /ˈkʌmpəs/; *gloves* /ɡlʌvz/; *torch* /tɔːtʃ/

Extra activity

Tell students they are going on holiday in the mountains for the weekend, but they can only take three objects from the rucksack. In pairs, students must choose three things, then tell the class which ones they chose and why.

Grammar plural nouns

3 Ask students to look at the words in Exercise 2 and find plural nouns. Read the grammar box with the students. Refer students to the information and practice on page 158.

Grammar notes

Note that if words end in -y after a vowel, the y does not change, e.g. *bays, monkeys* and *toys*.

There are some exceptions when a noun ends with -f, so *knives, wives, halves* follow the rule but *roofs* does not.

Irregular nouns often involve people or animals (*women, sheep, deer*).

4 💿 [1.9] Ask students to write the plurals. Let them compare their answers in pairs Play the recording. Students listen and check their answers.

Audioscript and key 💿 [1.9]

1 maps
2 mobile phones
3 compasses
4 hats
5 cameras
6 knives
7 countries
8 boxes

Extra activity

Write some other words on the board and ask students to write plurals, e.g. *city, wife, boy, watch, glass, prince*.

Listening

5 💿 [1.10] Start by reminding students who Andy is. Refer them back to his website and ask what he does.

Ask students to read the questions and options, and check any words that students don't know. Play the recording. Students listen and choose the answers.

ANSWERS

1 a
2 d
3 a hat, a first-aid kit, a camera, gloves

Audioscript 💿 [1.10]

I = interviewer, **A** = Andy

I: Hello. Today I'm in the north of Scotland. We're at the bottom of a mountain. It's very beautiful but it's very cold and I'm here with Andy Torbet. Andy, are you from Scotland?

A: Yes, I am. I'm from Aberdeen.

I: Now Andy. You're a professional climber so you've got a rucksack with you today. What's always in your rucksack?

A: Well, this is my hat. It's good because it's cold today, but it's also important when it's hot because of the sun.

I: I see. And what's this?

A: It's a first-aid kit. It's always in my rucksack.

I: Good idea. And what's that?

A: It's my camera. I take it everywhere. And these are my climbing boots.

I: Right. And over there. What are those?

A: My gloves.

I: Right, they ARE important today! OK. So we've got everything. Let's start climbing.

A: Sure. Let's go.

Background notes

The United Kingdom is made up of four countries: England, Scotland, Wales and Northern Ireland.

Aberdeen is a coastal city in the north-east of Scotland.

Grammar *this, that, these, those*

6 💿 [1.11] Ask students to look at the extract from the interview, and guess which words are correct. Play the recording. Students listen and check. Read the grammar box with the students. Refer students to the information and practice on page 158.

ANSWERS

1 this   2 that   3 these   4 those

Audioscript 💿 [1.11]

I = interviewer, **A** = Andy

I: I see. And what's this?

A: It's a first-aid kit. It's always in my rucksack.

I: Good idea. And what's that?

A: It's my camera. I take it everywhere. And these are my climbing boots.

I: Right. And over there. What are those?

A: My gloves.

Grammar note

We use the demonstrative pronouns *this* and *these* to refer to things that are close to the speaker.

We use the demonstrative pronouns *that* and *those* to refer to things that are further away from the speaker.

7 Ask students to complete the questions and answers. Let students compare their answers in pairs.

ANSWERS

1 What's this?
  It's a camera.
2 What's that?
  It's my mobile phone.
3 What are these?
  They're my boots.
4 What are those?
  They're keys.

Pronunciation /ɪ/ or /iː/

8a 🔵 [1.12] Play the recording. Students listen to the sounds. In feedback, point out the longer sound in /iː/.

Audioscript 🔵 [1.12]

/ɪ/ /iː/

8b 🔵 [1.13] Play the recording. Students listen and note whether the vowel sound is short or long. In feedback, check the answers.

Play the recording again. Students listen and repeat.

ANSWERS			
1 /ɪ/	3 /iː/	5 /ɪ/	7 /ɪ/
2 /iː/	4 /ɪ/	6 /iː/	8 /iː/

Pronunciation note

Some nationalities have real problems with these sounds. If yours do, help them by showing them how to physically make the sound.

To make /iː/, spread your mouth wider and hold the sound longer than when you make the /ɪ/ sound. Ask students to copy the way you make the sound.

Extra activity

Write (or say) some tongue twisters, and ask students to try to repeat them. Try these:

She's got pink keys.

This is a big green ship.

Speaking

9 Organise the class into pairs to ask and answer questions about things in the classroom and in their possession. Model the activity first by asking one or two questions in open class.

Extra activity

Monitor students carefully and listen to how accurately they use the demonstrative pronouns. Note down five or six errors that they make and write them on the board. Elicit corrections from students.

Homework

Ask students to write a list of ten things that they always take in their rucksack or suitcase when they go on holiday. In the next lesson, ask students in pairs or groups to share their lists.

2b At home

Lead-in

Introducing the theme and using words: furniture
Write *furniture* on the board, and check its meaning by eliciting examples. Then put students in pairs to write a list of all the furniture they can see in the classroom. After a couple of minutes, elicit words and write a list on the board (e.g. *table, chairs, desks, stools, board*).

Reading

1 Ask students to look at the photos. Ask: *What can you see?* Elicit any vocabulary in the picture that students know. Then put students in pairs to discuss the questions. Elicit similarities and differences.

SAMPLE ANSWERS

The apartments look the same size with the same walls, windows and lights. They all have a sofa on the right, and a TV on the left.

The families are different, they have different furniture, and the sofas are different colours.

2 Students read the article and answer the questions. Let them compare their answers in pairs before discussing as a class.

ANSWERS				
1 S	2 S	3 S	4 D	5 D

Vocabulary furniture

3 Ask students to look at the words in the table, and ask them to find the items in the first photo that are ticked in the table. Students can work in pairs. In feedback, use the picture to check any new words, and then check the other four words (*blinds, rug, carpet, plant*) by using mime or drawing pictures on the board. Drill the words for pronunciation (see the Pronunciation notes below).

Pronunciation notes

Note the stress in these words: *sofa, armchair, television, mirror, computer, carpet*

Note the stress and difficult pronunciation in these words: *picture* /ˈpɪktʃə/; *cupboard* /ˈkʌbəd/; *drawer* /ˈdrɔːə/

Extra activity

Mime using the different pieces of furniture. For example, mime working at a computer, switching on a lamp, watering a plant, straightening a picture. Students must guess the word. Then divide the class into pairs or groups to mime and guess words.

4 Students work in pairs to complete the table. In feedback, elicit and check the answers.

ANSWERS

	1	2	3	4
sofa	✓	✓	✓	✓
armchair		✓		
chair	✓		✓	
television (TV)	✓	✓	✓	✓
mirror	✓			
desk	✓			
lamp	✓			
computer	✓			✓
pictures	✓	✓	✓	✓
blinds			✓	
curtains	✓	✓		✓
cupboards and drawers	✓	✓	✓	✓
rug				✓
carpet		✓		
plant				✓

Extra activity

Ask students to describe their living rooms in groups of four. Model the task first by describing your living room in simple terms, e.g. *In my living room, there is a TV and a sofa but there isn't a computer. There are two lamps …*

They must find five similarities between all four of their living rooms.

Grammar *there is / are*, prepositions of place

5 Read through the grammar box with the class. Ask students to look at the sentence and discuss the question as a class. Refer students to pages 158 and 159 for further information and practice.

ANSWERS

After *there is*, the noun is singular. After *there are*, the noun is plural.

Grammar notes

Note also that after *there is* and *there isn't*, we use the indefinite article *a* with singular nouns. After *there are*, we use a number with plural nouns.

Note the question forms:

Are there any …? requires a *yes / no* answer, e.g. *Yes, there are. / No, there aren't.*

How many … are there? is asking for the number of objects, and requires a number in the answer, e.g. *There are three.*

6 Students complete the sentences. Do the first as an example with the class, and tell them to refer to the grammar box. Let students compare their answers in pairs.

ANSWERS

1 's	3 are	5 Is, is	7 are, 's
2 isn't	4 aren't	6 Are, aren't	8 Are, aren't

7 🔘 [1.14] Play the recording. Students listen and check their answers to Exercise 6. Play the recording again for students to listen and repeat.

Audioscript 🔘 [1.14]

1 There's a desk.
2 There isn't a rug, but there's a carpet.
3 There are three pictures on the wall.
4 There aren't any curtains.
5 Is there a plant? Yes, there is.
6 Are there any chairs? No, there aren't.
7 How many chairs are there? There's one.
8 Are there any books? No, there aren't.

8 In pairs, students practise asking and answering the questions. Model the activity first by getting students to ask you questions and getting them to guess the apartment you are thinking about.

Extra activity

An alternative task, to practise affirmative and negative sentences, is to get one student to describe one of the apartments from Exercise 1 (e.g. *In this apartment, there is a rug and a TV but there aren't any …*), and have the other student listen and guess which one.

9 🔘 [1.15] Read through the grammar box with the class. Ask students to look at picture 4 and choose the correct prepositions in the text. Let them compare their answers in pairs. Then play the recording for students to check. Refer students to page 159 for further information and practice.

ANSWERS

1 on	5 in the middle
2 under	6 in front of
3 opposite	7 behind
4 on the right	

Audioscript 🔘 [1.15]

There are two pictures on the wall and the sofa is under them. There's a TV opposite the sofa and there's a plant on the right of the TV. There's a large rug in the middle of the room. The family is in front of the window. The parents are behind the children.

Vocabulary notes

Some students get confused between *opposite* and *in front of*. In latin languages, *in front of* is a false friend as it looks similar to the word for *opposite*.

Opposite has the idea of facing something across a room, a street, etc. *In front of* has the idea of being positioned with your back to something – it's the opposite of *behind*. Draw two heads facing each other on the board, and another two heads, next to each other but facing in the same direction, in order to get across the idea.

10 Students complete the description. Let them compare their answers in pairs.

ANSWERS
1 in the middle	3 on	5 on
2 between	4 under	6 next

Extra activity

Tell students to choose an apartment and write about it. Monitor and check that they are using *there is / are* and prepositions correctly. When students are ready, ask them to read out their description in pairs or small groups.

11 Organise the class into pairs. Ask them to find the pictures of the empty rooms, and draw six items of furniture. You could model the activity on the board first by copying a picture and drawing one or two items of furniture in it.

When students are ready, they take turns to describe their rooms. Their partner must draw what they are describing. At the end, find out who drew pictures accurately.

Extra activity

Do this activity first as a whole-class picture dictation task. Before class, draw the diagram in the activity on a sheet of A3 paper, and add five or six pieces of furniture. In class, draw the diagram in the activity on the board without the furniture. Ask one student to come to the board with a marker pen. Hold up the piece of A3 paper so that the class (but not the student at the board) can see it. The class describe the drawing. The student must draw the items of furniture in the plan on the board.

Writing and speaking

12 Students write their description. Monitor and help with ideas and vocabulary. When they are ready, students exchange their descriptions, then discuss similarities and differences. Put the descriptions on the walls of the classroom so students can walk round and read other students' work.

Extra activity

Students read their partner's description of their room then draw it on a piece of paper. They compare drawings and say how close the drawings are to reality.

Homework

Ask students to write a description of a different room in their house, or the living room in their grandparents' or aunt and uncle's house.

Alternatively, they could write a description of the perfect living room of their dreams.

2c Global objects

Lead-in

Introducing the theme: cars and nationalities

Write the names of some famous car brands on the board, e.g. *Ferrari, Mercedes, Fiat, Rolls Royce, Renault, Ford.*

Ask students to say where these cars are from, and what they know about them. Elicit adjectives to describe the cars (*fast, beautiful, expensive, cheap, popular*).

Answers: Ferrari (Italy), Mercedes (Germany), Fiat (Italy), Rolls Royce (UK), Renault (France), Ford (US)

Reading

1 Ask students to look at the picture. Discuss the questions as a class.

2 Ask students to read the article and choose the correct answers. Let them compare their answers in pairs.

ANSWERS
1 A	2 C	3 B

Critical thinking close reading

3 Explain that close reading means reading a part of the text very carefully to find a very specific piece of information. Give students a moment to read through the sentences and answers. Then look at sentence 1, and ask students where in the text they can find the answer. Ask students to read the text closely to find the other answers. Let them compare their answers in pairs.

ANSWERS
1 A
2 A (Japanese engine)
3 A
4 C (parts are from Brazil but it doesn't say that the car is famous there)
5 A
6 B (they are made in Britain by an American company)
7 B (the glass is French but the factory is Belgian)
8 A

Background notes

The Mini is a small economy car first manufactured in 1959 by BMC (the British Motor Corporation). It became a design icon and was manufactured in Britain and in other countries all over the world (including Australia, Belgium, Spain, South Africa, Uruguay and Venezuela!). It appeared in the classic 1969 movie *The Italian Job*. BMW took over the production of the Mini from 2000. It is assembled at the large Cowley plant in east Oxford. The BMW Mini retains the look of the original car but is technically completely different.

Vocabulary countries and nationalities

4 Ask students to look at the article and find countries to complete the table.

Let them compare their answers with a partner before discussing as a class. In feedback, elicit the different suffixes (-*(i)an*, -*ese*, -*ish*) used in words for nationalities. Read through the *Wordbuilding* box with the class, and elicit other examples from the students. Refer students to page 19 of the Workbook for further information and practice.

ANSWERS

1 Britain	5 Canadian	9 Brazilian
2 German	6 Italian	10 England
3 Austrian	7 Japanese	11 Spanish
4 the Netherlands	8 Belgium	12 France

Background notes

The Netherlands is often also referred to as Holland in English. (Great) Britain is comprised of three countries: England (English), Scotland (Scottish) and Wales (Welsh).

Pronunciation word stress

5a [1.16] Play the recording. Students listen and underline the main stress.

Audioscript and key [1.16]

1 Britain	British
2 Germany	German
3 Austria	Austrian
4 The Netherlands	Dutch
5 Canada	Canadian
6 Italy	Italian
7 Japan	Japanese
8 Belgium	Belgian
9 Brazil	Brazilian
10 England	English
11 Spain	Spanish
12 France	French

5b [1.16] Play the recording again. Students listen and repeat.

Pronunciation notes

Note that when nationalities end with -*ian*, the stress tends to be on the syllable before the suffix. When nationalities end with -*ese*, the suffix tends to be stressed.

6 Ask students to answer the questions in pairs.

ANSWERS

1 Asia, Europe, the Americas (north and south)
2 Students' own ideas.

Speaking

7 Model the activity first, e.g. *My shoes are Italian, my car is from France*. Organise the class into pairs. Students take turns to tell each other about their objects.

2d At the shop

Lead-in

Using words: shops
Draw two horizontal lines on the board to signify a street, and write HIGH STREET between the lines. Ask students: *What type of shops do you find in a High Street?* Elicit some of the following and write them on the board: *clothes shop, shoe shop, chemist, supermarket, coffee shop, greengrocer,* etc.

Ask: *What do you buy in each shop? What do you say when you are in a shop?*

Real life shopping

1 Ask students to look at the picture. Discuss the question as a class and elicit any useful vocabulary.

2 [1.17] Check that students understand how to say the prices in the task (€21.00 = *twenty-one euros*; $19.35 = *nineteen dollars thirty-five*; £3.50 = *three pounds fifty*).

Play the recording. Students listen and match the conversation to the item and price. Let students check their answers in pairs.

```
ANSWERS
Conversation 1  coffee     £3.50
Conversation 2  bags       $19.35
Conversation 3  football    €21.00
Conversation 2 is shown in the photo.
```

Audioscript [1.17]

Conversation 1

A: Hello, can I help you?

B: Yes, I'd like a coffee, please.

A: Large or small?

B: A large one, please.

A: That's three pounds fifty.

Conversation 2

A: Hello. Can I help you?

B: Yes. These bags are nice but they're very small. Are there different sizes?

A: Yes, there are. … These ones are large.

B: Right. Is there a medium size?

A: No. Only two sizes.

B: OK. And are there other colours?

A: Yes, these ones are red.

B: Oh yes, those are nice! How much are they?

A: They're nineteen dollars thirty-five cents.

Conversation 3

A: Hello, can I help you?

B: Hello, I'd like a ball, please.

A: A football? A tennis ball?

B: Sorry, a football.

A: Well, the footballs are here.

B: Are they all black and white?

A: Err, no. There are also ones for different football teams. So this one is red and blue for Barcelona.

B: Is there a red one for Manchester United?

A: No, there isn't … sorry.

B: Oh. OK, that one, please.

A: This one?

B: Yes, please. How much is it?

A: It's twenty one euros.

3 [1.17] Give students a moment to read through the sentences. Explain the difference between *small*, *medium* and *large*.

Ask students to work in pairs to decide who says which phrase. Play the recording again. Students listen and choose, then listen again and check their answers. Let students compare their answers in pairs before discussing as a class.

```
ANSWERS
Can I help you? S
I'd like a coffee, please. C
Large or small? S
A large one, please. C
These ones are large. S
Is there a medium size? C
Are there other colours? C
These ones are red. S
Those are nice! C
How much are they? C
Are they all black and white? C
This one is red and blue. S
OK, that one, please. C
How much is it? C
```

4 Organise the class into pairs. Tell them to prepare a conversation from the prompts. Do the first sentence as an example, and monitor and help students with the activity.

When students are ready, ask them to practise reading out the conversation in pairs. Monitor carefully and make sure they are attempting a good intonation pattern.

```
ANSWERS
S: Hello. Can I help you?
C: Yes, I'd like a T-shirt, please.
S: Large or medium?
C: Medium. Are there other colours?
S: These ones are green and blue.
C: How much are they?
S: They're $7.50.
```

Extra activity

Ask students to improvise similar conversations with different objects: a bag, a ball, a shirt, etc.

Word focus *one / ones*

5 Ask students to underline *one* or *ones* in the expressions in Exercise 3, then complete the sentences 1–4. Let students compare their answers in pairs before discussing as a class.

ANSWERS

A large <u>one</u>, please.   This <u>one</u> is red and blue.

These <u>ones</u> are large.   OK, that <u>one</u>, please.

These <u>ones</u> are red.

1 one   2 ones   3 one   4 ones

Grammar notes

One is a pronoun used to refer to something when that type of thing has already been mentioned or when it is obvious what you are talking about. The plural is *ones*. It is often used with demonstrative adjectives (*this one, that one*, etc.).

Pronunciation *contrastive stress*

6 💿 [1.18] Play the recording. Students listen and note the stress, then listen again and repeat.

Audioscript 💿 [1.18]

3 <u>This</u> ball is <u>nice</u> but <u>that</u> one is <u>horrible</u>!

4 <u>These</u> gloves are <u>small</u> but <u>those</u> ones are <u>large</u>.

Extra activity

Write the following words on the board and ask students to prepare and practise saying sentences with them, using *one* and *this, that, these, those*.

book / interesting // terrible   *cars / fast // slow*

T-shirt / comfortable // uncomfortable

songs / boring // great

7 Organise the class into pairs to act out the situations. Ask students to decide who is A, and who is B, then to look at their roles on pages 154 and 155. Tell them to think about which phrases to use in the conversation.

When students are ready, tell them to practise the conversation, then change roles.

Extra activity

Alternatively, make this a whole-class fun activity. Students in pairs will roleplay running a market stall. They must write a list of products to sell, with prices.

Ask one student from each pair to walk round the class, visiting different 'stalls'. The other student remains at their stall and explains the products and prices to customers.

2e For sale

Lead-in

Using words: adjectives

Write the following sentence on the board:

In the classroom, there are some desks and some students.

Divide the class into two teams. Team A must add one adjective to one of the nouns in the sentence, e.g. *In the classroom, there are some large desks and some students.*

Then Team B must add another adjective. Team A add another. And so on until one team can't think of another adjective. Write words up as students give them to you. After a while, the sentence will look something like:

In the cold, white, modern, Spanish classroom, there are some large, white desks and some friendly, young, Spanish students.

Writing *adverts*

1 Ask students to look at the adverts. Discuss the question as a class. Follow up by asking: *Where do you see these ads?* (in newspapers or online) *Do you buy things from ads in newspapers or on websites? Why? Why not?*

ANSWERS

A computer desk and chair; a car (a 1965 British Mini); a rucksack

---

Vocabulary notes

Adverts or *ads* are short for 'advertisements'. You may need to check these words and *for sale* (= you can buy it) in feedback to Exercise 1.

Vocabulary *adjectives*

2 Ask students to find the opposites in the adverts. Do the first word as an example. Let students compare their answers in pairs.

ANSWERS

1 modern, new   4 fast

2 good   5 large

3 useful   6 cheap

Pronunciation notes

Note the stress: <u>mod</u>ern, <u>use</u>ful, ex<u>pen</u>sive

Writing skill *describing objects with adjectives*

3 Students read the example and rewrite the sentences. Let them compare their answers in pairs before discussing as a class.

ANSWERS

1 It's an old car.
2 They're modern computers.
3 It's a brown sofa.
4 They're fast roller blades.

4 Ask students to complete the table. Tell them to find the adjectives in the text. Let them compare their answers with a partner before discussing as a class.

ANSWERS

Opinion	Size	Age	Colour	Nationality	Noun
useful		modern	white		desk
			red, white, blue	British	Mini
fast		new			engine
	large		green		rucksack

Grammar notes

When we place adjectives before a noun, they tend to go in the order shown in the table. Other categories include shape, which goes after size (e.g. *a big, round table*), and material, which goes after colour (e.g. *a green plastic bottle*).

Adjectives are separated by a comma when there is more than one.

5 Students write the adjectives in order. Do the first as an example. Let them compare their answers in pairs.

ANSWERS

1 It's a fast, new, Japanese motorbike.
2 They're lovely, red gloves.
3 There are two beautiful, old, Italian chairs for sale.
4 A nice, small, grey computer desk for sale.
5 A large, modern, white house.

Extra activity

Organise students into pairs and ask them to write sentences to describe three objects in the classroom.

6 Ask students to think of an object in their home to describe. Elicit ideas from the students. Once students have decided on an object, ask them to write an advert. Monitor and help with language and ideas.

7 Put the adverts on the walls. Students walk round and read them. Ask students to note any adjectives that they think are in the wrong order. In feedback, ask for any corrections.

Homework

For homework, ask students to find online ads in English for something they are interested in (cars, mobile phones, cameras).

Tell them to note the adjectives used to describe the item then write their own ad using the words.

2f Coober Pedy's opals

Before you watch

1 Ask students to look at the photo and read the caption. Pre-teach *precious stone* and elicit the answer to the question.

ANSWERS

green, blue, yellow and red

2 Ask students to work in pairs, and answer the questions.

While you watch

3 Students watch the video and check their answers.

ANSWERS

1 Y   2 Y   3 Y

4 Ask students to number the things in the order they seem them while they watch the video.

ANSWERS

1 c   2 b   3 d   4 a   5 e

5 Students watch the video again. Tell them to choose the correct word to complete the sentences.

ANSWERS

1 southern	4 Red	7 always
2 under	5 tunnels	8 don't find opals
3 opals	6 a house	

6 Ask students to watch the video again. Tell them to complete the sentences from the video with the words.

ANSWERS

1 45	3 3,000	5 95
2 90	4 300,000	6 millions

After you watch

7 Organise the class into pairs. Ask students to prepare their roles, then act out the conversation. You could get some pairs to come to the front of the class to act out their roleplays.

8 Ask students to match the words to the photos.

ANSWERS

1 oil	3 diamonds	5 gas
2 gold	4 coal	

9 Students discuss the questions in groups.

Videoscript

00.02 This is southern Australia. It's very hot here.

In the summer, the temperature is over 45 degrees.

But under the ground, there is something very special.

In every hour of every day, there are people down here.

Why are they here? For one thing. For opals.

00.37 About 90 per cent of the world's opals are from Australia.

Peter Rowe is an Australian opal miner. His dream is a big, beautiful opal.

A lot of the miners live in the town of Coober Pedy. In Australia, Coober Pedy is famous for its opals. About 3,000 people live here and they all want to find opals. Opals like these.

These opals are worth about 300,000 dollars, maybe more.

01.36 The colour of the opal is very important.

These are green, blue, yellow and red. Red opals are very expensive.

But 95 per cent of opals have no colour. And these are worthless.

There were no expensive opals in these tunnels under Coober Pedy.

02.02 Afterwards, people use the tunnels for other things.

This family's home is in a tunnel.

So why do people like Peter Rowe work here?

Because they always believe they are near opals in the ground and that these opals are worth millions of dollars.

But after another day under the ground, these miners found nothing – again.

UNIT 2 Review

Grammar

1 Ask students to write the singular form of the nouns.

ANSWERS			
2 shelf	4 woman	6 child	8 shoe
3 family	5 knife	7 boot	

2 Ask students to complete the questions with *this*, *that*, *these* or *those*.

ANSWERS			
1 that	2 this	3 those	4 these

3 Ask students to read the description of the photo and choose the correct options.

ANSWERS	
1 is	5 in front of
2 are some	6 on
3 isn't	7 between
4 aren't any	8 behind

Vocabulary

4 Students delete the word that does not belong in each category.

ANSWERS		
2 map	4 hat	6 France
3 Dutch	5 blinds	7 age

5 Ask students to complete the sentences with a word from Exercise 4.

ANSWERS		
2 desk	4 roller blades	6 Brazilian
3 Austria / France	5 rug	7 slow

6 Ask students to write their own sentences using seven words from Exercise 4.

Real life

7 Ask students to match the questions to the responses.

ANSWERS					
1 c	2 a	3 e	4 f	5 d	6 b

8 Ask students to roleplay a conversation in a shop, using an object from page 22.

9 Students work in pairs to describe objects in their home.

Unit 3 Places

Lead-in

Test before you teach: times
Write the following digital times on the board: *7.00, 11.30, 4.15, 8.40*. Ask students in pairs to think of ways of saying the times. In feedback, elicit suggestions and find out how well students can use times.

1 Ask students to look at the photo. Ask the questions and elicit responses. Students will check their answers in Exercise 2.

2 🔘 [1.19] Ask students to read through the questions and predict what's in the listening. Check the words for the seasons. Then play the recording. Ask students to listen and answer the questions. Let students compare their answers in pairs.

ANSWERS
1 It's 12 o'clock at night (midnight).
2 The Midnight Sun Restaurant in the north of Norway.
3 The food is great.
4 Summer
5 Twenty-four hours

Audioscript 🔘 [1.19]

It's twelve o'clock at night and I'm in the Midnight Sun Restaurant in the north of Norway. It's very busy and very popular with Norwegians and tourists because the food is great here. It's called the Midnight Sun Restaurant because in the summer in Norway, the sun is always in the sky. There's light for twenty-four hours a day and so this restaurant is open all day and all night.

3 🔘 [1.20] Students complete the times. Then play the recording again. Students listen and check. Play the recording again for students to repeat the times.

Audioscript and key 🔘 [1.20]

1 It's six **o'clock.**
2 It's **half** past three.
3 It's twenty-five **past** nine.
4 It's quarter **to** four.
5 It's three **minutes** past two.
6 It's two minutes to **twelve**.

Vocabulary notes

Note that we always say *It's half past three* but we can say either *It's a quarter past three* or *It's quarter past three.*
Midnight is 12 o'clock at night. *Midday* or *noon* is 12 o'clock in the middle of the day.

4 Students work in pairs to ask and answer questions. Elicit feedback from the whole class.

3a No-car zones

Lead-in

Using words: describing cities
Write the names of the four cities that feature in this section on the board: *London, Tokyo, Bogotá, Melbourne.*

Ask students in pairs to think of 'facts' and 'opinions' about some or all of the cities, e.g. *London is the capital of the UK* (fact); *It's a very exciting city* (opinion).

After one minute, match each pair with another pair and ask them to share ideas. Then take feedback on the ideas from the class. You could build up a list of facts and opinions about the cities on the board.

Reading

1 Ask students to look at the photos. Ask: *What can you see?* Elicit ideas and vocabulary. Ask students to read the article and match the cities to the photos.

ANSWERS
1 Melbourne   3 Tokyo
2 London   4 Bogotá

2 Students read the article again and answer the questions. Let them compare their answers in pairs before discussing as a class.

ANSWERS
1 pollution
2 because of the traffic
3 eight million
4 parks
5 the no-car zones
6 half a million
7 There are lots of great shops and no cars.
8 in the cafés

Background notes

London is the capital of the UK, and Tokyo is the capital of Japan. Bogotá is the capital of Colombia in South America. Melbourne is Australia's second-largest city. It's on the southern coast of the country.

Vocabulary adjectives about cities

3 Ask students to underline the adjectives in the text. Let students compare their answers in pairs. Then ask students to work in pairs to match the adjectives to the definitions and opposites.

ANSWERS
1 free   5 great   9 expensive
2 crowded   6 noisy   10 small
3 polluted   7 beautiful   11 modern
4 popular   8 clean

Pronunciation notes

Point out the strong stress in these words: _crowded_, _polluted_, _popular_, _noisy_, _beautiful_, _expensive_

Extra activity

Before doing Exercise 4, brainstorm parts of your city, or cities in general, that could be described with the adjectives, e.g. the shopping centre, the old / historic district, the river, the park. That way, when they come to describe the city, they have specific places to describe.

4 Organise the class into pairs. Ask students in their pairs to decide on a city that they both know about. Then give them two minutes to think of how to describe the city and the different places in it, using the adjectives provided. In feedback, ask a few pairs to describe cities to the class.

Extra activity

Write some well-known international places on the board that your students might know, e.g. Trafalgar Square (London), Montmartre (Paris), Fifth Avenue (New York).

Ask students in pairs to choose one of these places and think of adjectives to describe them.

Grammar present simple (_I / you / we / they_)

5 Ask students to look at the sentences and discuss the questions as a class. Read the grammar box with the students. Refer students to the information and practice on page 159.

> **ANSWERS**
> The main verb is _have_ (used with _I, you, we_ and _they_).
> We add _don't_ (the auxiliary verb _do + not_ or _n't_) to make the verb negative.

Grammar note

With _I, you, we_ and _they_, the verb in the present simple is identical in form to the infinitive.

6 Ask students to prepare true sentences. Then ask them to work in pairs to compare their sentences. In feedback, ask students to tell the class about things they have in common with their partner. Encourage them to use _we_.

7 Ask students to prepare true sentences about their city. Start them off by referring to the example or by eliciting one or two sentences beginning _Most people_ .... Elicit sentences from the students.

Extra activity

When students have prepared sentences, have a class discussion. Ask for sentences from students and ask the rest of the class for their opinions. If your students are all from the same city, this will lead to a discussion about whether they agree or not. If students are from different places, this will lead to a discussion about whether life in their cities is similar or not.

Listening

8 🎧 [1.21] Lead in by asking: _What is life like in London?_ Elicit ideas from students. Refer them to their 'facts' and 'opinions' if students did the suggested lead-in at the start of this section. They can also refer back to the information in the article in Exercise 2.

Ask students to read the information on the notepad and predict what the student will talk about.

Play the recording. Students listen and complete the notes.

> **ANSWERS**
> 1 expensive   4 popular
> 2 free   5 crowded
> 3 great   6 quiet

Audioscript 🎧 [1.21]

A = journalist, B = student

A: Do you have a car in London?

B: No, I don't. I go everywhere by bicycle.

A: Really? Where do you live?

B: In the city centre.

A: Is it expensive?

B: Yes, it is. Well, the shops are expensive, but there are lots of free places like art galleries and museums.

A: Sounds great. Do you like art?

B: Yes, I do. And I like the theatre. This city has great theatres!

A: I'm sure. And what do you do?

B: I'm a student at university and I work in a restaurant at lunchtimes. It's popular with tourists so it's crowded every day.

A: So you're very busy! What time do you finish work?

B: At about three o'clock. After work I go home or in the summer, I go to the parks. I really like the parks in London. They're beautiful and quiet. I often meet friends there.

9 🎧 [1.21] Ask students to look through the questions and answers first, and see if they can match any from memory. Play the recording again. Students listen and match questions to answers.

> **ANSWERS**
> 1 b   2 e   3 d   4 a   5 c

Extra activity

Ask students to prepare true answers for the questions in Exercise 9. Tell them to interview a partner, asking and answering the questions.

Grammar present simple questions

10 Ask students to look at the questions from the interview, and answer the grammar questions. Let them discuss ideas in pairs. Read the grammar box with the students and refer them to the information and practice on pages 159 and 160.

> **ANSWERS**
> 1 1 have 2 live 3 like 4 do 5 finish
> 2 do (the auxiliary verb)
> 3 1 and 3

Grammar notes

We use *do* + the infinitive form of the main verb in questions. Note the form:

auxiliary verb + subject + main verb

| *Do* | *you* | *like* | *shopping?* |

11 Ask students to complete the questions. Let students compare their answers in pairs.

> **ANSWERS**
> 1 What do you do?
> 2 Where do you live?
> 3 Do you like shopping?
> 4 What time do you finish work?
> 5 Do you have a car?
> 6 Do you eat in cafés at lunchtime?
> 7 What time do you eat dinner?
> 8 Do you meet friends after work?

Speaking

12 Organise the class into pairs to ask and answer the questions from Exercise 11. Model the activity first by asking one or two questions in open class.

Extra activity

Make this a mingle. Ask students to stand up, walk round, and meet different students. They must ask three questions of each student they 'meet' before moving on to another student. In feedback, find out what they discovered about their classmates.

Homework

Ask students to write a blog based on the answers to the questions in Exercise 11.

3b Working under the sea

Lead-in

Introducing the theme and using words: jobs and work
Write the first five letters of the alphabet on the board (A, B, C, D, E) and ask students to give you a job for each letter (e.g. *artist, baker, chemist, doctor, engineer*). Then divide the class into groups of three or four. Tell them to continue thinking of jobs for each letter of the alphabet. In feedback, find out which letters they couldn't think of a job for.

Vocabulary places of work

1 Ask students to match the jobs to the places of work. Let students compare their answers in pairs.

> **ANSWERS**
> 1 an accountant   5 a doctor
> 2 a sailor   6 a waiter
> 3 a photographer   7 a teacher
> 4 a pilot   8 a student

Extra activity

Ask students to give you other jobs in each of the places, e.g. *nurse* (hospital), *cook* (restaurant), *artist* (studio), *secretary* (office).

2 Lead in by telling students about your job, e.g. *I'm a teacher. I work in a school / classroom.* Elicit the jobs of students in your class – help them to think of how to say the jobs in a simple way.

Students take turns to tell their partner about their job.

Listening

3 Discuss the questions about Beverley Goodman as a class.

> **ANSWER**
> She is a marine archaeologist and works on a ship.

Background notes

Dr Goodman is American but lives in Israel. She describes herself as a geoarchaeologist and explores the effects of ancient events such as tsunamis on the seabed.

4 🔊 [1.22] Give students a moment to read through the questions and predict what the answers might be.

Play the recording. Students listen and number the questions in the correct order.

> **ANSWERS**
> 1 c   2 b   3 e   4 a   5 d

Audioscript 🎧 [1.22]

I = interviewer, **B** = Beverly Goodman

I: Today I'm with Beverley Goodman. Beverley, what do you do exactly?

B: I'm a marine archaeologist. I work for *National Geographic* and I study places under the sea.

I: Where do you work? In an office?

B: I have one but I don't work in an office very often. I'm usually on a boat or under the sea.

I: What time do you start work?

B: Well, it depends. On the boat, I get up at just after five o'clock. I work with a team of other marine biologists and I meet everyone for breakfast at about seven. During breakfast we talk about the day. After breakfast, I start work. It's a long day.

I: Do you work late?

B: On the boats, yes, but I don't finish late when I'm at home.

I: Do you have a family?

B: Yes, I live with my husband and my two children. Sometimes my children go to work with me. They love the boats!

5 🎧 [1.22] Play the recording again. Students listen and choose the correct words. Let them compare their answers in pairs before discussing as a class.

> **ANSWERS**
> 1 under the sea   5 start
> 2 don't work   6 don't finish
> 3 five   7 two children
> 4 seven

Extra activity

Divide the class into A and B pairs. Tell student Bs to close their books. Student As ask the questions in Exercise 4 in the correct order. Student Bs remember and improvise Beverley's answers.

Word focus *work*

6 Ask students to complete the sentences. In feedback, check when *for* and *with* are used (see below).

> **ANSWERS**
> 1 for
> 2 with

Vocabulary notes

work for + a company or an employer (a person who gives you a job and pays you)

work with + people (colleagues)

7 Students write their own personalised sentences then read them to their partner. Ask a few questions in open class: *Who do you work for? Who do you work with?*

Grammar present simple (*he / she / it*)

8 Ask students to read the text quickly, and ask one or two focus questions to check understanding, e.g. *Where does Beverley work? How many children does she have?*

Students underline the verbs. Let them check answers and discuss the questions in pairs. Read the grammar box with the students. Refer students to the information and practice on page 160.

> **ANSWERS**
> Verbs: *is, studies, has, doesn't work, 's, gets up, meets, starts, finishes, doesn't finish, lives, go, love*
> 1 You add *-s* or *-es*
> 2 doesn't

Grammar notes

In the third person (*he, she, it*) forms, we usually add *-s*. After *-s, -z, -ch, -sh* or *-x*, we add *-es* (*washes, watches*, etc.). *Go* and *do* also add *-es*. If a verb ends with a consonant + *-y* the *-y* changes to *-i* before adding *-es*.

Note that the auxiliary verb *doesn't* takes the third person ending (*-es*), so the main verb does not take an ending. Watch out for errors such as *He don't works* … and *He doesn't works*.

9 Ask students to complete the text. Let them compare their answers in pairs before discussing as a class.

> **ANSWERS**
> 1 comes   5 prefers
> 2 studies   6 doesn't have
> 3 speaks   7 travels
> 4 has   8 doesn't get

Extra activity

Ask students to imagine that they are James and to rewrite the text using *I*. In feedback, ask students what they notice about the auxiliary verbs and verb endings.

Pronunciation *-s* endings

10 🎧 [1.23] Play the recording. Students listen and write the phonemic symbol next to each verb to show the sound they hear. Do the first three as an example. Let students compare their answers in pairs before discussing as a class. Make sure you drill the words for pronunciation or play the recording again so that students can listen and repeat.

> **ANSWERS**
> 4 /ɪz/   7 /s/   10 /ɪz/
> 5 /s/   8 /z/   11 /z/
> 6 /s/   9 /s/   12 /z/

Pronunciation notes

We use /s/ after verbs that end with unvoiced consonants (e.g. *p, f, t, k, th*), and /z/ after verbs that end with voiced consonants (e.g. *b, v, d, g, l*) and vowels (that are always voiced).

We only use /ɪz/ after *-sh, -ch, -s, -z* and *-x.*

11 🔊 [1.24] Ask students to match the questions to the answers. Do the first as an example. Play the recording so that students can listen and check. Read the grammar box with the students. Refer students to the information and practice on page 160.

ANSWERS				
1 d	2 e	3 c	4 a	5 b

Audioscript 🔊 [1.24]

1 What does Beverley do?
  She's a marine archaeologist.
2 Where does James come from?
  England.
3 When does Beverley start work?
  After breakfast.
4 Does James have an office?
  Yes, he does.
5 Does Beverley finish work early?
  No, she doesn't.

Grammar notes

In the third person (*he, she, it*) forms, we make questions with *does* and the infinitive of the main verb. Note the sentence order:

Question word	auxiliary verb	subject	main verb
What	*does*	*she*	*do?*

In short answers, we use the auxiliary verb, e.g. *Yes, she does* NOT *Yes, she lives.*

Extra activity

Divide the class into an equal number of A pairs and B pairs. Ask A pairs to look back at the text about Beverley and make as many *Does she … ?* questions as they can. Ask B pairs to look back at the the text about James and prepare *Does he … ?* questions.

Mix the pairs. Students take turns to ask and answer questions about the texts.

Speaking

12 Start the activity by asking students to look at the picture. Ask: *What's his name? What does he do? Where does he work?* Elicit ideas.

Divide the class into pairs. Students decide who is A and who is B then read their information on pages 153 and 154 in the Student's Book.

Tell students to prepare their questions then take turns asking and answering questions to complete the fact files.

ANSWERS

Student A

1 Who does he work for?
2 Where does he work?
3 Does he speak English?
4 What time does he start work?

Fact file

1 *National Geographic Magazine*
2 all over the world
3 English
4 nine o'clock

Student B

1 What does he do?
2 Where does he live?
3 Does he have children?
4 What time does he finish work?

Fact file

1 photographer
2 Lincoln Nebraska
3 He has three children.
4 six o'clock

Extra activity 1

Ask students to complete their own personal fact file using the headings in Joel's. Organise the class into pairs then ask each pair to exchange their fact files with another pair. In their pairs, students ask and answer questions about the information on their classmates in the fact files.

Homework

Ask students to write a fact file about a famous person or an interesting person in their family. In the next lesson, students ask and answer questions to find out about the information in the fact files.

3c Places and languages

Lead-in

Using words: numbers

Practise numbers by playing *buzz*. Students count round the class but they cannot say *three* or *five* or multiples of three or five. Instead, they must say *buzz*. So, the first student says *one*, the second student says *two*, but the third student must say *buzz*. The fourth student says *four*, but the fifth and sixth students must both say *buzz*. The seventh student says *seven*. Then *eight*. Then the ninth and tenth students must both say *buzz*. The eleventh student says *one* and the count starts again. If a student makes a mistake, he or she is 'out'. Continue the game until there is a winner or the students get so good that they stop making mistakes.

Reading and vocabulary

1 Discuss the questions as a class. Encourage students who speak more than one language to share their experiences with the class.

2 Ask students to read the article and choose the correct answer. Let them compare their answers in pairs.

ANSWER
a

3 Ask students to read the article again and find what the numbers refer to. Do the first as an example. Let them compare their answers in pairs.

ANSWERS

2 languages
3 speakers of Mandarin Chinese; people who speak English for doing business, reading the news or studying science and medicine
4 native English speakers
5 Spanish speakers
6 different languages in London
7 of the world's population speak Chinese, Hindi, Spanish and English
8 different islands in Vanuatu
9 different languages in Vanuatu
10 speaker of Amurdag

4 Students match the words to the definitions. Encourage students to guess the meaning from the context in the article. Read through the information in the *Wordbuilding* box with the class. Refer students to page 27 in the Workbook for further information and practice.

ANSWERS	
1 second	3 official
2 first	4 ancient

5 Ask the questions in open class and encourage a class discussion.

Critical thinking relevance

6 Read through the sentences with the class then ask students to look back at the text and decide which sentence goes at the end of which paragraph. Let students compare their answers in pairs.

ANSWERS	
Paragraph 1: d	Paragraph 3: b
Paragraph 2: a	Paragraph 4: c

Extra activity

In feedback, ask what helped students find the answers. For example, c is talking about the last speaker of a language (Charlie Muldunga), and in d, the word *Spanish* must refer to the paragraph which is about Spanish-speaking countries.

Vocabulary cardinal and ordinal numbers

7 Ask students to look at the examples and answer the questions. Let them compare their answers with a partner before discussing as a class.

ANSWERS	
1 the order	2 how many

8 Students work in pairs to complete the sequences of numbers.

ANSWERS	
1 5, 9, 11, 13	3 61st, 71st, 81st
2 11, 31, 61	4 1st, 2nd, 4th

Pronunciation saying numbers

9 🔊 [1.25] Play the recording. Students listen and check their answers. Then play the recording again so that students can listen and repeat.

Audioscript 🔊 [1.25]

1 1 3 5 7 9 11 13

2 11 21 31 41 51 61 71

3 21st 31st 41st 51st 61st 71st 81st

4 1st 2nd 3rd 4th 5th 6th 7th

Vocabulary and pronunciation notes

Note that with ordinal numbers, *one* becomes *first*, *two* becomes *second*, *three* becomes *third*, but the other numbers simply add *th* with some slight variations in spelling.

Pronouncing ordinal numbers can be difficult, particularly because of the use of the unvoiced /θ/ sound *th* at the end of many ordinal numbers. If students find this hard, tell them to place a finger in front of their mouth, put their tongue out to touch the finger, then try to say the /θ/ sound.

Extra activity

Write these more demanding number puzzles on the board and ask students to say the missing numbers:

| 3 | 6 | 9 | _ | 15 | 18 |

(12 – add 3 to each number)

| 3 | 6 | 7 | _ | 11 | 14 |

(10 – add 3 then 1, 3 then 1)

| 31st | 28th | 31st | 30th | _ | 30th |

(31st – number of days in each month from January to June)

Speaking

10 Model the activity first, e.g. *My favourite age is 30, because I'm 30 now. My house number is 22.*

Organise the class into pairs. Students take turns to tell each other about their favourite numbers.

Extra activity

Do a number quiz. Read out the following and ask students to write the numbers (add other questions to the list). In feedback, ask for the answers and the correct pronunciation of the numbers.

1 players on a football team (11)
2 seasons (4)
3 months (12)
4 Christmas Day (25th)
5 Olympic silver medallist (2nd)
6 days in a week (7)
7 New Years Day (1st)

3d The city of Atlanta

Lead-in

Using words: places in a city

If your students come from the same city, or are studying in the same city, ask them to make a list of the five most interesting places in the city centre. After one minute, elicit lists from the class and write any interesting words on the board. Agree on a class list of the five most interesting places in the city.

Introducing the theme: Atlanta

Alternatively, if you think your students have enough general knowledge to talk about Atlanta, put them in pairs to think of five things they know about Atlanta. Elicit ideas from the class in feedback (for example, it's a city in the state of Georgia, the 1996 Olympics were in Atlanta, it's the home city of Coca-Cola®).

Vocabulary places in a city

1 Discuss the questions as a class and write any useful vocabulary on the board. Point out the difference between a map (a plan of a city's streets) and a travel guide (a description of interesting places to visit).

2 Ask students to look at the map. Ask: *Which city is it? What places can you see?* Ask students to match places on the map to the activities. Let students check their answers in pairs.

ANSWERS

1 visitors' centre	5 parking
2 Children's Museum	6 library
3 Centennial Park	7 business district and offices
4 theatre	8 aquarium

Background notes

Atlanta is the capital of the state of Georgia which is in the south-eastern US. It has a population of 420,000 people and is a major transport hub. It is economically successful, with major industries in logistics, and professional and business services. It is best-known as the HQ of Coca-Cola® and CNN and as the host city of the 1996 Olympics.

Real life giving directions

3 [1.26] Give students a moment to look at the map and locate the visitors' centre.

Play the recording. Students listen and note the places mentioned. Let students compare their answers in pairs before discussing as a class.

ANSWER

The aquarium, Centennial Olympic Park, World of Coca-Cola®

Audioscript 🎵 [1.26]

T = tourist, G = guide

T: Hello. We'd like to go to the aquarium. Is it near here?

G: It's about fifteen minutes away, but you go past some interesting places on the way. So, look at this map. Go straight up Decatur Street and then up Marietta Street. Go across Spring Street and take the first street on the right. Centennial Olympic Park is on the corner. It's very nice. Go across the park and on the right there's the World of Coca-Cola®.

T: Oh, that sounds interesting.

G: Yes, it is. Go past it and the aquarium is opposite.

T: Great. Thanks a lot.

4 🎵 [1.26] Divide the class into pairs. Ask them to complete the conversation with the expressions. Play the recording again for students to check.

ANSWERS	
1 near here	4 Go across
2 about, away	5 on the right
3 straight up	6 Go past

Grammar notes

Note that we use the imperative (*Go, Take*, etc.) to give directions, along with prepositions of movement (*up, down, along, across, through*, etc.).

Extra activity

Revise prepositions of movement by drawing a line drawing of a street on the board and eliciting *across, down, up* and *along* and showing them with an arrow (we use *up* the High Street when it's going towards the centre, and *down* when it's going away).

5 Organise the class into pairs. Tell them to prepare a conversation using the expressions from the language box. Do one first as an example, and monitor and help students with the activity.

When students are ready, ask them to practise reading out the conversation in pairs. Monitor carefully and make sure they are attempting a good intonation pattern when asking the questions.

Extra activity

Bring in tourist maps of the city you are in. Hand them out in pairs or small groups and ask students to take turns playing the tourist and the local. Tell them to ask for directions from the school or from a well-known place in the centre to different places.

Homework

Ask students to write directions to send by email to a friend, describing how to get from the school to their house.

3e Describing a place

Lead-in

Using words: days, months, seasons and places

Write the following categories on the board: *seasons, months, days, places in a city.*

Ask students in pairs to write four things for each category. Monitor and note whether students are using capital letters appropriately. Find out which pair completes their lists first.

Writing a travel website

1 Discuss the question as a class. Elicit a list of places to find information on the board.

ANSWERS
A possible list: a travel website, a tourist information office or visitors' centre, a travel guide, guidebook or map, friends who have already been to the place, travel blogs.

2 Read through Bella's checklist with students and ask focus questions, e.g. *What are good places to visit in a city? What are good ways to travel around a city?* Elicit ideas.

Ask students to read the text and tick the items she describes.

ANSWER
Bella mentions 1, 2, 3 and 4.

Extra activity

Ask students to find two famous places, two types of building, two seasons, two months, one time of day and one sport in the text.

Writing skill capital letters

3a Students read the website again and find the item that is not written with a capital letter. Let them compare their answer in pairs before discussing as a class.

ANSWER
6

Grammar notes

In English we always use a capital letter at the start of a sentence. Many proper nouns, notably names of people, cities, countries, states, continents, use capitals.

Although days and months use capitals, seasons and parts of the day don't, e.g. *in March* but *in spring* or *in the afternoon*.

The names of buildings and streets always have capitals, e.g. *The National Theatre, Covent Garden* and *Oxford Road.*

Other situations where capitals are used include titles, e.g. *Sir, Mr, Mrs* and *Ms*, and *Queen Elizabeth*, and the names of companies.

3b Ask students to look at the picture. Ask: *What can you see? Which city is the blog about?* Students read the description quickly to check their prediction.

Ask students to rewrite the description. Let them compare their answers with a partner before discussing as a class.

ANSWER

I'm from Australia and I love Sydney! There are over four million people here but it's never crowded. That's because there's the harbour with the famous Sydney Opera House and there are beautiful beaches. My favourite season is summer because of the surfing. Lots of people go to Bondi Beach but on Saturdays I go with my friends to Narabeen Beach. It's quiet and relaxed. Afterwards we go to the centre of the city. There are over three thousand restaurants with every type of food from Japanese to Lebanese.

Extra activity

Ask students to look at the reading text on page 39 of the Student's Book. Tell them to find five different examples of capital letters and say why they are used in the text.

4 Start by eliciting favourite towns or cities on the board. Ask students why they like the cities they mention. Then brainstorm information students could include in their description. Tell them to look back at the texts about Sydney and Moscow to help.

Build up a list like this one: *location, population, famous buildings and places, places to meet friends, favourite season, favourite month, favourite time of the day, things to do, places to eat.*

Ask students to decide which information they want to include and in what order. Then tell students to write their descriptions.

5 Collect the descriptions and put them on the walls round the class. Ask students to walk round and read each other's descriptions. Tell them to mark any errors with capital letters on the descriptions as they read them.

Extra activity

As students perform this task, walk round yourself and note down any sentences with capital letter errors in them. In feedback, at the end, write three or four sentences on the board for students to correct.

Homework

For homework, ask students to write about their favourite holiday destination or about a place that they often visit.

3f Cowley Road

Before you watch

1 Ask students to look at the photo. Ask: *What city is it? Where is it?* Organise the class into groups of four to discuss the questions.

2 Students prepare questions in pairs. Take feedback from the whole class and write good questions on the board.

While you watch

3 Ask students to watch the video and tick the places.

ANSWERS

1, 2, 4, 5, 6, 8, 10, 11, 13

---

4 Organise the class into pairs to make questions. Play the video again. Students watch and check.

ANSWERS

1 Is there a post office near here?
2 Is there a good place to eat near here?
3 Is there a park round here?
4 How do I get to the supermarket from here?

---

5 Students watch the video again and choose the correct answers to the questions.

ANSWERS

1 c
2 c
3 a
4 c
5 b
6 b, c, e, f
7 b
8 a
9 c
10 a, b, d, f

After you watch

6 Organise the class into pairs. Ask students to decide on their roles and prepare them. When students are ready, tell them to act out the conversation. You could get some pairs to come to the front of the class to act out their roleplays.

7 Ask students to work in pairs to write paragraphs. Pass the paragraphs round the class for students to read and comment on.

Videoscript

The city of Oxford is famous because of its university and its history. But there are other interesting places to visit in Oxford.

For example, the Cowley Road is in East Oxford. It's a busy road with a lot of shops and places to visit.

00.21   There are lots of different communities here, including Asian, Caribbean, Chinese and African.

Is there a post office near here?

00.37   'Yes, there is. If you go to the end of the road and turn left and then cross over the road at the traffic lights, keep going about 50 metres and the post office will just be on your right.'

Is there a good place to eat near here?

01.00   'Yeah, there are some places. I mean, there are some choices, which is … Italian, Turkish, Greek and … burger, pizza places.'

'There are several good places to eat round here. It's a good road for it. There's the Greek place just there. There's the Italian over the road. There is the American-style Atomic Burgers down there, who also have a pizzeria at the other end.'

Is there a park round here?

01.45   'Yes, there is. There's a park just up the road here on Manzil Way. So if you just keep walking straight up here for about five minutes, probably across six or seven streets and then you'll see the park on your left just after the medical centre and it's a park for, well, for pre-schoolers or for older children so there's, you know, swings and slides and roundabouts and a seesaw, that kind of thing.'

How do I get to the supermarket from here?

02.23   'Sure … there are a couple of big supermarkets.

If you just go back up Manzil Way and turn right onto Cowley Road, there's one on the right and then one directly opposite on the left. There are also a number of smaller supermarkets which sell foods from different countries. So there's a Greek supermarket, two Polish supermarkets, a Russian supermarket and there's a fantastic one called the Oriental Store which sells Chinese ingredients and all sorts.

That's … I think it's 188 Cowley Road.'

UNIT 3 Review

Grammar

1   Ask students to complete the sentences with the verbs from the box.

ANSWERS				
1 live	2 eat	3 like	4 work	5 have, go

2   Ask students to complete the conversation with *do* or *don't*.

ANSWERS		
1 do	3 Do	5 don't
2 Do	4 don't	6 don't

3   Ask students to read the sentences and choose the correct option to complete them.

ANSWERS		
1 come	3 speaks	5 doesn't
2 lives	4 don't	6 does

Vocabulary

4   Ask students to say the times.

ANSWERS	
1 five o'clock	4 quarter to twelve
2 quarter past seven	5 three minutes past three
3 twenty-five past nine	6 four minutes to ten

5   Students match the places to the descriptions.

ANSWERS			
1 restaurant	3 hospital	5 office	7 car park
2 library	4 hotel	6 park	8 museum

6   Ask students to read the article and complete the adjectives.

ANSWERS			
1 big	3 crowded	5 modern	7 clean
2 popular	4 beautiful	6 polluted	8 quiet

Real life

7   Students complete the missing word in each sentence about directions.

ANSWERS		
1 Where	3 away	5 Take
2 near	4 across	6 Turn

Speaking

8   Students work in pairs to describe six things from their normal day, and say when they do them.

Unit 4 Free time

Lead-in

Introducing the theme: free time

Write *Saturday* and *Sunday* on the board and ask students to think of all the things they do on those days and write them down in a list. After two minutes, tell students to compare their list with a partner. They must find three things they both do on Saturdays and three things they both do on Sundays.

1 🎵 [1.27] Ask students to look at the photo. Ask: *What can you see? Where are they?* Elicit responses. Pre-teach *fishing* and *river*.

Play the recording. Students listen and answer the question. In feedback, check students understand *gym*, (e.g. *a place you go to do exercise, use running or cycling machines*, etc.). Ask the class if any of them go to a gym.

> **ANSWER**
> 2

Audioscript 🎵 [1.27]

1 Well, in my free time I go shopping. I go every Saturday with friends and we go to the city centre. It's fun!

2 In my free time, I go fishing with my brother. We get up early in the morning and drive for about two hours. It's quiet and very relaxing.

3 After work I go to the gym. I go about three times a week. After a long day with lots of other people it's nice to go on your own and it's good for you, of course.

2 🎵 [1.27] Ask students to read through the table. Check the meaning of *on my own* (= alone, not with anybody). Then play the recording. Ask students to listen and match the speakers to the information. Let students compare their answers in pairs.

ANSWERS

	Free-time activity?	When?	Who with?	Why?
Person 1	go shopping	every Saturday	friends	It's fun!
Person 2	go fishing	early in the morning	my brother	It's quiet and relaxing.
Person 3	go to the gym	after work	on my own	It's good for you.

3 Students prepare notes about their own free-time activities, using the bullet points as a guide.

Model the activity by telling students about your free-time activity. Make sure you mention when, who with, and why so that students have a clear understanding of what to say. Monitor and help with ideas.

4 Divide the class into groups to talk about their free-time activities. Encourage the other students in the group to ask follow-up questions. Monitor and note errors for an error feedback at the end.

Extra activity

Make this a Q & A mingle. Ask students to look back at the questions in the table in Exercise 2 and expand them:

What's your favourite free-time activity?
When do you do it?
Who do you do it with?
Why do you do it?

Tell students to walk round the class and ask at least three people about their activities.

4a 100% identical?

Lead-in

Test before you teach: *go, do* and *play*

Write *go, do* and *play* on the board and ask students in pairs to think of as many words that collocate (or go) with the adjectives as they can.

Students may come up with sports (*go swimming, running, do aerobics, play tennis*, etc.) or activities (*go shopping, play the piano*) or other phrases (*go home, do homework*, etc.).

In feedback, elicit phrases from students and put any interesting ones on the board.

Reading

1 Ask students to look quickly at the photos. Ask: *What can you see? What is the relationship between the people? What do they do?* Elicit ideas and vocabulary. Check *identical twins* (= brothers or sisters born on the same day who look the same). Ask students to discuss the questions in Exercise 1 in pairs. In feedback, ask any student with an interesting story to tell the class.

2 Ask students to read the article and answer the question.

> ANSWER
> It's about both: their work and their free time.

3 Students read the article again and complete the table. Let them compare their answers in pairs before discussing as a class. Make sure students understand that Bob and Mike do some things together (watch films and play computer games), and some things on their own (Bob goes to the gym) or with friends (Mike goes to the beach).

ANSWERS			
	The Mulgray Twins	**The Kitt Twins**	**The Bryan Twins**
Job?	*writers*	actors and musicians	professional tennis players
Free-time activity?	gardening, walking	Tae Kwon Do, swimming	*Bob goes to the gym.* Mike meets friends at the beach. Bob and Mike both watch films and play computer games.
Who with?	together	together	on their own / with friends / together

Background notes

Bob and Mike Bryan are one of the world's top doubles pairs. They have won four grand slams and the gold medal at the 2012 London Olympics.

Tae Kwon Do is a martial art and an Olympic sport. It originated in Korea.

Extra activity

Ask students to close their books. Then ask questions and ask students to shout out answers.

How old are Morna and Helen? (73)

What do they do at the weekend? (go walking)

What's Camille's sister's name? (Kennerley)

What sport do they both like? (Tae Kwon Do)

What instrument do they play? (the harp)

What do Mike and Bob play in their free time? (computer games)

Who likes going to the gym? (Bob)

Vocabulary free-time activities

4 Ask students to match verbs and nouns. Let students compare their answers in pairs. Tell them to check their answers in the article. Read the *Wordbuilding* box with the class. Refer students to page 35 in the Workbook for further information and practice.

ANSWERS	
1 go walking	5 watch films
2 play a musical instrument	6 play tennis
3 do Tae Kwon Do	7 go to the gym
4 play computer games	8 meet friends

Vocabulary notes

We use *play* with sports that involve a ball (*play tennis, football, golf, basketball*, etc.). We use *go* with an activity that ends with *-ing* (*go swimming, running*, etc.). We use *do* with a martial art and an activity or sport that involves exercise (*do exercise, yoga, aerobics, judo*, etc.).

Extra activity

If students didn't do the lead-in task at the start of this section (or didn't do it very well), ask them to think of as many sports and activities that go with *play, do* and *go* as they can.

5 Organise the class into pairs. Ask students to work together to think of ideas and prepare their questionnaires. Monitor and help with ideas and vocabulary.

6 Ask students to work with a new partner. They take turns to interview one another, using the questions on their questionnaires.

Grammar *like / love + -ing*

7 Ask students to look at the underlined words in the sentences and discuss the questions as a class. Read the grammar box with the students. Refer students to the information and practice on page 160.

ANSWERS	
a 1 and 2	b 3 and 4

Grammar notes

Note that, in English, it is possible to say, for example, *I like dancing* and *I like to dance* with little difference in meaning. We use *-ing* to emphasise the activity and the infinitive to emphasise a specific action. At this level, it is best to just teach the more common use with *-ing*.

Pronunciation /ŋ/

8 🔘 [1.28] Ask students in pairs to say the *-ing* form of the verbs. Play the recording. Students listen and repeat.

Pronunciation notes

The nasal sounds /m/ and /n/ are common in many languages, but the velar nasal /ŋ/ is uncommon, and therefore hard for some students to say. It is produced by blocking the airflow in the vocal tract and redirecting it through the nose.

Speaking

9 Introduce the activity by writing three sentences of your own on the board. Ask students to guess which one is false. Then tell students to write their own sentences. Monitor and check that they are using the *-ing* form correctly.

10 Organise the class into pairs to take turns reading out their sentences and guessing which one is false.

11 Model the activity first by asking one or two questions in open class. Give students a minute or two to prepare questions. Then put them in pairs to interview each other.

Extra activity

Make this a mingle. Ask students to stand up, walk round, and meet different students. They must ask three questions of each student they 'meet' before moving on to another student. In feedback, find out what they discovered about their classmates.

Homework

Ask students to write about their likes and dislikes.

4b Free time at work

Lead-in

Using words

Write the following words on the board: *Arctic, photographer, polar bears, national parks, hobby, summer, nature.*

Check students understand the meaning of the words then ask them to decide how the words might be connected. (All the words are key words from the text about Norbert Rosing.)

Reading

1 Check the meaning of the activities. A good way of doing this is to use a mixture of mime, examples and check questions. Ask students to discuss the questions in pairs.

Extra activity

Ask students to take turns miming the activities in Exercise 1. Their partner must guess which activity they are miming.

2 Ask students to look at the photos. Ask: *What can you see? What's his job? What type of photographs does he take?* Ask students to discuss the questions about Norbert Rosing in pairs (note that there are no correct answers, these are questions for discussion).

3 Students read the text and answer the questions. Let them compare their answers in pairs.

ANSWERS			
1 Yes		4 No	
2 No		5 Yes	
3 Don't know		6 No	

Extra activity

Read out the definitions below and ask students to give you a word from the text with the same meaning (answers in brackets):

An activity you do in your free time (hobby)

A place where there are trees and animals (a national park)

A verb that describes what the sun does when it is bright (shines)

A large white animal (polar bear)

Background notes

Norbert Rosing was born in 1953 and is a renowned wildlife photographer who has published many books. Many of his photos are taken in the national parks of Germany and North America.

Grammar adverbs of frequency

4 Students look at the examples and discuss the questions in pairs. Read the grammar box with the students. Refer students to the information and practice on pages 160–161.

> ANSWERS
> 1 after
> 2 before
> 3 1 usually   2 often   3 sometimes   4 not often

Grammar notes

Frequency adverbs go before full verbs but they go after the verb *be* and after auxiliary verbs, e.g. *I often go ...* but *I am often ...* , *I don't often go ...* , *I have often seen ...*

5 Give students two or three of your own examples to get them started. Then ask them to put adverbs of frequency in the sentences. Ask students to compare their sentences in pairs before discussing as a class.

Extra activity

Ask students to add frequency adverbs to the sentences below, then discuss them:

I get up early at the weekend.

I go swimming in the summer.

I am bored in class.

Ask fast finishers to write and discuss their own sentences.

Listening

6 🎧 [1.29] Give students a moment to read the topics. Then play the recording. Students listen and number the topics in the correct order. Let students compare their answers in pairs before discussing as a class.

> ANSWERS
> 1 c   2 b   3 a

Audioscript 🎧 [1.29]

I = interviewer, N = Norbert Rosing

I: So Norbert. How often do you go to the Arctic?

N: I go once a year.

I: How long do you spend there?

N: I'm sometimes there for a few weeks and sometimes for a few months.

I: Why do you like the Arctic so much?

N: Because it's one of the last places in the world with no human impact. There aren't many people and no roads …

I: So how do you travel to these places?

N: I usually travel by car to the end of the road and then I go by snow mobile or sometimes by boat. And I walk, of course.

I: I love your photos of polar bears. How often do you see them?

N: Between August and November, you see polar bears every day. Also at this time in the Arctic the sun shines twenty-four hours a day so I can work at night.

I: What do you do in your free time?

N: That's a good question! I go out every night so I always sleep during the day. And I read a book or I often go for a walk. But yes, it's sometimes boring and you need a lot of patience!

7 🎧 [1.29] Play the recording again. Students listen and decide if the sentences are true or false. Let them compare their answers in pairs. Ask students to correct the false sentences.

> ANSWERS
> 1 T   4 F (You see polar bears every day)
> 2 T   5 F (He takes photos at night)
> 3 T   6 F (It's sometimes boring)

8 Discuss the question as a class.

Extra activity

Write the following phrases from the interview on the board and ask students to say what they mean:

no human impact (humans haven't changed the place)

the sun shines twenty-four hours a day (the sun is in the sky all day)

you need a lot of patience (you must wait a lot and not get angry)

Grammar expressions of frequency

9 Ask students to look at the extract. Discuss the question as a class. Read the grammar box with the students. Refer students to the information and practice on page 161.

> ANSWER
> They go at the end of the sentence.

Grammar notes

Expressions of frequency usually go at the end of the sentence. However, it is possible to put the expressions at the start of the sentence, especially when you want to give them emphasis, e.g. *Every Christmas, Jack and Louise come from Australia to visit us.*

Note that in the expressions in Exercise 10, *a* has the same meaning as *per* or *every*.

10 Ask students to rewrite the sentences with frequency adverbs. Let them compare their answers in pairs.

> ANSWERS
> 2 twice a year
> 3 once a day
> 4 once a year / every year
> 5 three times a day
> 6 once a month / every month

Pronunciation linking

11 🎧 [1.30] Ask students to look at the sentences. Ask: *What do the lines show?* (linking between consonants and vowels). Play the recording. Students listen and repeat. Ask them to practise saying the sentences in pairs.

Pronunciation notes

When a word ends with a consonant and the next word starts with a vowel, they 'link'. A way of thinking about it is that the consonant sound leaves the end of its word and joins the start of the next word, e.g. *How often* becomes /haʊ ˈwɒfən/.

Speaking

12 Start the activity by asking students two or three *How often* questions, e.g. *How often do you go to the gym? How often do you work on Saturdays? How often do you visit relatives at the weekend?*

Organise the class into pairs. Tell students to choose a topic and prepare their questions. Monitor and help with ideas and vocabulary.

13 Divide the class into groups of four. Make sure you split up the pairs who prepared questions together. Students take turns asking and answering questions.

Homework

Ask students to write a blog about how often they do things under the heading of one of the topics in Exercise 12.

4c Extreme sports

Lead-in

Using words: sports (on flashcards)

At this level, it is a good idea to bring the lesson off the page, especially when eliciting or introducing new words. Draw ten or more of the sports in Exercise 1 on pieces of A4 paper (ideally backed by a piece of card). Alternatively, find pictures of the sports in magazines or on the Internet and glue them on to card or use them on an interactive whiteboard or on slide presentation software. In class, show the pictures in turn and ask: *What sport is it?* Elicit the sports, say them, and ask students to repeat. By eliciting the sports from flashcards, learning words becomes a whole-class activity, and you get a good opportunity to do some oral repetition work and develop pronunciation.

Vocabulary sports

1 Organise the class into pairs. Ask them to discuss the sports and answer the questions.

> ANSWERS
> 2
> a baseball, basketball, cricket, football, tennis, (ice hockey uses a flat type of ball called a *puck*)
> b sailing, surfing, swimming
> c skiing
> d baseball, basketball, cricket, football, ice hockey
> e baseball, basketball, cricket, football, ice hockey, tennis
> f go cycling, running, sailing, skiing, surfing, swimming (note that we say *do boxing*)
> g boxing – box, cycling – cycle, running – run, sailing – sail, skiing – ski, surfing – surf, swimming – swim

Pronunciation note

The stress in all these sports words is on the first syllable.

Background notes

In American English, the word *football* is used to refer to the American game which involves an oval ball and helmets, so Americans tend to use the word *soccer* for the game known in Europe as *football*.

Reading

2 Ask students to look at the photos. Ask: *What sports are they?* Elicit the names of the sports and check that students are clear about their meanings.

Students discuss the photos in pairs and match them to the adjectives. In feedback, ask students to tell the class which adjectives they used to describe which pictures.

3 Ask students to read the article and match the sentences to the sports. Let them compare their answers in pairs.

ANSWERS

1 A, B, C, D
2 A, D
3 B, C
4 A
5 A, B, C, D

Critical thinking fact or opinion

4 Read through the sentences with the class then ask students to look back at the text and decide whether they are fact or opinion. Let students compare their answers in pairs.

ANSWERS

1 F   2 O   3 F   4 O   5 O   6 F

5 Ask students to find other facts and opinions in the article. Elicit their ideas in feedback.

SAMPLE ANSWERS

Facts: there are lots of facts in the text
Opinion: 'I don't like soccer'; 'I like the adrenaline'; 'it's very peaceful'

Extra activity

Ask students to write two facts and two opinions about a sport that they like doing. Tell them to read out their facts and opinions to a partner. Their partner must say which sentences are facts and which are opinions, and must then guess which sport their partner is describing.

Grammar can / can't

6 Ask students to look at the examples and answer the questions. Let them compare their answers with a partner before discussing as a class. Read the grammar box with the students. Refer students to the information and practice on page 161.

ANSWERS

1 before   3 no
2 no   4 well

Grammar notes

Can is a modal auxiliary verb used here to talk about general abilities. The negative is formed by adding '*t* (an abbreviation of *cannot*), and the question is formed by moving *can* before the subject.

In statements, *can* is weakly stressed and pronounced /kən/. The negative is strongly stressed and pronounced /ka:nt/. In questions and short answers, *can* is strongly stressed and pronounced /kæn/.

Adverbs of manner such as *high* and *well* (the irregular adverb of *good*), and adverbs of degree such as *a bit* and *a lot*, generally go after the verb at the end of the sentence.

7 Students work in pairs to complete the sentences and discuss the question.

ANSWERS

1 can   4 can
2 can   5 can
3 Can, can't   6 can

1, 2, 4 and 6 contain adverbs.

Extra activity

Ask students to practise reading out the sentences in pairs. Pay attention to the weak and strong stresses when pronouncing *can* and *can't*.

Speaking

8 Model the activity first. Ask the questions in the speech bubbles and elicit responses from different students in the class. Then ask students to prepare their own sentences. Organise the class into pairs. Students take turns to ask each other their questions.

Extra activity

Play *Find someone who …* . Elicit ten phrases that students can use in *Can you … ?* questions, and write them on the board, e.g. *play basketball, play tennis, do an extreme sport, cook Italian food, play the guitar, ride a horse,* etc. Encourage students to think of interesting things to ask. Once you have ten, ask students to stand up and walk round the class. They must interview different class members, asking *Can you … ?* questions with the phrases on the board. They must find as many people as they can who say *yes* to the questions.

4d In your gap year

Lead-in

Using words: gap years

Write the following words on the board:
gap year, volunteer, university, a break, travel, a job, enthusiastic

Check the meaning of the words, or ask students to look them up in their dictionaries. Check the pronunciation. Then ask students to say what connects the words, and what they think this section is going to be about.

Reading

1 Ask students to look at the picture. Ask: *What can you see? What is the person's job?*

Ask students to read the website and answer the questions. Let students check their answers in pairs.

> **ANSWERS**
> 1 volunteer jobs for a student's gap year
> 2 helping lions in Zambia; writing for an English-language newspaper in Bolivia; teaching English

2 Discuss the questions as a class.

Background notes

A gap year is a year that people take off work or study to do something interesting, usually involving travelling to distant parts of the world. In the UK, taking a gap year between finishing school at the age of eighteen and starting university is very common. Other people take a gap year after finishing university, before committing to a career. Young people often do voluntary work in the UK or abroad, especially in the developing world. There are a lot of agencies advertising in newspapers or on the web which offer jobs.

Zambia is a country in southern Africa. Bolivia is in South America.

Real life talking about abilities and interests

3 🎧 [1.31] Give students a moment to look at the website and find the number. Ask students how to say it.

Play the recording. Students listen and answer the question. Let students compare their answers in pairs before discussing as a class.

> **ANSWER**
> 1 Help the lions

Audioscript 🎧 [1.31]

T = travel adviser, **S** = student

T: Hello, Gap Year Volunteer Work. Can I help you?

S: Yes, hello. I'd like some information about your gap year jobs. I'm a student and I want to travel next year. Do you have any interesting volunteer jobs?

T: Sure. We have a job for English teachers. Are you good at teaching?

S: Err. I don't know. I can speak English well, but what other jobs are there?

T: Can you write? There's an English newspaper in Bolivia. They need journalists. But it's for eighteen months.

S: No, I can't go for eighteen months. And I'm not very good at writing. Is there anything else?

T: Do you like animals?

S: Yes, I love them.

T: Well, we have a job in Zambia. It's with lion cubs.

S: Wow! That sounds interesting. What's the job exactly?

4 🎧 [1.31] Ask students to read through the expressions. Play the recording again. Students listen and tick the ones they hear.

> **ANSWERS**
> Students should tick:
> Are you good at teaching?
> Do you like animals?
> I can speak English well.
> I can't go for eighteen months.
> I'm (not very) good at writing.
> I love them!

Vocabulary notes

Note that we use *I'm good at* + *-ing* as well as *I can* to talk about abilities.

lion cub = a baby lion (*cub* is also used for the young of other animals, particularly big cats, e.g. *tiger cub, bear cub*)

Pronunciation sentence stress

5 🎧 [1.32] Play the recording. Students listen and pay attention to the stressed words. Play the recording again. Students listen and repeat.

Audioscript 🎧 [1.31]

1 Are you <u>good</u> at <u>writing</u>?
2 I'm <u>good</u> at <u>writing</u>.
3 <u>Can</u> you <u>teach</u>?
4 How <u>well</u> can you <u>teach</u>?
5 I <u>can't</u> speak <u>English</u> very <u>well</u>.
6 Do you <u>like</u> <u>animals</u>?
7 I <u>love</u> <u>animals</u>!

Extra activity

Ask students to find the audioscript of the conversation from Exercise 3 on page 171 of the Student's Book. Ask students to practise saying the conversation in pairs, paying careful attention to the sentence stress.

6 Organise the class into pairs. Ask students to improvise a conversation using the information on the website and the phrases to talk about abilities and interests. With weaker classes, tell them to prepare a conversation first. When students are ready, ask them to practise reading out the conversation in pairs. Monitor carefully and make sure they are attempting good sentence stress.

Homework

Ask students to write a letter to the gap year company asking for one of the jobs. Tell them to write about their abilities and interests.

4e You have an email

Lead-in

Using words: ways of communicating
Write *Talking and writing to people* on the board. Elicit as many different ways of talking and writing as you can and put them on the board. Use mime to elicit suggestions (e.g. hold an imaginary phone to your ear) if students aren't sure what to say. Build up the following list: *by phone, by text, by email, online chat, on a social networking site, with blogs, by letter, postcard, memo.*

Ask students to say which method they use to contact different people in their family, their friends and their colleagues.

Writing short emails

1 Discuss the questions as a class. Elicit ideas.

2 Students read the emails and discuss the question in pairs.

> **ANSWERS**
> 2, 5 and 6 are about work. 1, 3 and 4 are about free time.

Extra activity

Ask: *Who wrote the emails? Who did they write them to? What words told you the email was about work?* (e.g. *receptionist, busy, photocopiers, customers*) *Which words told you the email was about free time?* (e.g. *film, party, eat out*)

Writing skill reference words

3a Students read the emails again and find the answer. Let them compare their answer in pairs before discussing as a class.

> **ANSWER**
> The new Spielberg film

Grammar notes

English uses reference words to replace and refer back to nouns and phrases that have already been used. This avoids repetition. Reference words can be subject or object pronouns (*it, him, they, them*, etc.), possessive adjectives and pronouns (*her, its, their, theirs*, etc.), and other pronouns such as *one* and *here* and *there*.

3b Ask students to look at the emails and find what the pronouns refer to. Let them compare their answers with a partner before discussing as a class.

ANSWERS
2 her = the receptionist
3 it = the party; him = Omar
4 it = sushi; there = to the restaurant on Brooke Street
5 one = the photocopier
6 it = the email from Paris; them = the two customers in Paris

4 Start by doing the first sentences as an example with the class. Ask students to rewrite the rest of the sentences. Let them compare their answers in pairs.

ANSWERS
2 I have your letter. Can you come and get <u>it</u>?
3 Do you like Mexican food? The café downstairs does <u>it</u> at lunchtime.
4 I'm in my office so meet me <u>there</u>.
5 Olav can't finish his work. Can you help <u>him</u>?
6 Matt and Suki are late. Please call <u>them</u>.
7 I like the new nightclub. Can we go <u>there</u>?
8 Can you buy a new computer? This <u>one</u> is very old.

5 Start by brainstorming a few ideas from students about what they could write. Then ask students to write their two emails. Monitor and help with ideas and vocabulary, and make sure students are using at least one reference word.

6 Organise the class into pairs. Students exchange emails and write a reply.

Extra activity

Write the following words on the board: *it, her, one, there*. Challenge fast finishers (or the whole class in pairs) to write one email containing all four reference words.

Homework

Copy the email below on to small pieces of paper and hand them out at the end of the lesson. Ask students to write a reply to the email for homework.

Hi

There's a party on Friday. It's at 8 at Paula's house. Bring her a present. See you there.

Alternatively, you could write the email on the board for students to copy, or, if you have your students' email addresses, you could email it to them.

4f In my free time

Before you watch

1 Ask students to look at the photo. Ask: *What does it show?* Then organise the class into pairs to discuss the photos.

ANSWERS
The photo shows a basketball hoop from an odd angle.
1 By bouncing a ball and throwing it.
2 a ball, a hoop, a court

2 Ask students to match the activities with the pictures.

ANSWERS
1 E   2 B   3 A   4 C   5 D

While you watch

3 Ask students to watch the video, and note the questions. Let them compare answers in pairs.

ANSWERS
1 What do you do in your free time?
2 How often do you do it?
3 Why do you enjoy doing it?

4 Play the video again. Students complete the tables. Let them compare answers in pairs.

ANSWERS
Question 1
Caroline: going to concerts, playing the ukulele
Maureen: gardening
Ben: going snowboarding, playing golf

Question 2
Caroline: every day for about 10 or 15 minutes; every week on a Monday
Maureen: In the spring, quite often; in the summer less often
Ben: snowboarding for two weeks; disc golf once a week; competitions some weekends

Question 3
Caroline: loves making music, getting together with friends
Maureen: fresh air, eating fresh vegetables
Ben: beautiful mountain scenery; hang out with friends; see some interesting locations

5 Divide the class into groups of four to compare answers and add more information. Play the video again so that students can check.

After you watch

6 Students match the phrases to the speakers.

ANSWERS

1 B 2 M 3 C 4 M 5 B 6 B 7 B

7 Students match the phrases. Do the first one as an example.

ANSWERS

1 combination of 5 more energy
2 prepare it 6 spend time with
3 meeting 7 places
4 clean

8 Organise the class into threes. Ask students to decide on their roles and to prepare them. When students are ready, tell them to act out the conversation. You could get some groups to come to the front of the class to act out their roleplays.

Videoscript

What do you do in your free time?

0.06 Caroline: I really like music, so in my free time I like going to concerts and I really like playing the ukelele.

00.16 Maureen: I love gardening and so I have an allotment.

00.27 Ben: In my free time, I really like going snowboarding in the winter. And during the summer, I play quite a lot of disc golf. Disc golf is essentially a mix between Frisbee and golf. It's a lot of fun.

How often do you do it?

01.00 Caroline: I practise the ukelele every day for about ten or 15 minutes. And then every week on a Monday, a group of us go to a café together to play the ukelele.

01.14 Maureen: In the spring, I go quite often because I have to dig the soil and get it ready.

In the summer, when I plant, I go less often and in the autumn, I pick the vegetables and I have to go less often still.

01.35 Ben: During the winter, I'll maybe go snowboarding for two weeks on a holiday. And during the summer, I will usually play disc golf once a week and some weekends I go away for competitions.

Why do you enjoy doing it?

01.53 Caroline: I enjoy playing the ukelele because I love making music and it's a really easy instrument to play. And I really like getting together with friends and we've got a very good teacher who teaches us some really good songs.

02.07 Maureen: I enjoy doing it because I like the fresh air and enjoy eating the vegetables we grow.

02.19 Ben: I enjoy snowboarding because you get to spend time in really beautiful mountain scenery. It's also a nice way to take a holiday and you come back feeling very refreshed. Disc golf is a nice way for me to hang out with my friends during summer and also going to competitions at the weekends takes me to some quite interesting locations.

UNIT 4 Review

Grammar

1 Ask students to complete the sentences with the -*ing* form of the verbs from the box.

ANSWERS

1 swimming 4 listening
2 playing 5 watching
3 going

2 Ask students to write the sentences about what the people do in their free time.

ANSWERS

2 Chris often watches TV.
3 Annette goes to the cinema once a month.
4 Shelly sometimes plays computer games.
5 Chris plays computer games every day.
6 Chris sometimes goes to the cinema.
7 Annette doesn't often play computer games.
8 Shelly usually goes to the gym at the weekend.

3 Students match the questions with the answers.

ANSWERS

1 c 2 b 3 e 4 a 5 d

Vocabulary

4 Ask students to decide which word cannot be used after the verb in capital letters.

ANSWERS

1 running 4 the guitar 7 the gym
2 camping 5 a musical instrument 8 sport
3 football 6 TV

5 Ask students to complete the sentences with the words from the box.

ANSWERS

1 skis 4 gloves 7 mountain
2 ball 5 ice 8 sky
3 water 6 teams

Real life

6 Ask students to read the conversation and choose the correct options to complete it.

ANSWERS

1 at 2 well 3 play 4 very well 5 Do

7 Students complete the sentences for themselves, then compare them with a partner.

8 Students complete the questions to ask their partner, then work in pairs to ask and answer.

Unit 5 Food

Lead-in

Introducing the theme: food

Write the following nationalities on the board: *Chinese, Japanese, Thai, American, French, Italian, Mexican, Indian, Turkish* (adapt these according to your students' knowledge)

Ask students to discuss these questions in pairs:

Can you name two dishes for the cooking of each nationality?

What's typical about the food from these countries?

What's your favourite type of food?

1 Ask students to look at the photo. Ask: *What can you see? What's cooking?* Elicit responses. Discuss the questions as a class.

> **ANSWER**
>
> He's a noodle chef and he cooks noodles in a street café in Chinatown, Thailand.

2 💿 [1.33] Play the recording. Students listen and answer the questions.

> **ANSWERS**
>
> 1 Because he travels to different countries.
> 2 Because he tastes lots of different types of food.
> 3 He always goes to the local restaurants and cafés.
> 4 Because there are lots of street cafés and they're really cheap. All the street chefs make the food by hand and then they cook it on a real fire. You can smell the food in the distance.
> 5 His favourite dish is noodles.

Audioscript 💿 [1.33]

I have a great job because I travel to different countries, I meet new people and visit new places. But I really love travelling because I taste lots of different types of food. So when I arrive in a new city, I always go to the local restaurants and cafés. I'm in Thailand at the moment and my favourite place is Chinatown in Bangkok. There are lots of street cafés and they're really cheap. All the street chefs make the food by hand and then they cook it on a real fire. So when you walk up the street you can smell the food in the distance. My favourite dish is noodles. The chefs serve the noodles with a hot sauce. They taste delicious. I can eat them at any time of day – for breakfast, lunch or dinner!

Background notes

Chinatown is centred around Sam Peng Market near the Yaowarat Road in the heart of Bangkok, the capital city of Thailand in Southeast Asia. It has been the trading centre of the Chinese community in Thailand for over 200 years.

Vocabulary notes

Check the following types of food used in the article:

noodles = a staple food in parts of Asia made from unleavened dough in long, thin strips

sauces = liquid, creamy or semi-solid types of food served or used in preparing other foods

3 💿 [1.33] Ask students to complete the sentences. Then play the recording again. Ask students to listen and check. Let students compare their answers in pairs.

> **ANSWERS**
>
> | 1 make | 3 smell | 5 taste |
> |--------|---------|---------|
> | 2 cook | 4 serve | 6 eat |

4 Organise the class into pairs or small groups to talk about their favourite dishes. Monitor and note errors for an error feedback at the end.

Extra activity

Ask students to talk about their favourite café or restaurant. Ask them to discuss the following questions: *How do they cook and serve the food? What sauces do they use? What's a typical dish? How does the food taste?*

5a Famous for food

Lead-in

Test before you teach: food

Write the letters of the alphabet on the board then organise the class into groups of five or six. Ask students to say types of food beginning with each letter of the alphabet. So, student 1 says 'apple', 2 says 'banana', 3 says 'carrot', 4 says 'duck' or 'dessert', 5 says 'eggs', etc. If a student can't think of a word, he or she is out, and so is that letter. The next student starts with the next letter. Continue until one student has won in each group.

Vocabulary food

1 Lead in to this task by organising students into pairs, telling them to close their books, and asking them to tell their partner the names of as many types of food as they can.

Students match the words to the pictures and check with their partner. In feedback, model and drill the words, pointing out the strong stress (see below).

```
ANSWERS
1  rice         6  chicken    11  prawns    16  eggs
2  peppers      7  lamb       12  onions    17  lemons
3  potatoes     8  fish       13  oranges   18  lentils
4  chips        9  raisins    14  salt      19  cheese
5  pasta       10  juice      15  nuts      20  pepper
```

Vocabulary notes

In American English, picture 4 is called *fries* or *french fries*. Americans use the word *chips* for the snack that we can buy in bags at the supermarket (*crisps* in UK English).

Raisins are dried grapes.

Prawns are also called *shrimps* and the two words are used interchangeably. Brits and Australians tend to use the word *prawns*, while Americans tend to say *shrimps*.

Lentils are a type of edible pulse – they are seeds grown in pods.

Note that the uncountable word *pepper* is used to describe ground black peppercorns, whereas the countable word *peppers* is used for red, green, yellow and chilli peppers.

2 Ask students to complete the sentences then compare with a partner. In feedback, ask some individuals to say what they have in common with their partner.

Extra activity

Ask students to categorise the words in Exercise 1 under the headings *meat, fruit and vegetables, dairy* and *carbohydrates*. Ask them to add one more word to each category (e.g. *beef, bananas, milk* and *bread*).

Pronunciation /tʃ/ or /dʒ/

3 🎧 [1.34] Lead in by pointing out the phonemic symbols and modelling how to say the sounds.

Students listen and note which sound they hear. Let them compare their answers in pairs before discussing as a class.

Play the recording again. Students listen and repeat.

```
ANSWERS
1  /tʃ/          3  /tʃ/
2  /dʒ/          4  /dʒ/
```

Pronunciation notes

Both these sounds are pronounced in a similar way. They are *palato-alveolar affricates*, which means that you make the sound by pressing the end of your tongue against the spot where your palate meets your alveolar ridge, then, as the air flows through, you release your tongue. The difference between the sounds is that /tʃ/ is unvoiced, but /dʒ/ is a voiced sound.

Extra activity

Ask students to think of other words they know with these sounds.

Speaking and listening famous for food

4 Ask students to match the foods with the countries. Let students compare their answers in pairs. Tell them to check their answers on page 153.

```
ANSWERS
1 a      2 c       3 b       4 f       5 d       6 e
```

5 In a class of mixed nationalities, encourage students to tell the class about popular or national dishes in their countries.

6 🎧 [1.35] Lead in by asking students to look at the dishes on page 59. Ask: *What can you see? What type of food is it? What is in each dish?* Elicit ideas.

Play the recording. Students listen and match the speakers to the photos. Let students compare their answers in pairs.

```
ANSWERS
1 B              2 C              3 A
```

Audioscript 🎧 [1.35]

1 This is Kabsa. It's a popular dish in my country and also in other countries like Yemen. You need some chicken or some people make it with fish. Cook the chicken with an onion, some salt and pepper and other seasoning. Some tomatoes are good with it as well. We eat it with rice. And I put some nuts and raisins on the top. It tastes delicious.

2 Ceviche is popular in Peru but also in countries like Chile. It's easy to make. It's fish but you don't cook it. You put some juice from a lemon on the fish and this cooks it. Sometimes we eat it with onions and maybe some salad as well. You eat it cold.

3 Spaghetti Bolognese is a famous dish all over the world but the real Bolognese comes from my city of Bologna in Italy and our city's dish is pasta with Bolognese sauce. People put different things in the sauce and every Italian has their favourite recipe. For example, some people use carrots. I don't use any carrots but you always need some meat, onions and tomatoes. You eat it hot but when we have some left, I eat it cold for lunch the next day.

7 🔊 [1.35] Play the recording again. Students listen and match the dishes to the sentences. Let students compare their answers in pairs.

ANSWERS

2 B, K	4 B, K, C	6 K	8 B, K
3 C	5 B, K	7 C	

Extra activity

Ask students to look at the audioscript on page 171 and use the three descriptions as models for them to write a description of a popular dish from their country. Ask students to read out their descriptions to the class.

Grammar countable and uncountable nouns (*a, some* and *any*)

8 Ask students to look at the highlighted words in the sentences and discuss the questions as a class.

9 Read the grammar box with the students, and check the answers to the questions in Exercise 8. Refer students to the information and practice on pages 161 and 162.

ANSWERS

You can count onions, lemons, carrots and tomatoes
You can't count juice or meat.

Grammar notes

Countable nouns are so called because you can count them. In general, these words add -s or -es to form the plural.

Uncountable nouns can't be counted – these include liquids (*milk, water*, etc.) and substances or materials (*meat, bread,* etc.).

Of course, this can be much trickier than it looks. Many languages have no concept of countability, and other languages use countable nouns when English uses uncountable ones. Be careful with words like *rice* and *fruit* which may be countable in some languages, but are uncountable in English.

10 🔊 [1.36] Ask students to choose the correct options. Do the first as an example. Let students compare their answers in pairs.

Play the recording. Students listen and check.

ANSWERS

1 some	3 an	5 some	7 any
2 a	4 some	6 some	8 some

11 Organise the class into pairs. Tell students to decide who is A, and who is B, then tell them to read their recipes on pages 154 and 156 of the Student's Book. Monitor and help with vocabulary and question forming.

When students are ready, ask students to take turns asking and answering their questions. The idea is that if their partner has a spare ingredient, they exchange it.

In feedback, ask students, *What ingredients do you have from your partner? What ingredients do you need now?*

ANSWER

Student A needs mushrooms. Student B needs butter and mushrooms.

Speaking

12 Introduce the activity by describing a special meal that you know, and saying what ingredients you need.

Organise the class into pairs. Tell them to think of their own special meal and make a list of ingredients. Ask students to talk about what they need, using *a / an, some* and *any*. Monitor and help with ideas.

13 Ask students to tell the class about their special meals. As students tell the class about their meals, note any errors with *a / an, some* or *any*. Do an error feedback at the end.

Extra activity

Play 'make a pizza'. Tell students to think of their three favourite pizza ingredients (apart from cheese and tomato sauce). Monitor and help with ideas and vocabulary. Then organise the class into groups of five. Tell the groups that they must agree on a pizza with a maximum of five ingredients (plus cheese and tomatoes). Tell them that they all have to share and eat the pizza. After students have discussed and agreed on their pizzas ask them to present them to the class. Ask students to decide whose pizza is great, and whose pizza is terrible!

Homework

Ask students to write about their national dish.

5b Food markets

Lead-in

Using words: food and markets
Play a chain memory game. Say: *I went to the market and bought apples.* The next student must add a type of food you buy in a market, e.g. *I went to the market and bought apples and fish.* The next student must remember what has been said and add their own type of food, e.g. *I went to the market and bought apples, fish and potatoes.* Continue round the class. Students are 'out' if they can't think of a word. If your class is very large, get students to play the game in groups of five or six.

Reading

1 Ask students to choose an answer. Then discuss the question as a class.

Extra activity

Ask students some follow-up questions: *What do you usually buy in a supermarket? What do you buy in a market? How often do you go shopping?*

2 Ask students to look at the photo and the title. Ask: *What can you see? What is the article about?* Elicit ideas. Students then read the text and answer the questions. Let them compare their answers in pairs.

> **ANSWERS**
> 1 They are good for everyday shopping.
> 2 They are great for fresh food and local dishes.
> 3 It is 200 years old.
> 4 meat and seafood
> 5 the local sauce
> 6 a great restaurant
> 7 live music – musicians play and sing
> 8 from Thursday to Saturday (early)

Background notes

National Geographic named St Lawrence Market the world's best food market in April 2012. It is contained in two large buildings, and has restaurants, delis, farmer's markets and antique markets as well as areas for different types of food.

Castries Market dates from 1894 and is the largest market on the Caribbean island of St Lucia.

Kreta Ayer Wet Market is called a wet market because the floor is kept wet for hygiene reasons. It sells turtles, frogs and snakes for cooking.

La Vucciria in Palermo on the island of Sicily is over 700 years old.

Borough Market is in Southwark in central London. It began in 1756, and its present buildings were designed in 1851.

3 Discuss the questions as a class or in small groups.

Extra activity

This article is based on an original *National Geographic* article which listed ten top food markets, including markets in France, Finland and the US. Ask your students to find further information online about famous markets by searching for 'top ten markets', including their names, locations and what they sell.

Grammar *a lot of* and *not much / many*

4 Students look at the sentences and complete the rules. Let them compare their answers in pairs. Read the grammar box with the students. Refer students to the information and practice on page 162.

> **ANSWERS**
> 1 a lot of   2 not many   3 not much

Grammar notes

We use *a lot of* (or, more colloquially, *lots of*) in affirmative sentences with both countable and uncountable nouns. It is also possible to use *a lot of* with the negative or in questions.

We can only use *much* (with uncountable nouns) and *many* (with countable nouns) in negative sentences or with questions.

5 Do the first two sentences as examples to get students started. Then ask them to rewrite the rest of the sentences. Ask students to compare their sentences in pairs before discussing as a class.

> **ANSWERS**
> 3 There aren't many local markets in my region.
> 4 Do you buy many sweets for the children?
> 5 There isn't much milk in the fridge.
> 6 (no rewrite possible)
> 7 She doesn't put much salt on her food.
> 8 Do you eat many strawberries in the summer?

6 Say some sentences about yourself first to get students started. Ask them to prepare their own sentences then tell their partner.

Extra activity

Play the same chain game as in the lead-in to this section (see above). Say, *I don't eat many apples.* The next student must add a countable food, e.g. *I don't eat many apples or carrots.* The next student must remember what has been said and add their own type of food, e.g. *I don't eat many apples, carrots or potatoes.* Continue round the class. Students are 'out' if they can't think of a word or use a singular or uncountable noun in error. Play the same game with *I don't eat much …*

Listening and vocabulary quantities and containers

7 [1.37] Remind students of the markets in Exercise 2. Ask: *Which market is in London? Which market has a restaurant upstairs?* etc. Then play the recording. Students listen and say which market the shopper is in.

> ANSWER
> Castries Market

Audioscript [1.37]

M = market trader, **C** = customer

M: Hello, can I help you?

C: Yes. I'd like some bananas, please.

M: These are nice and fresh.

C: OK.

M: How many do you want?

C: Err. They're quite big so six, please.

M: OK. Anything else?

C: Yes. Some rice, please.

M: How much do you want? A kilo?

C: Yes, a kilo.

M: Here you go. And what about some of this sauce. It's local.

C: Is it hot?

M: Yeah, it's hot but it goes with anything.

C: Yes. OK.

M: How many do you want?

C: Just one bottle … oh actually, two. I can take one back to England. And I also need some bread. Do you sell any?

M: No, but there's a place on the other side of the market. So that's six bananas, a kilo of rice, two bottles of sauce. That's …

8 [1.37] Play the recording again. Students listen and answer the questions. Let them compare their answers in pairs.

> ANSWERS
> 1 six   2 one   3 two

9 Ask students to look at the pictures first. Elicit the names of any containers they already know. Then ask students to match the containers to the nouns. Let them compare their answers in pairs.

> ANSWERS
> 1 a bottle of sauce   5 a packet of pasta
> 2 a piece of chocolate   6 a tin of tuna
> 3 a slice of bread   7 a kilo of flour
> 4 a glass of water   8 a bag of rice

Grammar *how many / how much*

10 Ask students to look at the question forms. Discuss the questions as a class. Read the grammar box with the students. Refer students to the information and practice on page 162.

> ANSWERS
> *How many* asks about countable nouns.
> *How much* asks about uncountable nouns.

Speaking

11 Start the activity by acting out the first conversation with a reliable student.

Organise the class into pairs. Tell students to take turns to play the different roles and to act out the conversations. Monitor and prompt and note any errors for a correction feedback at the end.

With weaker classes you could get students to prepare and write conversations first.

5c The seed vault

Lead-in

Using words: growing plants

Write the following words on the board:

seeds, plants, flowers, grow, water

Ask students to look up the words or guess their meanings. Then ask them to say what connects the words.

Reading

1 Organise the class into pairs. Ask them to discuss the questions. Then take feedback and have a discussion as a class.

2 Ask students to look at the photos and the title and predict what the text is about. Ask them to guess what a 'seed' and a 'vault' might be.

Students read the text and answer the questions.

> ANSWER
> storing

3 Ask students to read the article again and answer the questions. Let them compare their answers in pairs.

> ANSWERS
> 1 because of bad weather or disease
> 2 farmers
> 3 no
> 4 Norway
> 5 It's on Spitsbergen in Norway
> 6 below (inside a mountain)
> 7 half a million
> 8 2.2 billion

Word focus *of*

4 Ask students to look at the underlined phrases, then complete the sentences with *of*.

> ANSWERS
> 1 A lot of people in China eat rice for breakfast.
> 2 The United States of America is famous for burgers.
> 3 I'd like a bottle of water, please.
> 4 A friend of mine is vegetarian.
> 5 I eat my main meal in the middle of the day.
> 6 There are many varieties of potato.

Grammar notes

There are many expressions that use *of* in these categories.

Quantity: *a lot of, a bit of, a number of, some of*

Parts of things: *types of, varieties of, examples of*

With people, we generally use the saxon genitive possessive 's to show possession (*John's coat*), but with places and things we use *of*, e.g. *the capital of France, the end of the road, the front of the picture.*

Pronunciation linking *of*

5 🔊 [1.38] Play the recording. Students listen and notice the link between the consonant sound and the vowel sound at the start of *of* (for the audioscript see the answer key to Exercise 4).

Play the recording again. Students listen and repeat.

Pronunciation note

Note the weak pronunciation of *of*: /əv/

Critical thinking summarising

6 Read through the sentences with the class then ask students to look back at the text and match them to the paragraphs. Let students compare their answers in pairs.

> ANSWERS
> a 2   b 4   c 3   d 5   e 1

Speaking

7 Ask students to work in pairs to summarise the main points of the article, using the phrases in the box, and without looking at the article. Take feedback from the class.

> SAMPLE ANSWERS
> It's is important to store different types of seed for the future. Svalbard Global Seed Vault is the biggest seed vault in the world. It is a very cold place. The vaults are one hundred and thirty metres inside the mountain, on the island of Spitsbergen. There are three large areas and there are about half a million varieties of seeds here. They can live here for thousands of years.

Extra activity

Ask students in groups of four to choose the seeds of five plants to put in the seed vault. In feedback, ask different groups to describe and give reasons for their choices.

5d At the restaurant

Lead-in

Introducing the theme: menus

Bring in some real English language menus. Ideally, bring in enough so that there is one for each pair in the class. Even if you aren't in an English-speaking country, it's easy to download them from the Internet. Pass them round the class and ask students, *What type of restaurant is it? What type of food do they have? Is it cheap or expensive?*

Then do a quick scanning task. Say: *Find a dish with meat in it. Find a vegetarian dish. Find a type of fruit. Find a dessert.* Students shout out answers. You can give points for correct answers if you wish.

Speaking and vocabulary

1 Discuss the questions as a class or in small groups. Make sure students understand *starter* (the first, small course), *main course* (the second, big course) and *dessert* (the last, sweet course).

2 Ask students to look at the photo. Ask: *What can you see? What type of food does it serve?* Elicit ideas.

Organise the class into pairs. Students look at the menu and choose dishes to order. In feedback, check the meaning and pronunciation of the dishes and the prices (see below).

Vocabulary notes

soup of the day = many restaurants serve a different type of soup every day

garlic fries = fries (or *chips*) flavoured with garlic

seafood special = restaurants use the word 'special' as a general word for a dish that they serve

Caesar salad = a salad with lettuce, parmesan cheese and croutons

ice cream sundae = ice cream with a topping of sauce, syrup or other toppings such as nuts or fruit

$2.50 = two dollars fifty

Background notes

Calzone's is a real restaurant in North Beach, San Francisco. A *calzone* is a type of pizza that is folded over so that all the ingredients are inside the pizza base.

Real life ordering a meal

3 [1.39] Give students a moment to look at the questions. Play the recording. Students listen and answer. Let students compare their answers in pairs before discussing as a class.

ANSWERS
1 a bottle of sparkling water, a seafood special, and a four-cheese pizza
2 $27.40 (plus tip)

Audioscript [1.39]

A = man, B = woman, C = waiter

A: This is a nice place.

B: Yes, it's one of my favourite restaurants. They have great pizzas.

C: Good afternoon. How are you today?

B: We're great, thanks.

C: Great. My name's Arthur and I'm your waiter today. So here is the menu. Can I get you anything to drink first?

A: Err, I'd like a bottle of water, please. Sparkling.

B: Yes, good idea.

C: One bottle or two?

B: One between us, thanks.

C: OK.

B: Well, the garlic fries are really good. Do you call them *chips* in England?

A: Yes, they look good. But I don't want a starter. I'll have a seafood special.

B: Really? Are you sure?

A: Well, I'd also like a dessert …

B: Right.

C: Hi. Here's your water. Are you ready to order?

A: Yes, I'd like the seafood special.

C: OK. Good choice.

B: And I'd like a four-cheese pizza.

C: OK. Any starters?

B: No, thanks. We're fine.

C: OK. So one seafood special and one four-cheese pizza. …

A: That was delicious.

B: Good. Are you ready for dessert?

A: Actually, I'm full.

C: Hi. How was that?

B: Very nice, thanks.

C: Can I get you anything else? Some dessert?

A: No, thanks. Could we have the bill, please?

C: The bill?

B: He means the check.

C: Oh, sure.

4 [1.39] Ask students to read through the expressions and decide whether the waiter or customers say them. Let them compare their answers in pairs.

Play the recording again. Students listen and write C or W next to the phrases. Read through the *Wordbuilding* section with your class. Refer them to page 43 of the Workbook for further information and practice.

ANSWERS

Here is the menu. W

Can I get you anything to drink first? W

I'd like a bottle of water, please. C

I don't want a starter. C

I'll have a seafood special. C

I'd also like a dessert. C

Are you ready to order? W

I'd like a four-cheese pizza. C

That was delicious. C

Can I get you anything else? W

Could we have the bill, please? C

Vocabulary notes

Note that in restaurants, people use *I'd like + noun* and *I'll have + noun* when ordering food and drink.

When asking for permission, we use *Can I … ?* or *Can we … ?* It is also possible to use *could* (as in *Could we have the bill, please?*) This is a little more formal and polite.

When ordering or asking for permission in a polite, formal situation, English speakers tend to use *please* a lot.

Extra activity

Ask students to tell you any other words that are different in British and American English. Here are some relevant to your students' level (US English first): *cookie / biscuit; fall / autumn; truck / lorry; apartment / flat; drugstore / chemist; freeway / motorway; movie / film; movie theater / cinema; closet / cupboard; main street / high street; elevator / lift; zip code / postcode; gas / petrol; store / shop; pants / trousers; subway / tube; cab / taxi; candy / sweets*

Pronunciation contracted forms

5 [1.40] Play the recording. Students listen and repeat the contracted forms.

6 Organise the class into threes. Ask students to improvise a conversation using the menu and the phrases for ordering a meal.

With weaker classes, tell them to prepare and write a conversation first. When students are ready, ask them to practise reading out the conversation in pairs. Monitor carefully and make sure they are attempting to contract *I'd* and *I'll* correctly.

Extra activity

Ask students in pairs to prepare their own menu. Tell them to decide what type of restaurant they have, and what dishes to write on the menu.

When students are ready, ask them to change partners with another pair. Students take turns to 'visit' each other's restaurant and order food from the menu.

Homework

Ask students to imagine they are going to open a new restaurant in London with food from their country. Tell them to write a menu with popular dishes from their country, and a brief description of each dish.

5e What do I do next?

Lead-in

Using words: food

Write *a cake* and *a pizza* on the board. Organise the class into two groups of three to six students (in a large class divide them into four groups). Tell Group A to write a list of as many ingredients that could go in a cake as they can think of in one minute. Tell Group B to do the same for a pizza. After one minute, find out which group has most words.

Cake: *flour, sugar, eggs, jam, chocolate, fruit (oranges, lemons, bananas, apples, raisins, etc.), milk, cheese, nuts, cream.*

Pizza: *flour, salt, pepper, peppers, fish, salmon, seafood, prawns, meat (chicken, lamb, beef, pork), tomatoes, cheese, onions, pineapple, eggs.*

Writing instructions

1 Students read the texts and match them to where they read them. Let them check their answers in pairs.

ANSWERS

1 b   2 a   3 c

Extra activity

Follow up by asking: *What products are in texts 1 to 3? What types of food can you see?* Ask students to write one extra instruction for each text.

Grammar notes

We use the imperative form when writing (or saying) instructions. Note the following:

Heat the oven.

Do not use the barbecue …

Never leave children …

Writing skill punctuation

2a Students read the instructions again and find the types of punctuation. Let them compare their answers in pairs before discussing as a class.

2b Ask students to match the punctuation to the uses, and find examples. Let them compare their answers with a partner before discussing as a class.

ANSWERS

2 full stop: *… in about fifteen minutes.*

3 comma: *a cool, dry place*

4 colon: *… follow these instructions:*

5 comma: *First of all,*

6 comma: *After you open the bottle, use the sauce within three months.*

2c Start by doing the first sentence as an example with the class. Ask students to add the punctuation in the rest of the text. Let them compare their answers in pairs.

ANSWERS

Fortune cookies are nice at the end of a meal in a Chinese restaurant, and they're easy to make.

You need the following: pieces of paper, three eggs, sugar, salt and flour.

First of all, write your messages on the pieces of paper. After you mix the eggs, sugar, salt and flour, pour the mixture onto a tray.

---

3 Organise the class into pairs. Start by checking the meaning of the verbs. Use mime and the pictures to do this. Then ask students to write their favourite recipe. Monitor and help with ideas and vocabulary, and make sure students are using the imperative to write instructions, and using the correct punctuation.

4 Students exchange instructions and comment on the punctuation and the content of their partner's instructions.

Extra activity

Write the following words on the board: *knife, spoon, bowl, jug, board.* Use the pictures on page 65 to check their meaning. Then ask students to say which verbs go with each kitchen utensil, e.g. *knife (chop, slice, cut), spoon (mix), bowl (mix, put), jug (mix, pour), board (chop, put, slice, spread).*

Homework

Ask students to write instructions for their national dish or for a dish that is popular at particular times of year in their country.

5f Gelato University

Before you watch

1 Ask students to look at the photo. Ask: *What flavours can you see?* Discuss the questions as a class.

2 Ask students to look at the pictures and match the pictures and the words.

ANSWERS

1 A	3 G	5 C	7 F
2 D	4 B	6 E	

---

3 Have a class discussion.

While you watch

4 Ask students to number the topics in order while they watch the video.

ANSWERS

1 a   2 c   3 b

---

5 Ask students to watch the video again, and answer the questions.

ANSWERS

1 in Bologna in Italy
2 from countries all over the world, including Australia, Sierra Leone and Saudi Arabia
3 they learn how to make 'gelato'
4 35 to 40
5 Madagascar
6 800 euros
7 management and marketing
8 about 120,000 euros

After you watch

6 Give students some time to read through the sentences. Play the video again for students to match the speech with the people. Point out that Kaori Ito is the first speaker in the video.

ANSWERS

1 b   2 a   3 d   4 c

---

7 Ask students to read through the phrases and expressions. Tell them to choose the correct answer.

ANSWERS

1 c   2 a   3 d   4 b

---

8 Organise the class into pairs. Ask students to decide on their roles and prepare them. When students are ready, tell them to act out the conversation. You could get some pairs to come to the front of the class to act out their roleplays.

9 Students discuss the questions in groups.

Videoscript

This is a university near the city of Bologna in Italy. The students come from countries all over the world, including Australia, Sierra Leone and Saudi Arabia. And what's the subject? How to make Italian ice cream, or gelato.

Kaori Ito These students want a new career. The average age is 35 to 40.

They're ready to stop doing their old jobs and to open a new chapter in their lives.

Holly works in the textile industry. But she wants to start a gelato factory in her country of Madagascar.

Holly I want to open an Italian gelato parlour in Antananarivo, the capital of Madagascar. The shop is for a certain class of people. It isn't for everyone.

Students pay about 800 euros a week.

They learn how to make gelato, but they also learn about management and marketing.

Kevin Koh is 25 and from Singapore. He works for his father's fruit import company. After only a few days of training, he can make strawberry ice cream.

01.25 Kevin It's not until I attended, started attending, this course that I realised that there's actually a lot about the ingredients, a lot about understanding about the building blocks, about how, how … what goes in the gelato.

Students learn a lot about the gelato business. A modern gelato machine costs about 120,000 euros, but the profits are high. A litre of ice cream costs two to three euros, but customers pay around 20 euros per litre. That's a tasty profit!

UNIT 5 Review

Grammar

1 Students match the sentence beginnings to the endings.

ANSWERS					
1 c	2 d	3 b	4 e	5 a	6 f

2 Ask students to read the conversation and choose the correct options to complete it.

ANSWERS		
1 much	3 a lot of	5 a lot of / many
2 A lot of	4 a lot of / much	6 not many

3 Ask students to write the words from the box in the correct place in the table.

ANSWERS
How much: rice, soup
How many: eggs, oranges, bottles of water

Vocabulary

4 Ask students to write the words from the box in the correct category.

ANSWERS		
1 oranges, raisins	3 chicken, lamb	5 pierogi, satay
2 peppers, potatoes	4 juice, milk	6 bag, tin

5 Ask students to think of one more word for each category in Exercise 4.

6 Students read the text about mint tea and complete it with words from the box.

ANSWERS				
1 make	2 tastes	3 put	4 pour	5 mixes

Real life

7 Students replace the phrases in bold in the sentences with phrases from the box.

ANSWERS	
1 Would you like	3 Are you ready to
2 I'd like	4 Can we have

Speaking

8 Students work in pairs to describe their favourite café and say what they normally order there.

Unit 6 Money

Lead-in

Introducing the theme: giving money

Write the following on the board:

a child, a musician, a homeless person

Ask students: *Do you give money to all or any of these people when you see them in the street? What do you give and why?* Have a class discussion.

1 Ask students to look at the photo. Ask: *What can you see? Where is he?* Discuss the questions as a class.

> **ANSWER**
>
> He plays music in the street. Passers-by give him money.

2 [1.41] Play the recording. Students listen, check their answers to Exercise 1, and answer the questions.

> **ANSWERS**
>
> 1 Oxford Street is a famous shopping area in London.
> 2 A lot of people come shopping here and spend money.
> 3 Because people go in and change their money, then give their small coins to the busker.

Audioscript [1.41]

Oxford Street is a famous shopping area in central London. Every day, thousands of people spend money on food, clothes and electronics. It's also a good place for buskers to earn money. This Scottish bagpiper often plays on Oxford Street because people give him coins and small amounts of money. But after a few hours, that can add up to a lot of money. One of the best places on the street for buskers is near to a currency exchange office. Tourists go there and change their money. Then, when they come out, they often give their small coins to the busker before they go shopping.

3 [1.41] Play the recording again. Ask students to listen and say which collocations they hear.

> **ANSWERS**
>
> spend money, earn money, give … coins / money, change money

4 Students match the verbs to the places. Let them compare their answers in pairs before discussing as a class.

> **ANSWERS**
>
> You change money at a currency exchange.
> You spend money in the shops.
> You give / spend money in the street.
> You earn money at work.

5 Organise the class into groups to talk about the questions. Note errors for an error feedback at the end.

6a The face of money

Lead-in

Introducing the theme: money

Write the following questions on the board:

How much money do you have?

What notes do you have?

What coins do you have?

Who is on the notes?

Who or what is on the coins?

Organise the class into pairs or small groups. Tell them to ask and answer the questions without looking at their money. After their interviews, ask students to check their answers.

Reading

1 Students match the countries to the currencies. Let students compare their answers in pairs.

> **ANSWERS**
>
> Canada: dollar   Mexico: peso
> China: renminbi   Pakistan: rupee
> Egypt: pound   Russia: rouble
> France: euro   Saudi Arabia: riyal
> Japan: yen   Switzerland: franc

2 Tell students to check their answers on page 154 of the Student's Book. Discuss the question as a class in feedback.

Background notes

Dollars

A lot of countries use the dollar, including Australia, Belize, Canada, Hong Kong, New Zealand, Singapore, Taiwan, the USA, and many Caribbean countries.

Euros

This is the currency of the eurozone of the EU (Austria, Belgium, Cyprus, Estonia, Finland, France, Germany, Greece, Ireland, Italy, Luxembourg, Malta, the Netherlands, Portugal, Slovakia, Slovenia, and Spain). Since 2002, France has used the euro, which replaced the franc.

Francs

Switzerland, Liechtenstein and most francophone African counties continue to use francs as their currency.

Pesos

This is the name of the currency of the following Spanish-speaking countries in central and South America: Argentina, Chile, Colombia, Cuba, Dominican Republic, Mexico and Uruguay. It is also used in the Philippines.

Pounds

This is the currency of the United Kingdom and its dependent territories. Egypt, Lebanon, Syria, Sudan and South Sudan also use the term to describe their currencies. Before the nineteenth century, Egypt used a currency called piastres. When the country came under the influence of the UK, the word pound was introduced to refer to 100 piastres.

Riyals
Riyals or rials are used in Iran and in some of Saudi Arabia's neighbouring countries including Yemen, Qatar and Oman.

Rupees
India, Pakistan, Sri Lanka, Nepal, Mauritius, Seychelles, Maldives and Indonesia all use the rupee.

Roubles
Russia and Belarus use roubles.

Only China uses **renminbi** (it means 'people's currency'), and only Japan uses **yen**.

3 Ask students to look at the photos. Ask: *What can you see?* Check the meaning of *coins* (hard, round metal money) and *notes* (paper money).

Discuss the questions as a class.

> **ANSWER**
> Queen Elizabeth II's face is on the notes.

4 Students read the article and answer the question. Let them compare their answers in pairs before discussing as a class.

> **ANSWERS**
> Over thirty countries including Canada, Cyprus, Fiji, Bermuda, the Bahamas, Scotland.

5 Students read the article again and complete the notes. Let them compare their answers in pairs.

> **ANSWERS**
> 2 1936   3 1960   4 1977   5 1992   6 2002

Vocabulary age

6 Students read the article again and do the vocabulary tasks in pairs.

> **ANSWERS**
> 1 ten years old; in her mid-twenties; middle-aged; in her late fifties; in her seventies
> 2 29 = late twenties; 35 = mid-thirties; 41 = early forties; 55 = mid-fifties; 61 = early sixties; 89 = late eighties
> 3 Students' own ideas.

Extra activity

Ask students to guess the ages of well-known celebrities and express them with the new language. Try the following (their ages in July 2013 are given):

Tom Cruise (51); Brad Pitt (48); Julia Roberts (45); Meryl Streep (64); Sir Paul McCartney (71)

Grammar *was / were*

7 Ask students to look at the highlighted words in the sentences and discuss the questions as a class.

Read the grammar box with the students. Refer students to the information and practice on pages 162 and 163.

> **ANSWERS**
> 1 The two sentences in a are about the present (the present simple form of *be*).
>   The sentence in b is about the past (the past simple form of *be*).
> 2 There are many occurrences of *was*, *wasn't*, *were* and *weren't*. The negative forms are *wasn't* and *weren't*.

Grammar notes

We use *was* in first and third person forms, and *were* in second person and plural forms. The abbreviated form of *not* (*n't*) is added to *was* and *were* to make the negative. Questions are formed by inverting *was* and *were* with the subject.

8 Ask students to look at the photos. Ask: *What are the currencies? Who are the people on the notes? What do you know about them?*

Students choose the correct forms. Let them compare their answers in pairs.

> **ANSWERS**
> 1 was   3 was   5 were   7 weren't
> 2 wasn't   4 were   6 was   8 were

9 Write the names Arthur Honegger and Ichiyu Higuchi on the board. Ask students: *What do you know about these people? What can you guess? What do you want to know?* Elicit ideas.

Organise the class into pairs. Ask students to find their relevant information and complete the questions with *was* and *were*. When students are ready, they take turns to ask and answer questions to complete their texts.

Extra activity

In a mixed nationality class, ask students to tell the class about famous people on their banknotes.

Writing and speaking

10 Introduce the activity by writing two or three sentences about the life of someone in your family. Tell students to ask questions to find out more about them.

Then ask students to prepare their own sentences.

11 Students take turns to read out their sentences. Their partner must ask questions to find out more information.

Homework

Ask students to write a biography of a famous person on one of their banknotes.

6b Discover the past

Lead-in

Using words: treasure

Write the following words on the board: *gold, silver, coins, metal, jewellery, rings, treasure*

Check the meaning of the words or ask students to check them in their dictionaries. Ask students to say what connects the words (their value; the fact that they are all metal). Ask students to show you any examples of these things that they have in their possession.

Listening

1 Ask students to look at the photo and read the text quickly to find the answers to the questions. Discuss the questions as a class.

ANSWERS
1 It is Birmingham Museum and Art Gallery, in central England. Visitors go to find out about local history and see old archaeological objects.
2 Students' own answers

2 💿 [1.42] Ask students to look at the questions before they listen. Play the recording. Students listen and note answers to the questions. Let them compare their answers in pairs.

ANSWERS
1 To help improve the museum.
2 one exhibition
3 She read an article about it in the newspaper.
4 Because his children have a school project about history and archaeology.
5 No, it's his first visit to a museum.

Audioscript 💿 [1.42]

A = interviewer, **B** = woman, **C** = man

A: Hello, I work for the museum and we'd like to interview visitors. Your answers can really help the museum in the future.

B: Yes. OK, then.

A: Great! So, my first question is: Are you here to visit all of the museum or are you here to see one exhibition?

B: Actually, I'm interested in the exhibition of Anglo-Saxon objects.

A: Oh, that's good.

B: Yes, it's very exciting because I read a lot of history books about the Anglo-Saxons.

A: OK. And how do you know about the exhibition?

B: I read an article about the exhibition in the newspaper …

A: Excuse me, I work for the museum. Can I ask you some questions about your visit today?

C: Err, sure. What kind of questions?

A: Well my first question is this: Are you here to visit all of the museum or are you here to see one exhibition?

C: I don't know, really. My children have a school project about archaeology and history so we came here. It's my first time in a museum.

A: Really? Is it interesting?

C: Not for me. I think history's boring but my children are excited.

A: Oh. Well, are they interested in a special period of history?

C: I don't know. I'll ask them. Kids! Kids!

Vocabulary *-ed* / *-ing* adjectives

3 💿 [1.42] Read through the sentences with the class, and ask them to listen to the recording again and choose the adjective they hear for each sentence. Let them check their answers in pairs.

ANSWERS
1 interested	4 boring
2 exciting	5 excited
3 interesting	

4 Students look at the sentences in Exercise 3 again, and answer the questions about the use of *-ed* and *-ing* adjectives. Discuss the answers as a class.

ANSWERS
1 interested, excited
2 exciting, interesting, boring
-*ed* adjectives describe how the person feels, -*ing* adjectives describe the thing or situation.

5 Students complete each sentence in the pairs with the correct form of the adjective (*-ed* or *-ing*).

ANSWERS
1 interesting	4 bored
2 interested	5 excited
3 boring	6 exciting

Extra activity

Write the following sentence starters on the board and ask students to complete them with their own personal information.

I'm interested in …

The last boring film I saw was …

I feel bored when …

English lessons are interesting when …

Put students in pairs or small groups to share their sentences.

6 Ask students to think about the questions about history for a minute or two, then discuss their opinions about history as a class.

Reading

7 Ask students to look at the photo and read the article, then answer the questions. Let students compare their answers to the questions in pairs before discussing as a class.

ANSWERS
1 one thousand years ago
2 metal work and jewellery
3 under the ground in a field
4 1,500
5 Yes, thousands of visitors came and the exhibition had to move to a bigger building.
6 £3,285 million

Background notes

The treasure that was found is now known as the Staffordshire Hoard (named after the county it was found in). It is the largest hoard of Anglo-Saxon gold and silver metalwork ever found. Experts believe that the objects date back to the seventh and eighth centuries.

The Anglo-Saxons were a Germanic people who first came and settled in the southern half of Britain in the 6th century AD. They pushed out the Celtic inhabitants. As well as bringing their metalwork and jewellery skills, they also brought their language and their poetry. Anglo-Saxon English or Old English is the root of modern English. In fact, England is a corruption of Angle Land (named after the Angles, one of the many Anglo-Saxon tribes that colonised the country).

Grammar past simple (affirmative) regular and irregular verbs

8 Ask students to read the newspaper story again, underline the past form of the verbs and answer the questions. Let students compare their answers to the questions in pairs before discussing as a class. Read the grammar box with the students. Refer students to the information and practice on page 163.

ANSWERS
1 past
2 lived, worked, made
3 *lived* and *worked* are regular; *made* is irregular

Grammar notes

We form the regular simple past by adding -ed to the infinitive of the verb. There are exceptions (add -d to verbs ending in -e, e.g. lived; change y to i and add -ed to verbs ending with a consonant followed by -y, e.g. carried; note that say and pay become said and paid).

There are many irregular forms in English. The most common verbs tend to be irregular.

9 Give students an example to get them started. Then ask them to find and underline the past forms.

Ask students to compare their answers in pairs before discussing as a class.

ANSWERS
Regular: *received, studied, showed, moved, wanted*
Irregular: *were, took, came, was*

Extra activity

Ask students to think of other present tense verbs that they know and write them up on the board. Find out if students can change the verbs into past forms.

10 Ask students to look at the photos and the title. Ask: *Who was Tutankhamen? What do you know about Howard Carter?* Elicit ideas. Use the pictures to pre-teach *mask, tomb* and *archaeologist*.

Students read the text and write the past forms. Let students compare their answers in pairs. In feedback, ask what they found interesting about the text.

ANSWERS
1 lived   5 became
2 went   6 died
3 worked   7 made
4 discovered   8 had

Extra activity

Write the eight past forms from Exercise 10 on the board. Tell students to close their books and retell the story of the mask of Tutankhamen in pairs, using the past forms as prompts.

Background notes

Tutankhamen (or Tutankhamun) was an Egyptian pharoah who ruled Egypt between 1332 BC and 1323 BC. He died young (he was 19) and was buried in a pyramid. When Howard Carter discovered his tomb, it was a worldwide sensation, and interest in ancient Egypt grew in Europe as a result. Artefacts from the tomb have toured the world on display.

Pronunciation -ed endings

11a [1.43] Give students a moment to read through the past forms and predict which ones add an extra syllable. Play the recording. Students listen and write the number of syllables.

ANSWERS
3 like = 1; liked = 1
4 want = 1; wanted = 2
5 work = 1; worked = 1
6 start = 1; started = 2
7 play = 1; played = 1
8 visit = 2; visited = 3
9 travel = 2; travelled = 2

11b [1.43] Play the recording again. Students listen and repeat.

Pronunciation notes

When verbs end with a /t/ or a /d/ sound, we add an extra syllable and -ed is pronounced /ɪd/. Otherwise, there is no extra syllable.

Note that -ed is pronounced /t/ after unvoiced sounds and /d/ after voiced sounds.

Speaking

12 Start the activity by writing two years on the board that are important for you, and asking students to guess why.

Then ask students to prepare five years of their own.

13 Organise the class into pairs. Ask students to share their years with a partner and ask them to guess what happened in them.

Extra activity

Write the following verbs on the board: *live, work, start, visit, travel, play.* Ask students to write five sentences about their lives using five of the verbs. Tell them to write four true sentences and one false one.

When students are ready, divide them into groups of four. Ask students to read out their sentences. Students must guess which one isn't true.

Homework

Ask students to write their life story using *was born* and the verbs in the extra task above.

6c A cashless world?

Lead-in

Using words: money
Write the following word pairs on the board:

coins / notes

cash / cheques

a credit card / a debit card

a purse / a wallet

a pocket / a handbag

Ask students in pairs to discuss the difference in meaning between the words in each pair. Tell them to look in dictionaries, but also tell them to use any objects in their possession to show the meaning. In feedback, use mime or realia to check the meaning of these words (see Vocabulary notes below).

Reading

1 Ask students the questions and discuss the issues as a class.

Vocabulary notes

Cash is the general word for paper and metal money that you carry with you.

A *credit card* is a plastic card that allows you to borrow money in order to make purchases. In contrast, a *debit card* takes money directly from your bank account in order to pay for something.

In British English, a *purse* is a small bag for carrying money, with a zip or clip at the top, usually carried by a woman in a handbag, whereas a *wallet* is a smaller, flatter leather holder, more typically used by men, and carried in a pocket.

In American English, the word *purse* has a different meaning. It is used to mean the same as *handbag*; a larger bag generally used by women for carrying umbrellas, make-up, etc.

In American English, *cheque* is spelt *check*.

Extra activity

Ask students to show you examples of cash, credit cards, purses, wallets, pockets, etc. which they have with them.

2 Ask students to look at the words and the timeline. Explain that the words in the box are different ways of buying or paying for things, and ask them to guess when each of the payment methods appeared. Then ask students to read the article and check and complete their answers. Read through the *Wordbuilding* box with the students. Refer them to page 51 of the Workbook for further information and practice.

ANSWERS

1 animals	5 cheque book
2 seashells	6 credit card
3 metal coins	7 mobile phone
4 paper money	

Critical thinking relevance

3 Read through the sentences with the class then ask students to look back at the text and decide which sentences go at the end of which paragraphs. Let students compare their answers in pairs.

ANSWERS

1 b   2 f   3 a   4 d   5 e   6 c

Extra activity

Ask students to say what clues tell them which sentence goes with which paragraph in the article. For example, the linkers *but* and *also* contrast or add similar information. Pronouns such as *it* and *they* refer back to nouns in the last sentences of the relevant paragraphs. And lexical clues such as *Emperor* and the repetition of the words *cash* and *credit card* give clues.

Speaking

4 Organise the class into pairs. Ask students to read the questions in the survey and prepare their own personal answers. Then ask them to take turns asking and answering the questions. They should make a note of their partner's answers.

5 Students join another pair to compare their answers. In feedback, ask different groups to tell the class what they found out.

Extra activity

Ask students to look back at the exercises and text in 6c and find as many words connected with money as they can. As well as the words in Exercise 1, they should find the following: *payment, income, bank account, bills, cheque book, bank card, cash machine, PIN, buy, sell, pay, spend, save.*

Tell students to think of definitions for five of the words. Put them with a new pair to read out their definitions. The other pair must guess which word is being defined.

6d Help!

Lead-in

Introducing the theme: collecting money
Write the following situations on the board:

Your teacher is leaving.

The local hospital needs money.

There is a natural disaster on the other side of the world.

Tell students that people are collecting money for these three situations. Divide them into pairs or small groups to decide how much to give in each situation. Then have a class discussion and find out when your students give money and how much.

Listening

1 Ask students to look at the charities' logos. Ask: *What can you see? What do you know about the charities?*

Ask students to discuss the questions in pairs. Let students check their answers on page 156 of the Student's Book.

ANSWERS

The WWF (World Wildlife Fund) helps animals in the wild and works on conservation and environmental projects.

Save the Children helps children around the world in emergency situations and in long-term relief.

The Red Cross and Red Crescent give food and medicine to people in wars.

Background notes

These days, WWF actually stands for World Wide Fund for Nature, although it is still called the World Wildlife Fund in the US and Canada. It started in Switzerland in 1961 and was initially interested in protecting endangered species. As the organisation has become larger, it has become concerned with biodiversity, reducing pollution and climate change as well. It uses an image of a giant panda as its logo.

The International Committee of the Red Cross was founded in Switzerland in 1863. The International Federation of Red Cross and Red Crescent Societies was founded in 1919 and it is responsible for organising massive humanitarian relief efforts during wars or large-scale emergencies. It operates as the Red Crescent in Muslim countries where the term Red Cross might be inappropriate.

Extra activity

Ask students to name and talk about other charities that they know of which do similar work.

2 🔊 [1.44] Ask students to look at the photo. Ask: *Where are they? What are they doing?* (collecting money) *Why?* Elicit reasons why people collect money.

Play the recording. Students listen and match the conversations to the topics. Discuss the question as a class.

ANSWERS

1 b	2 a	3 c

Audioscript 🔴 [1.44]

Conversation 1

A: Hi? Hello? I'm collecting for a charity.

B: Err. What's it for exactly?

A: It's for poor children in different countries. We use the money for food and hospitals and also for new schools. So could you give us something?

B: Yes, certainly. Here you are.

A: Thanks very much.

B: You're welcome.

Conversation 2

A: Hey. Can I ask you something?

B: Yes, of course. What is it?

A: Well, I don't have any money until tomorrow. Could you lend me some money?

B: I'm sorry, but I can't.

A: Don't worry. I can ask someone else.

B: OK. Sorry.

Conversation 3

A: Oh no! It's two pounds for the car park. I only have a five-pound note.

B: So what's the problem?

A: The machine takes coins. You can't use notes. Can I borrow the money?

B: Actually, I'm afraid I don't have any coins. I only have a ten-pound note! But look. It takes credit cards.

A: I haven't got a credit card.

B: Don't worry. I have.

Real life requesting

3 🔴 [1.44] Ask students to look at the conversations and try to remember or guess where the words go.

Play the recording. Students listen and check their answers. Let students compare their answers in pairs before discussing as a class.

ANSWERS

Conversation 1	Conversation 2	Conversation 3
1 could you	3 Can I	7 Can I
2 Yes, certainly	4 Yes, of course.	8 I'm afraid
	5 Could you	
	6 I'm sorry	

4 Ask students to complete the list with phrases from the conversations in Exercise 3.

ANSWERS

Requests

2 Can I ask you something?
3 Could you lend me some money?
4 Can I borrow the money?

Responses

Yes, certainly.

Yes, of course.

I'm sorry, but I can't.

I'm afraid I don't have any coins.

Grammar and vocabulary notes

We use *Can I ... ?* or *Could I ... ?* to request permission to do something. We use *Can you ... ?* or *Could you ... ?* to ask someone else to do something. Using *could* is more polite, and, importantly, more tentative than using *can*. That's why English speakers tend to use *can* when it is not a 'big' request and they are not tentative (*Can I open the window? It's a bit warm in here.*) They are expecting the answer *yes*. They use *could* when it's a 'big' request (*Could you carry this bag upstairs for me, please? I have a bad back.*)

I'm sorry, but ... and *I'm afraid (that) ...* are both polite ways of refusing.

Point out the meaning of *lend* and *borrow*. You could check that students understand by 'lending' a book to a student, making it clear that you want it back.

Extra activity

This section has lots of verbs that collocate with money. Elicit as many as you can from the class, e.g. *ask for, give, collect, lend, borrow, take, have, use*. You can also take the opportunity to revise the verbs from previous sections: *pay, spend, win, lose, earn*.

Pronunciation stress in questions

5a 🔴 [1.45] Play the recording of the four requests from Exercise 4. Students listen and note the stress.

Audioscript and key 🔴 [1.45]

1 Could you <u>give</u> us <u>something</u>?

2 Can I <u>ask</u> you <u>something</u>?

3 Could you <u>lend</u> me some <u>money</u>?

4 Can I <u>borrow</u> the <u>money</u>?

Pronunciation notes

In requests, we tend to use clear stress patterns. The greater the stress, the politer and more tentative the request. The intonation also tends to rise in the middle and then fall. A flat intonation sounds rude. However, an over-exaggerated intonation can sound grovelling or insincere.

5b 🔴 [1.45] Play the recording again. Students listen and repeat. Encourage them to imitate the stress patterns and intonation on the recording.

6 Organise the class into pairs. Ask students to practise the conversations in Exercise 3. Then ask them to improvise their own conversations.

With weaker classes, tell them to prepare a conversation first. When students are ready, ask them to practise reading out the conversation in pairs. Monitor carefully and make sure they are attempting good intonation.

Extra activity

Provide students with prompts to use to make conversations, e.g.

open the window

do my homework for me

lend me ten euros

borrow your car

lend me a thousand euros

6e Thanks!

Lead-in

Introducing the theme: thanks

Ask students: *When do you say 'thank you'? When was the last time you said 'thank you', and who to? Do you ever write 'thank you' letters? When was the last time, and why did you write?*

Writing thank you messages

1 Students discuss the questions in small groups or as a class. In feedback, ask students if they can think of other situations when people write 'thank you' letters.

2 Students read the card, email and letter. Discuss the question in feedback.

ANSWERS

A thanks someone for a graduation present
B thanks someone for their work
C thanks a customer for showing interest in their products

Vocabulary notes

Note that in a formal letter the recipient's title and surname (but not their first name or initials) are used, e.g. *Mr / Ms Smith*. The sender writes his or her name in full. If a letter begins *Dear Mr / Ms Smith,* it ends *Yours sincerely*. If it begins *Dear Sir / Madam,* it ends *Yours faithfully*.

Writing skill formal and informal expressions

3a Students read the messages again and complete the table. Let them compare their answers in pairs before discussing as a class.

ANSWERS

	A	B	C
Introduction	Hi!	Dear Nadia	Dear Mr Keeping
Thank the person	Thanks for…	Thank you for…	Thank you very much for…
Talk about future contact	See you soon!	See you again next year.	I look forward to hearing from you in the future.
End the writing	Love	Best regards	Yours sincerely

3b Ask students to look at the expressions in the table in pairs, and decide which messages use informal expressions, and which are more formal. Ask students to think about what this tells them about the people writing.

ANSWERS

A

The note in A is handwritten and very informal. Ginny is writing to a family member or close friend – and is probably quite young. Examples of high informality include abbreviations (*thanks*), dramatic punctuation (*!*), and very personal language (*Hi, Love*).

B

The email is still informal. Sanjit is writing to someone he knows well, but in a business context. The letter is warm and informal, but it avoids abbreviations and highly personal language.

C

The business letter is written to someone the writer does not know except in a business context. Consequently, it uses all the formalities of such a letter, including fixed expressions such as *Please find enclosed* and *I look forward to*.

---

4 Lead in by reading through the situations with the class and eliciting whether they think the situations require a formal or informal 'thank you' message, and whether they should write a note, an email or a letter.

Ask students to choose a situation and write their message. Monitor and help with ideas.

5 Organise the class into pairs. Students exchange messages and comment on the use of language in them.

Extra activity

If your class know each other well, elicit some situations from them involving class members which deserve a 'thank you' letter, e.g. one student may have given another a lift to class, another may have brought in a cake or biscuits at some time. Tell students to write a short thank you note to another class member.

Homework

Ask students to write a 'thank you' message to a friend or family member who has helped them recently.

6f Bactrian treasure

Before you watch

1 Divide the class into pairs to complete the text about Bactria with the past simple form of the verbs.

ANSWERS

1 was
2 travelled
3 bought and sold
4 became
5 made
6 discovered
7 called

---

2 Organise the class into groups of four to describe the photos.

While you watch

3 Ask students to watch the video and match the descriptions to the photos.

ANSWERS

1 page 78
2 photo 6
3 photo 5
4 photo 4
5 photo 3
6 photo 1
7 photo 2

---

4 Play the video again. Students watch and choose the correct option.

ANSWERS

1 c   2 a   3 b   4 a   5 c   6 c

After you watch

5 Divide the class into groups to make their video. Tell them to choose seven objects and discuss why they are important.

6 Students present their seven objects to the class.

Videoscript

Over 2,000 years ago, the northern part of Afghanistan was called Bactria. Bactria was an important place because it was on the main route between the Mediterranean, China and India.

It became a rich region and famous for its kings and queens, their palaces and gold.

00.32 In 1978, a group of Russian archaeologists were in the region and discovered more than 20,000 gold items from the period. The treasure included this beautiful gold crown. A Bactrian queen wore it.

00.54 The archaeologists moved the treasure to the national museum in Kabul, the capital of Afghanistan. But this was a period of terrible war for the people of Afghanistan and the treasure disappeared.

Was it stolen? Many people thought so.

01.18 Then, in 2004, archaeologists discovered six underground vaults in Kabul. There were no keys, so they had to break open the doors one by one. Behind the first door, there was the gold and jewellery.

For example, these gold bracelets have lion heads on them.

And as they opened the next five doors to each vault they found more and more treasure, like this golden belt.

02.00 The treasure also tells us a lot about Bactrian history. These are faces of people from Bactria. And this statue of a cat and this animal tells us that animals were important in Bactrian culture.

Now the Bactrian treasure is travelling to museums all around the world so everyone can enjoy this amazing treasure and learn about the history of Bactria.

UNIT 6 Review
Grammar

1 Ask students to read the article and complete it with the past simple form of the verbs in brackets.

ANSWERS		
1 became	4 sent	7 worked
2 wasn't	5 were	8 discovered
3 wanted	6 was	9 was

2 Ask students to read the questions about the text and complete them.

ANSWERS
1 Was there a route
2 Were Meriwether Lewis and William Clark
3 Was there a woman
4 Was she
5 Was her face

3 Students write five sentences using the verbs and places in the table.

ANSWERS
1 We change money at a currency exchange.
2 We earn money at work.
3 We spend money in shops.
4 We give money to charity.
5 We keep money in a purse or wallet.

4 Ask students to complete the sentences.

ANSWERS				
1 card	2 phone	3 shells	4 transfer	5 account

5 Ask students guess the ages of famous people.

ANSWERS			
1 -ed	2 -ing	3 -ing	4 -ed

6 Students guess the ages of famous people.

Real life

7 Ask students to order the words to make requests.

ANSWERS
1 Could you give me a dollar?
2 Can I ask you something?
3 Could you lend me your phone?
4 Can I borrow your car?

8 Students make the requests and respond in pairs.

Speaking

9 Students work in pairs to describe the events.

Unit 7 Journeys

1 Ask students to look at the photo. Discuss the questions as a class.

> **ANSWERS**
>
> You can see a sailing ship, small boats, an airship, the sea and a city on the skyline.
> It's the second Mayflower ship.

2 💿 [2.1] Ask students what they know about the Mayflower and elicit ideas. Play the recording. Students listen and answer the questions.

> **ANSWERS**
>
> 1 120   2 5

Audioscript 💿 [2.1]

In 1620, one hundred and twenty people travelled across the Atlantic Ocean. The ship was called the Mayflower. It left England on September the 6th. At first the weather was good but later, there were bad storms at sea. Eventually, after 2,750 miles, the Mayflower arrived in the 'New World' (now America) on November the 11th. The people on the ship were the first Europeans to live in the 'New World'. After this journey, the Mayflower sailed across the Atlantic Ocean four more times. On its final journey, it left England but it never arrived in America.

3 Ask students to choose the correct verbs. Let students compare their answers in pairs.

> **ANSWERS**
>
> 1 sailed   3 arrived in
> 2 left   4 travelled

4 Divide the class into pairs or small groups to ask and answer the questions. Monitor and note errors for an error feedback at the end.

7a Flight of the Silver Queen

Reading

1 Ask students to look at the photo and the map. Discuss the questions as a class. Use the pictures to pre-teach useful words (*plane, silver, flight, non-stop, take off, land, pilots*).

> **ANSWER**
>
> From England to South Africa

2 Ask students to read the article and put the paragraphs in the correct order. Let students check their answers in pairs before discussing as a class.

> **ANSWERS**
>
> 1 C   2 A   3 D   4 B

3 Ask students to read the article and decide if the sentences are true or false. Let students check their answers in pairs before discussing as a class. Ask early finishers to correct the false sentences.

> **ANSWERS**
>
> 1 T
> 2 F (*four aeroplanes didn't finish the journey*)
> 3 T
> 4 F (*they left Italy and landed the next day in Cairo*)
> 5 F (*they had a lot of mechanical problems with the plane and its engine*)
> 6 F (*The Silver Queen couldn't take off so in the end they changed their plane for a different one.*)
> 7 T
> 8 F (*the newspaper didn't give them £10,000 but only £5,000.*)

4 Discuss the questions as a class.

> **SAMPLE ANSWERS**
>
> for the money, for the adventure, to become famous, to show they were strong and brave, to get future work as a pilot, to test the technology of the planes, to develop their skills as pilots, to see the world, to explore new places

Extra activity

Write key verbs from the story on the board: *offer, enter, take off, fly, not stop, land, win, not give.*

Ask students in pairs to close their books and to try and remember and retell the story from the verb prompts. Tell them to use the past tense.

Grammar past simple (negatives)

5 Ask students to look at the sentences and discuss the questions as a class. Read the grammar box with the students, and check the answers to the questions. Refer students to the information and practice on pages 163 and 164.

> ANSWERS
> 1 didn't (past of do)
> 2 no
> 3 base infinitive

Grammar notes

The past is formed with *didn't* + base infinitive. As many languages form the past with a word equivalent to *not* in front of the past form, watch out for errors from students which may include *I no(t) travelled, I don't travelled, I didn't travelled.*

6 Ask students to make sentences from the table. Do the first sentences as an example. Let students work in pairs, or work separately then compare their answers in pairs. In feedback, elicit some answers, and make sure students are using and saying the forms correctly.

> ANSWERS
> In the 1920s, people didn't travel into space. People travelled by train.
> People didn't pay by credit card, they paid with cash.
> People didn't play computer games, they played games.
> People didn't use satellite navigation, they used maps.

Extra activity

Fast finishers can write their own sentences about the 1920s using other verbs and ideas.

7 Start students off by producing one or two sentences of your own, e.g. *Ten years ago I didn't work in this school. I didn't have short hair.* Then ask students to write their own sentences. Monitor and make sure students are using the forms correctly. Put students in pairs to share their ideas.

Extra activity

Ask students to write two true past tense sentences and one false one. When they read them to their partner, he or she must guess which one is false.

Listening

8 🔘 [2.2] Ask students to predict what the speaker will talk about on the radio programme from the title and the three topics.

Play the recording. Students listen and order the topics.

> ANSWERS
> 1 b   2 c   3 a

Audioscript 🔘 [2.2]

I = interviewer, H = historian

I: This week's programme is about a famous journey nearly one hundred years ago. In 1920, an aeroplane called the *Silver Queen* travelled from England to Cape Town. It was the first aeroplane to travel on this journey. Here in the studio to tell us about this journey is travel historian Nigel Ross.

H: Hello.

I: So Nigel, in 1920, this was a small aeroplane and there weren't many airports in Africa at that time. How dangerous was this journey?

H: Oh, it was very dangerous for the two pilots.

I: Yes, the two pilots were Pierre Van Ryneveld and Quintin Brand. Did they have maps for this journey?

H: Yes, they did. Well, for some parts of the journey. For example, they had maps for Europe, Egypt and South Africa. But they didn't have maps for other parts of Africa.

I: And why did they go on this journey? Was it for the money?

H: All travellers and explorers go for different reasons. But Van Ryneveld and Brand didn't go for the money. I think they flew there because it was new. They wanted to be the first.

9 🔘 [2.2] Play the recording again. Students choose the correct options. Let them compare their answers in pairs before discussing as a class.

> ANSWERS
> 1 had   3 didn't go
> 2 didn't have 4 wanted

Grammar past simple: questions and short answers

10 Ask students to look at the sentences and discuss the question as a class. Read the grammar box with the students, and check the answer to the question. Refer students to the information and practice on pages 163 and 164.

> ANSWER
> did

Grammar notes

The past simple question is formed with *did,* which inverts with the noun or pronoun and is followed by the base infinitive of the main verb.

Q-word	*did*	noun / pronoun	infinitive
Where	*did*	*you*	*go?*

11 Divide the class into pairs. Tell them to decide who is A and who is B, and find and read their information on page 155 or 156.

Once students have prepared questions, tell them to take turns to ask and answer them. In feedback, ask students what was the same and what was different about this flight compared to the flight of the Silver Queen.

Extra activity

Ask students if they know about any other famous flights. Ask any well-informed students to tell the class what they know. You could prompt students by writing the names of famous aviators on the board, e.g. the *Wright Brothers, Amelia Earhart, Charles Lindbergh, Amy Johnson, Louis Bleriot, Chuck Yeager.* Ask students to research one of these aviators and tell the class about him or her in the next lesson.

Speaking

12 Introduce the activity by describing a journey that you made.

Tell students to prepare to speak by thinking of a journey and making notes to answer the questions. Monitor and help with ideas.

Extra activity

It is a good idea to lead in to this activity by briefly telling a story of a journey you made, then writing the following question prompts on the board:

Where / go?

Why / go there?

How / travel there?

Have / any problems?

How long / the journey take?

Students must ask questions, and you retell the story in response. This models the activity fully and gives students some good accuracy practice with question forms.

13 Organise the class into pairs. Ask students to take turns to ask questions and tell their partner about their journeys. In feedback, ask students to tell the class what they remember about their partner's journey. Note any errors students make with past forms and do an error feedback at the end.

Homework

Ask students to write about their journey.

7b Animal migrations

Lead-in

Test before you teach: comparing

Write the names of three types of animals on the board, e.g. *an elephant, a cheetah, a frog.*

Ask students in pairs to think of as many ways as they can to compare the animals. After two minutes, elicit ideas. Students may say, for example: *Elephants are very big but frogs are small,* or *Cheetahs are fast but elephants are big.* Alternatively they may attempt comparative forms. Either way, accept the ideas. Find out what adjectives students know, and whether they can already use comparative forms to some extent.

Vocabulary journey adjectives

1 Ask students to look at the photo. Ask: *What can you see?* (wildebeest) *Where are they going?* Ask students to read the text and answer the question.

> **ANSWER**
> migrations by animals

Background notes

The Serengeti is a geographical region in east Africa which covers 30,000km² of north Tanzania and southern Kenya. The migration of 1.2 million wildebeest each year takes place every July – it's the largest terrestrial mammal migration in the world.

2 Students find the opposite adjectives in the text. Let them check their answers in pairs.

> **ANSWERS**
> easy / difficult, fast / slow, safe / dangerous, short / long

3 Lead in by describing your own journeys. Then ask students in pairs to describe their journeys.

Extra activity

Ask students to describe other journeys they take, e.g. their summer holidays, visiting grandparents, journey to school, journey to the supermarket.

Listening

4 🔘 [2.3] Ask students to look at the photos. Ask: *What are the animals' names? What do you know about them? What do you want to find out?* Elicit ideas.

Check the words in the glossary. Then play the recording. Students listen and match the animals to the distances. Let them compare their answers in pairs.

> **ANSWERS**
> 1 b   2 c   3 a

Audioscript 💿 [2.3]

1 The saiga lives in Central Asia. In the spring it walks to higher places. A male saiga can walk thirty-five kilometres a day and it's faster than a female. The journey is more difficult for a female saiga because she has her calf in the spring.

2 Many turtles swim longer distances than other sea animals, but the loggerhead turtle has a longer journey than other turtles. It leaves the beach as a baby and it swims around fourteen thousand kilometres. Fifteen years later, the female turtle returns to the same beach and lays eggs.

3 Tree frogs go on shorter journeys than other animals, but for a small tree frog the journey isn't easier. Every spring it climbs down a tree. That's about thirty metres. It lays eggs in water and then returns up the tree. For a tree frog that's a very long journey.

5 💿 [2.3] Play the recording again. Students listen and answer the questions. Let students compare their answers in pairs.

ANSWERS	
1 Central Asia	4 the same beach
2 her calf	5 in water
3 the beach	

Extra activity

Write these verbs on the board: *swim, leave, lay, walk, climb.* Ask students to say which animal does which verb.

Grammar comparative adjectives

6 Students look at the sentences and answer the questions. Let them compare their answers in pairs. Read the grammar box with the students. Refer students to the information and practice on page 164.

ANSWERS	
1 -er	2 more

7 Complete the first two gaps in the table as examples to get students started. Then ask them to complete the rest of the table. Ask students to compare their sentences in pairs before discussing as a class.

ANSWERS	
1 bigger	6 more expensive
2 colder	7 longer
3 hotter	8 more interesting
4 more dangerous	9 easier
5 cheaper	10 higher

Extra activity

Ask fast finishers to write opposite comparatives to those in the table, e.g. *shorter, smaller, more difficult, more boring, lower.*

Word focus *than*

8 Do the first sentence as an example. Elicit suggestions such as *Australia is hotter / more interesting than Antarctica.*

Then ask students to work in pairs to write sentences. Elicit suggestions from the class.

SAMPLE ANSWERS
2 A car is more expensive than a bicycle.
3 Rock-climbing is more dangerous than surfing.
4 Travel by air is cheaper than travel by sea.
5 An elephant is bigger than a lion.
6 A holiday in the city is more expensive than camping in the countryside.
7 Paris is more expensive than New York.
8 Train journeys are longer than plane journeys.

Pronunciation stressed and weak syllables /ə/

9 💿 [2.4] Play the recording. Students listen and notice the use of the weakly-stressed schwa in the -er ending and *than*. Play the recording again. Students listen and repeat.

Speaking

10 Ask students to look at the sentences and discuss which is fact and which is opinion, then do the same with the other sentences in Exercise 8. They should then say the opinions with the phrases.

ANSWER
The first sentence is a fact, the second is an opinion.

11 Students write their own sentences. Remind them to use the opinion phrases from Exercise 10. Monitor and help with ideas.

12 Start the activity by acting out the first conversation with a reliable student.

Organise the class into pairs. Tell students to take turns to read out opinions and say if they agree or not.

Extra activity

Have a class discussion about one or two of the topics.

Homework

Ask students to write comparative sentences about two cities they know well.

7c The longest journey in space

Lead-in

Using words: space
Elicit nouns which are useful for this lesson from your students. You could bring in a picture or pictures of the sun or one or more planets, put them on the board, and ask students to say what they are. Alternatively, draw a big sun in the middle of the board, and elicit and draw the Earth, Moon and other planets.

Words to check are: *Sun, Moon, planet, Earth*, the names of all the planets, *solar system, spacecraft, rings, ice.*

Reading

1 Discuss the question as a class. Build up ideas on the board.

> **SAMPLE ANSWERS**
>
> Space travel is important so we can explore new worlds, find new minerals and materials, discover life on other planets, improve scientific understanding, improve technology.
>
> It's too expensive, there's nothing there.

2 Ask students to look at the photos and the caption and discuss the questions. Ask students to predict what the text is about from the photos and the title.

> **ANSWERS**
>
> Voyager 1
>
> It photographed planets and moons

3 Ask students to read the article and answer the questions. Let them compare their answers in pairs.

> **ANSWERS**
>
> 1 two
> 2 Jupiter and Saturn
> 3 Jupiter, Saturn, Uranus and Neptune
> 4 at the end of our solar system

4 Students read the article again and decide what the underlined words refer to. Alternatively, get students to replace the reference words before reading the article for a second time, thus testing their general knowledge and memory. Do the first sentence as an example. In feedback, ask students to say which reference words are used to replace the nouns or phrases.

> **ANSWERS**
>
> 1 Florida   5 Uranus
> 2 Voyager 2   6 Neptune
> 3 Saturn   7 outside the solar system
> 4 Jupiter's

Grammar notes

English uses subject and object pronouns (*he, him,* etc.), possessive adjectives and pronouns (*her, hers,* etc.), demonstrative adjectives and pronouns (*this, that, those,* etc.), and the adverbs *here* and *there* as reference words to replace (and refer to) nouns or phrases to avoid repeating them in a text.

Background notes

NASA (the National Aeronautics and Space Administration) is responsible for the space programme and aerospace research on behalf of the US government.

The solar system describes the 'system' of planets that orbit the Sun. Note that there used to be nine planets until Pluto was demoted to a dwarf planet in 2006.

Critical thinking fact or opinion

5 Read through the sentences with the class then ask students to answer the questions. Ask students to say which words helped them to differentiate fact from opinion.

> **ANSWERS**
>
> Fact: On 20th August and 5th September in 1977, two spacecraft took off from Florida, USA.
>
> Opinion: Voyager 1 and Voyager 2 started a long and difficult journey to the end of the solar system.

6 Students read the text again and find more sentences with the writer's opinions. Let them compare their answers in pairs.

> **ANSWERS**
>
> Paragraph 2: … the best photographs … ; … most famous
>   for its rings …
> Paragraph 4: … their most amazing journey …

Vocabulary notes

We can tell that a sentence contains an opinion when it uses phrases like *I think …, I believe …, It seems …,* and from opinion adjectives such as *difficult, good (best), famous* and *amazing.*

Grammar superlative adjectives

7 Compare the sentences and discuss the questions as a class. Read the grammar box with the students. Refer students to the information and practice on pages 164 and 165.

> **ANSWERS**
>
> a compares two things
> b compares more than two things

Grammar notes

We add -est to adjectives with one syllable and use *the* in front of the superlative form (because it is unique), e.g. *the smallest boy*. With longer adjectives, we use *most*, e.g. *the most interesting book*.

Note two syllable adjectives: *busy – busiest, modern – more modern* but *narrow – narrowest*

Note irregular superlatives: *good – best, bad – worst, far – farthest / furthest*

The fact that English has two types of comparative and superlative forms (betraying both its north Germanic and its Norman French roots) often confuses students. Speakers of romance languages often say: *more big, more young*, etc. while speakers of German often say, *intelligenter* or *moderner*. It is worth getting students to compare how their language forms comparatives and superlatives.

8 Students find and underline the forms, then answer the questions. Let them compare their ideas in pairs.

> **ANSWERS**
> (the) best, (the) most famous, (the) coldest, (the) furthest, (the) most amazing
> *good* and *far* have irregular forms. The word *the* comes before the superlative adjective.

9 Students complete the quiz questions with superlatives. Let them compare answers in pairs. Check that students have the correct answers, then let them discuss the answers in pairs.

> **ANSWERS**
> 1 Which planet is the nearest to the Sun? (Mercury)
> 2 Which planet is the easiest to see the in the sky? (Venus)
> 3 Which planet is the furthest / farthest from the Earth? (Neptune)
> 4 Which planet is the best for human life? (Earth)
> 5 Which planet is the hottest? (Venus)

Extra activity

Ask students to prepare other questions using the following words: *cold, beautiful, strange, small, wide, wet, dry*. They can then research the answers for homework.

Writing and speaking

10 Start by brainstorming subjects students could ask about (e.g. countries, cities, famous people, animals).

Then ask students to work in groups to prepare a quiz. When the groups are ready, ask them to try out their questions on another group.

In feedback, find out which group answers most questions correctly.

7d How was your trip?

Lead-in

Introducing the theme: trips

Write the word *trip* in the middle of the board. Then elicit words that go with it and write them up at random on the board, e.g. *day, business, work, round, bus, train, road, fishing, camping, sightseeing, field*. Ask students in pairs to give examples of some of these trips that they have made.

Vocabulary *journey, travel* or *trip*?

1 Ask students to match the words to definitions in pairs or small groups. Discuss the answers in feedback.

> **ANSWERS**
> 1 b   2 a   3 c

Vocabulary notes

Note that *travel* is an uncountable noun and describes the activity rather than individual events. It can also, of course, be a verb.

We often precede *trip* with other words (*day, business, work, round, bus, road trip*, etc.) (see lead-in).

Other words you could mention here are: *voyage* (a journey by sea), *excursion* (similar to *trip*, but always for pleasure, not work), *expedition* (a journey to find or explore a place).

2 Discuss the questions as a class. Elicit any interesting answers from students.

3 Ask students to look at the pictures. Ask: *What can you see? Where is the man? How do you know he is on a work trip?* Elicit ideas.

Organise the class into pairs. Students match the words to the pictures. In feedback, check the difference between *very* and *really* (see grammar notes below). Read the *Wordbuilding* box with the class. Refer students to page 59 of the Workbook for further information and practice.

> **ANSWERS**
> A tiring   D really useful
> B comfortable   E delicious
> C very interesting F terrible

Grammar notes

With core adjectives such as *comfortable, interesting, tiring* and *useful*, you can use *very* and *really* to make them stronger.

With extreme adjectives such as *delicious and terrible*, you can use *really* but you can't use *very*.

Extra activity

Ask students to give other adjectives you could use to describe the pictures.

Real life asking about a trip

4 [2.5] Give students a moment to look at the questions. Play the recording. Students listen and answer. Let students compare their answers in pairs before discussing as a class.

> **ANSWERS**
>
> Conversation 1
> 1 still on the trip
> 2 the flight, the airport hotel
> 3 the flight was tiring; the hotel was comfortable
>
> Conversation 2
> 1 in his own country
> 2 the local food; the weather
> 3 the food was delicious and the seafood was fresh; the weather was terrible

Audioscript [2.5]

Conversation 1

C = Dr Cunningham, E = Dr Egan

C: Doctor Egan? Doctor Egan?

E: Yes, are you Doctor Cunningham?

C: That's right. Nice to meet you. But please, call me Sonia.

E: Nice to meet you too, Sonia. I'm Charles.

C: How was your flight?

E: Not bad. A bit tiring because we were delayed for ten hours.

C: That's right. I got your message.

E: Oh, that's good. But I had a good night's sleep at the airport hotel.

C: Oh, was it comfortable?

E: Yes, very. I feel fine now.

C: Great! OK. My car is outside.

E: Right. Let's go.

Conversation 2

F = friend, E = Dr Egan

F: Hello Charles. How was your trip?

E: Very interesting. And I had some very useful meetings with Doctor Cunningham.

F: Good. Did you try the local food?

E: Yes, I did. It was delicious. I ate fresh seafood every night.

F: And what was the weather like?

E: Terrible! On the second day we couldn't travel anywhere.

F: Why? What happened?

E: There was a terrible storm. It rained for twenty-four hours and all the roads were closed.

5 [2.5] Ask students to read through the expressions and try to complete them. Let them compare their answers in pairs. Play the recording again. Students listen and complete the questions.

> **ANSWERS**
> 1 How was   4 was, like
> 2 Was it   5 happened
> 3 Did you

Vocabulary notes

Note the use of *How ... ?* and *What ... like?* when asking for descriptions about trips.

Pronunciation intonation in questions

6 [2.6] Play the recording. Students listen and pay attention to the intonation. Then they listen and repeat, imitating the intonation patterns.

Audioscript [2.6]

1 How was your flight?
2 Was it comfortable?
3 Did you try the local food?
4 What was the weather like?
5 Why? What happened?

Extra activity

Draw a rising arrow and a falling arrow on the board before students attempt the roleplays in Exercises 7 and 8. When students are speaking, listen carefully, and, if their intonation is flat or incorrect, point to the appropriate arrow on the board to correct them.

7 Organise the class into pairs. Ask student B to look at the pictures in Exercise 2 and think of questions to ask. Ask A to look at the pictures and think of responses. When students are ready, ask them to improvise a conversation.

Monitor carefully and make sure they are attempting the correct intonation in conversations.

8 Ask students to look at the pictures on page 155. Ask: *What can you see? Where is he? How does he feel?* Elicit ideas and vocabulary.

Students change roles and prepare questions and responses based on the pictures on page 155. When they are ready, they improvise conversations.

Homework

Ask students to write a dialogue about a trip they have made. Tell them to use questions from page 88 of the Student's Book but to use their own information to write responses.

7e The digital nomad

Lead-in

Introducing the theme: travel blogs
Write the following random phrases from the blog on page 89: *… the final day of … ; … a very long … ; … travel for … ; … ten kilometres from … ; … started to walk to … ; … felt sorry for … .*
Ask students to say what type of text these phrases might be from. Ask them to say how you could start or end any of these phrases. Ask them what story the text might tell.

Vocabulary online writing

1 Discuss the questions as a class.

Extra activity

Ask some follow-up questions: *What can you find out from reading blogs? What is good or bad about blogs? Do you prefer writing a diary to a blog?*

2 Students read the blog and answer the questions. Let them check their answers in pairs.

> ANSWERS
> 1 Because he travels all the time and is always online.
> 2 He writes about his journeys.

3 Students match words to definitions. Let them check their answers in pairs.

> ANSWERS
> 1 website   4 homepage   7 comment
> 2 blogs   5 blogger   8 posts
> 3 online   6 uploads

Writing a travel blog

4 Ask students to predict what the travel blog might be about from the photo. Then ask them to read the blog and answer the questions. Let students compare their answers in pairs.

> ANSWERS
> 1 ten kilometres from Kodari
> 2 three days
> 3 the north side of Everest
> 4 The bus stopped – the engine needed fixing.
> 5 He looked a bit sad.
> 6 He wanted a good hotel and a hot meal.

Extra activity

Check these new words: *final* (last); *border* (place where one country meets another); *engine* (machine that gives power to a vehicle); *passengers* (people on a bus); *fix* (repair)

Background notes

Lhasa is the capital of Tibet, which is an autonomous region of China. The region borders the independent country of Nepal. They are mountainous regions in the Himalayas.

Writing skill *so, because*

5a Students read the third paragraph of the blog again and find the conjunctions. Let them discuss their answers to the questions in pairs before discussing as a class.

> ANSWERS
> a because
> b so

Grammar notes

We use *so* to give a result or consequence. We use *because* to give a reason. Both words join two clauses.

5b Ask students to complete the sentences. Let them compare their answers with a partner before discussing as a class.

> ANSWERS
> 1 because   3 because   5 so
> 2 so   4 so   6 because

6 Start by reading out sentences from your own imaginary blog, e.g. *I was on holiday in Mexico so I decided to go sightseeing. I was with my friends …*

Give students time to prepare ideas for their blogs first. Monitor and help. Then ask them to put their ideas together in sentences.

7 Organise the class into pairs to exchange blogs and comment on the content and the use of conjunctions.

Extra activity

Write the following sentence starters and ask students to complete them with their own ideas.
I write a blog because …
I often read blogs about … because …
I spend a lot of time online so …
My hobbies are … and … so …

Homework

Ask students to write a travel blog about another journey they have made.

7f Women in space

Before you watch

1 Discuss the questions as a class.

2 Organise the class into pairs. Tell them to read the sentences and choose the correct option.

While you watch

3 Students watch the video and check their answers.

> **ANSWERS**
> 1 American woman in space
> 2 days
> 3 travelled
> 4 other women

4 Students watch the video again, and match the year to the events.

> **ANSWERS**
> 1 g   2 d   3 f   4 a   5 b   6 h   7 c   8 e

5 Students watch the video again, and choose the correct answers.

> **ANSWERS**
> 1 a   2 b   3 a, b   4 b   5 b   6 c

After you watch

6 Organise the class into pairs. Ask students to decide on their roles and prepare them. When students are ready, tell them to act out the conversation. You could get some pairs to come to the front of the class to act out their roleplays.

7 Organise the students into pairs. Give students time to prepare to speak. Then ask them to take turns to talk about their role-model.

Videoscript

NASA began in 1958.

It put a man on the Moon in 1969.

Spacecraft like Voyager 1 and 2 discovered new places in our solar system and the space shuttle flew into space and back again.

00.19 In the early days of NASA, space was a man's world.

But on the 18 June 1983, Sally Ride was the first American woman in space.

Sally was a doctor of physics and she was part of a group of six candidates to be the first female astronaut.

Sally soon got the job and went into space on the Challenger space shuttle.

00.51 The Russians sent the first women into space in 1963, but Sally Ride was the first for the USA.

She helped to launch two satellites and did scientific experiments over six days.

After she returned from the journey, Sally gave talks across the USA.

01.29 In particular, her journey was important for women and many travelled to listen to her.

Sally went into space one more time – in 1984.

And after her, there were other women astronauts and other 'firsts'.

01.59 Mae Jemison was a physician and became the first African-American woman in space with the space shuttle Endeavour in 1992.

Then, in 1995, Eileen Collins became the first female pilot, with the space shuttle Discovery.

And she flew two more times in 1999 and 2005.

02.33 So as a result of Sally Ride, and many more female astronauts after her, young women – as well as young men – now dream of becoming astronauts and a journey into space.

UNIT 7 Review

Grammar

1 Ask students to complete the text with the past simple form of the verbs in brackets.

> **ANSWERS**
>
> | | | |
> |---|---|---|
> | 1 began | 5 stayed | 9 didn't believe |
> | 2 travelled | 6 worked | 10 said |
> | 3 took | 7 didn't travel | |
> | 4 didn't return | 8 became | |

2 Ask students to write questions about Marco Polo from the prompts.

> **ANSWERS**
>
> 2 Where did he travel from?
> 3 How long did the journey take?
> 4 How long did he stay in China?
> 5 After 1295 did he travel to Asia again?

3 Students work in pairs to ask and answer the questions in Exercise 2.

> **ANSWERS**
>
> 1 He began his journey when he was seventeen years old.
> 2 He travelled from Venice through to Persia, to Afghanistan and along the Silk Road to Cambulac (now Beijing).
> 3 The journey took three years.
> 4 He stayed in China for seventeen years.
> 5 No, he didn't.

4 Ask students to read the information in the sentences, then write two comparative sentences using the two adjectives in brackets, as in the example.

> **ANSWERS**
>
> 2 A Porsche is faster than a Mini. A Mini is slower than a Porsche.
> 3 This house is more expensive than the apartment. This apartment is cheaper than the house.
> 4 London is bigger than Madrid. Madrid is smaller than London.
> 5 The Nile River is shorter than the Amazon. The Amazon River is longer than the Nile.

5 Ask students to read the sentences and compare them with the relevant sentences in Exercise 4 (e.g. sentence 1 in Exercise 5 and in Exercise 4), then write a superlative sentence.

> **ANSWERS**
>
> 2 It's the fastest car.
> 3 It's the most expensive home.
> 4 It's the biggest capital city.
> 5 It's the shortest river.

Vocabulary

6 Students write one type of transport for each category.

> **SAMPLE ANSWERS**
>
> | | | | |
> |---|---|---|---|
> | 1 a bike | 2 a plane | 3 a boat | 4 a car |

7 Ask students to choose the correct options to complete the sentences.

> **ANSWERS**
>
> | | | | |
> |---|---|---|---|
> | 1 journey | 2 trip | 3 take | 4 writes / blogs |

Real life

8 Students complete the sentences with words from the box.

> **ANSWERS**
>
> | | | | |
> |---|---|---|---|
> | 1 meal | 2 weather | 3 hotel | 4 flight |

Speaking

9 Ask students to work in pairs to remember as much as they can about the different journeys from the unit.

Unit 8 Appearance

Lead-in

Introducing the theme: festivals

Write the following international festivals on the board: *Mardi Gras in New Orleans, Carnival in Rio, Notting Hill in London, Venice Carnival*.

Ask students in pairs or small groups to share what they know about each of these carnivals. Take feedback from the class and find out if anyone has ever been to one of these festivals, or other famous festivals round the world (but note that they will talk about their own local festivals later in the lesson).

1 Ask students to look at the photo first. Ask: *What can you see? Who is the man?* Elicit *a festival, a dancer*. Then ask students to read the caption and answer the questions.

> **ANSWERS**
> 1 in the Philippines
> 2 colourful, crowded, exciting, fun, loud, popular, noisy

2 💿 [2.7] Give students a moment to read through the sentences and options. Check that students are familiar with this type of activity, and if necessary explain how it works (see Teaching notes below). Then play the recording. Ask students to listen and choose the correct option.

> **ANSWERS**
> 1 T   2 DK   3 DK   4 T   5 F

Audioscript 💿 [2.7]

I was in the city of Iloilo in the Philippines last month. I wanted to see the Dinagyang Festival. The festival is always on the fourth Sunday in January. It's the most famous festival in the Philippines and thousands of local people and tourists come to the city. Groups of local people wear colourful clothes and make-up. Then they dance through the streets. The music was really loud. I also ate lots of local food – it was delicious!

Teaching notes

Make sure students understand how to do this type of activity. Explain that the information on the recording (or in the text) must match the statement in the sentence if it is *true,* and contradict it if it is *false*. If the recording does not give any information about the statement, students should answer *don't know,* even if they know what the answer is from their own knowledge.

Background notes

The Dinagyang is a religious, cultural and thanksgiving celebration in Iloilo City, Philippines. It is held both to honour the Santo Niño and to celebrate the arrival of Malay settlers and the fact of selling of the island to them by the Ati tribe.

3 Organise the class into pairs or groups of four or five to share information about the festivals in their countries. If you have a range of nationalities in your class, mix students from different parts of the world.

They should look at the questions and prepare to answer them. They could make brief notes to help them, if they think they need to. Then they take turns to ask and answer the questions in their groups. In feedback, ask students to tell you about their partner's festival.

Extra activity

Ask students to research one of the festivals in the lead-in on the Internet before the next class. Tell them to find information to answer the questions in Exercise 3.

8a The faces of festivals

Lead-in

Test before you teach: *has got*

Ask students to look at the photo of the carnival dancer on page 93. Ask them to describe the young man using the structure *he's got ...* See how many sentences they can think of.

Listening

1 Ask students to look at the photos. Ask: *What can you see?* Elicit the word *masks*.

Get students in pairs to discuss the questions.

2 💿 [2.8] Ask students to listen to the recording. Students listen and number the children in the photo in the order the speakers discuss them.

> **ANSWERS**
> 1 boy on the right   2 boy on the left   3 girl in the middle

Audioscript 💿 [2.8]

A = woman, **B** = man

A: I've got some photographs here from my holiday in Spain.

B: Oh, let me see.

A: This one is from a town called Banyoles. It's in Catalonia.

B: What's this one?

A: This is of three children in masks. It was a special festival. They always have it in the summer. People come from all over for the food and music.

B: Why have they got these masks?

A: It's part of the festival. The masks are called *capgrossos* in the local language. I think they're a bit ugly.

B: Oh no! I don't think so. He's got a fantastic white face. And look at those red cheeks.

A: Yeah but he hasn't got any eyebrows.

B: Oh that's right. Well, he's got one. So are they brothers and sister?

A: Yes, that's right. I think this one's the oldest brother. Or maybe he's tall because he's got that big hat. And she's his little sister. She's got great big blue eyes.

B: She's similar to my daughter with that blonde hair and the red ribbon.

A: I hope she isn't!

3 💿 [2.8] Give students some time to read through the questions and help with any difficult vocabulary. You may want to pre-teach *similar* and *ribbon* by miming or drawing, or using the picture. Play the whole of the recording again for the students to listen and answer the questions. Let them check their answers with a partner before discussing as a class.

> **ANSWERS**
> 1 She was on holiday.
> 2 Three children were in the masks.
> 3 The festival is in the summer.
> 4 People travel there for the food and the music.
> 5 She thinks they are a bit ugly.
> 6 The white face of the third mask.
> 7 Yes, they are.
> 8 Because she's got blonde hair and a red ribbon.

4 Get students to discuss the questions in pairs. In feedback, ask students why they think the masks are beautiful or ugly.

Grammar *have got / has got*

5 Tell students to look at the sentences from the conversation in Exercise 2.

Go through the sentences with the students and ask them to choose the correct option. Read through the grammar box with the class. Refer students to the information and practice on page 165.

> **ANSWERS**
> 1 be   2 have got

Grammar notes

Have got is commonly used to express possession. In this structure, *have* is an auxiliary verb. It inverts with the subject to form questions (e.g. *Has he got ... ?*), and goes with *n't* to form a negative (e.g. *He hasn't got ... .*).

Note that it is possible to use *have* instead of *have got* (*I have blue eyes / Do you have brown eyes?*)

6 💿 [2.9] Ask students to look at the picture and ask: *Has he got a mask? Do you like it?* and collect students' ideas. Pre-teach *a string of seashells around his neck*, using the picture. Then give students some time to read through the text and complete it with a form of *be* or *have got*. Get students to check their answers in pairs. Play the recording for the students to check their answers.

> **ANSWERS**
> 1 is
> 2 are
> 3 have got / 've got
> 4 have got / 've got
> 5 has got / 's got
> 6 has got / 's got

Audioscript 💿 [2.9]

This Polga tribesman is a dancer at a festival in Papua New Guinea. All the men are tall and handsome and they've got colourful clothes with red hats over their short, dark hair. They've got white faces and black lines around their brown eyes, on their eyebrows and on their cheeks. The man in the photo has got red on his lips and nose, and he's got black on his chin and a string of seashells around his neck.

Vocabulary face and appearance

7 Get students to look at the highlighted words in the text in Exercise 6 and point at the parts of the face on their own face or in the photo.

Extra activity

Get one of the students to come to the front of the class. Call out the parts of the face at random. The student must touch each part on his or her own face. Alternatively, you could use this activity as a class competitive game between two teams. Each team must touch the parts of the face as you call them out. The team which does this most quickly and with no mistakes, gains a point. The team which gains the most points is the winner.

8 Ask students to look at the table. Explain or mime *general appearance* and *height*. Give students some time to go through the text in Exercise 6 again and complete the table. Check answers.

ANSWERS

General appearance: handsome
Height: tall
Hair: short, dark
Eyes: brown

Pronunciation groups of consonants

9 🔘 [2.10] Write *a, o, u* and *r, t, n* on the board and ask students: *Where are the consonants? Where are the vowels?* Ask students to look at the words in the box, listen to the recording and repeat the words, paying attention to the groups of consonants.

10 Ask students to look at the table. Give them some time to write true sentences about the three children in Exercise 1. Check answers.

SAMPLE ANSWERS

He's got brown hair and a hat.
He's handsome.
She's got a red ribbon.
She's got blue eyes.
She hasn't got a hat.
He's got a white face, red cheeks and red lips.
He's got one eyebrow. He's ugly.
They've got big heads.
They are beautiful / ugly.

Extra activity

Get students in pairs to look at the picture in Exercise 1 for a minute then close their book and say as many sentences describing the children as they can.

11 Give students some time to write a short description of their appearance on a separate piece of paper, using *be* and *have got*. Then students in pairs read out the sentences to each other and decide if it is a correct and accurate description.

Extra activity

Ask students to stand up and walk round the class. Call out a sentence, e.g. *Sit down if you've got blue eyes.* The students who have got blue eyes must sit down. Continue calling out the sentences, using the vocabulary in Exercise 10, until all the students are sitting down. Play two or three times.

Speaking

12 Write *The Secret Student* on the board and tell the students that the secret student is in the class. Get students to look at the questions in the speech bubbles, then choose a reliable student to ask you a couple of questions, e.g. *Is it a man or a woman? Has he got blue eyes? Is she tall?* until the students guess who this person is. Then organise the students into pairs and get them to ask and answer the questions together.

Homework

Ask students to write a description of a souvenir or a mask they have at home, using *be* and *have / has got*.

8b Global fashion

Lead-in

Using words: fashion
Write *Fashion* on the board and explain that it means the style of clothes which is popular now, and the business connected to it. You may want to teach the word *fashionable*. Ask: *Do you read fashion magazines? Do you buy fashionable clothes? Why / Why not? What is in fashion now?*

Reading

1 Pre-teach *price, size, brand* by talking about an item of clothing you are wearing. Then get the students to look at the questions. Students answer the questions in pairs. You may also want to prompt students to ask you the questions first to encourage them to talk more about themselves.

2 Ask students to look at the picture. Ask: *What does she do?* and elicit *a photographer*. Ask students to read the text and answer the questions. Let them compare their answers in pairs.

ANSWERS
1 She is a fashion photographer.
2 She works in the fashion capitals of the world.
3 She is in Sudan now.

3 Ask students to look through the questions. Then ask students to read the text again and answer the questions. Check the answers. Finally, ask students to look at the glossary and go through the words.

ANSWERS
1 b   2 b   3 a   4 a

Extra activity

Ask students to read the article again and find two more clothes words in it.
Answers: *jeans, T-shirts*

Word focus *like*

4 Ask students to look at the expressions from the article and elicit the answer to the first question. Ask students to look at the article again and find another phrase that uses *like* with the meaning 'similar to'.

ANSWERS
In sentence 1, *like* means 'similar to'.
The businessman's suit in Beijing is like the businessman's suit in Berlin.

5 Students in pairs discuss the question. Get class feedback.

Grammar present continuous

6 Ask students to look at the two sentences from the article and answer the questions. Let them compare their answers in pairs. Read through the grammar box with the class. Refer students to pages 165 and 166 for further information and practice.

ANSWERS
1 b   2 a, present simple

Grammar notes

In English, we use the present continuous when we talk about things which are happening now or at the time around now.

The form of the present continuous affirmative is subject + *be* (*am / is / are*) + verb + *-ing*.

The negative form is subject + *be* (*am / is / are*) + *not* + verb + *-ing*.

The question form is *be* (*am / is / are*) + subject + verb + *-ing*.

In short answers, English uses the present form of *be* and omits the main verb, e.g. *Yes, he is. No, I'm not.* Watch out for errors such as *You studying English? Yes, I studying.*

Language learners usually don't have many problems using the present continuous form, because they already know the forms of *be*, but they tend to have problems using it correctly, especially if they do not have an equivalent form in their L1. They often use the present simple instead of present continuous when they talk about things which are happening now or at the time around now e.g. *She talks to me now* instead of *She's talking to me now*, etc.

7 Find the first example as a class, and point out that students need to underline the other examples of the present continuous in the article in Exercise 2. Let them compare their answers in pairs.

ANSWERS
So, what is she doing there?
'I'm taking photographs, of course!'
'I'm not taking photographs for *Vogue* or anyone else.'
'But I'm visiting regions in the world with their own traditional clothes and their own fashions.'

Grammar notes

Language learners tend to confuse the present continuous with other uses of the *-ing* form of the verb, which can have different meanings. You might want to compare the phrase '*And I like looking at clothes*', from the article, with '*I'm taking photographs*' and point out that '*I like looking at clothes*' is not the present continuous. It is a gerund used to describe an activity, and there is no form of *be*.

8 🎵 [2.11] Ask students to look at the conversation. Elicit the answer to gap 1 as a class. Then ask students to go through the whole of the conversation and write the present continuous form of the verbs in brackets. Play the recording. Students listen and check.

ANSWERS

1 I'm calling
2 's speaking
3 'm not staying
4 'm waiting
5 are you going / 're you going
6 Are you travelling
7 are working / 're working
8 is not working / isn't working

9 Ask students to look at the sentences and choose the correct form of the verbs to complete them. Let students check their answers in pairs before discussing as a class.

ANSWERS

1 is travelling   5 is taking
2 doesn't go   6 doesn't take
3 she's visiting   7 Does she have
4 likes   8 is she taking

Vocabulary clothes

10 Ask students to look at the pictures and match the words with the pictures. Check answers and drill pronunciation.

ANSWERS

1 jumper   6 shoes
2 belt   7 socks
3 dress   8 tie
4 trousers   9 shirt
5 skirt   10 hat

Pronunciation notes

Draw the students' attention to the pronunciation and the stress of *skirt* /skɜːt/, *shirt* /ʃɜːt/, *shoes* /ʃuːz/, *tie* /taɪ/, *trousers* /ˈtraʊzəz/. Also note that students often confuse the pronunciation of *shirt* and *skirt*.

11 Divide the class into pairs or small groups and ask students to take turns to describe what they, or their partner, or you, are wearing today.

Extra activity

Describe what somebody in the classroom is wearing today without saying who it is. Students guess the person, then they take turns to describe somebody in the classroom for the others to guess.

Homework

Students find a photo of a celebrity, a famous person or even themselves and write what they are wearing in the photo.

8c In fashion or for life?

Lead-in

Test before you teach: parts of the body
Divide the class into pairs. Tell them to write down as many parts of the body as they can in one minute. Brainstorm answers and write all the answers students can think of on the board. Tell the class to put the words in order – from the top of the head to the bottom of the foot.

Reading

1 Ask students to look at the information box and discuss the questions in pairs first. If you have a range of nationalities in your class, mix students from different parts of the world. When students are ready, have a whole-class discussion.

2 Ask students to look at the photos of the two men and pre-teach *a tattoo*. Note that the plural of *tattoo* is *tattoos*. Get students to discuss the questions in pairs.

ANSWERS

Picture 1 (page 98) fashionable
Picture 2 (page 99) traditional

3 Pre-teach *put on*, *take off* (demonstrate *putting on* and *taking off* using mime). Ask students to read the article quickly and decide which paragraph talks about each section. Let students check their answers in pairs.

ANSWERS

a 3   b 4   c 2   d 1

Critical thinking close reading

4 Ask students to read the whole of the article again and decide if the sentences are true (T), false (F) or don't know (DK). Let them compare their answers in pairs or in small groups before discussing answers as a class.

Go through the *Wordbuilding* box about phrasal verbs with students. For more information and practice, refer them to page 67 of the Workbook.

ANSWERS

1 T   2 T   3 DK   4 T   5 DK   6 F   7 F   8 DK

Grammar notes

A phrasal verb consists of a verb and a preposition or an adverb that modifies or changes the meaning of the main verb: for example, *put* means to place in a specified location, but *put on* is a phrasal verb that means to dress oneself in something.

Extra activity

Ask students to go through the article again and find another phrasal verb in the text. Answer: *take (them) off*

Vocabulary parts of the body

5 Ask students to go through the article again and underline parts of the body in the article. Then ask students to label the pictures on page 98. Check answers and drill the pronunciation of the new words.

ANSWERS

1 shoulder	5 neck	8 leg
2 back	6 chest	9 knee
3 arm	7 hand	10 ankle
4 foot		

Pronunciation note

Draw the students' attention to the pronunciation of *ankle* /ˈæŋkəl/, *knee* /niː/, and *shoulder* /ʃəʊldə/. Explain that k in *knee* is not pronounced.

Extra activity

Say a sentence, e.g. *Touch your knees,* and ask students to follow your instructions. If a student makes a mistake, she / he has to sit out until the next round.

Speaking

6 Put students in pairs or small groups of three or four. If you have a range of nationalities in your class, mix students from different parts of the world. Get them to discuss the questions.

Extra activity

Ask students to draw the tattoo they would like to have on a piece of paper. Divide the class into small groups. They must describe their tattoo and say why the design is important to them.

8d The photos of Reinier Gerritsen

Materials

Ask students to bring in a photo that they like, to talk about in the lesson.

Lead-in

Introducing the theme: talking about photos
Before the lesson, go through a couple of glossy magazines and cut out six to ten interesting photos (depending on the size of your class). Alternatively, download some interesting photos from the Internet. At the start of the lesson, pass round the pictures and ask students in pairs to look at each photo as it goes through their hands and note any words or descriptions that come to mind. Collect in the photos and hold them up. Elicit comments and descriptions from the class. Find out which photos they like the best and why.

Real life talking about pictures and photos

1 Ask students to discuss the questions in pairs. In feedback, ask any student with an interest in art or photography to talk to the class.

2 Ask students to look at the photo. Pre-teach *underground*, *subway* (the underground train system). Divide the class into pairs or groups of three or four to discuss the questions.

ANSWERS

1 They are on the subway / underground. They feel tired, sleepy, bored, etc.
2 Students' own answers.

Background note

In American English, the *subway* is the underground train system, and in British English this is called the *underground* or *tube*.

Extra activity

To provide students with extra support before they listen, get students in pairs or groups of three or four to describe the people in the photograph first. Ask: *Who is on the right? Who is on the left? Who is in the middle? Who is at the back? What are they doing?*

3 [2.12] Tell students that they are going to listen to someone talk about Reinier Gerritsen and his photography. Ask students to read the questions first. Ask: *What do you think?* and get students in pairs or groups of three or four to make predictions about the photo (see Extra activity).

Play the recording once for students to listen and answer the questions. Let them check their answers in pairs before discussing the answers as a class.

ANSWERS

1 His photos are very interesting and the speaker likes them because normally she doesn't look at people in their everyday life very closely, but the photographer does.
2 on the New York subway
3 First: the man and woman on the right.
  Second: the woman in the middle reading her book.
  Third: the woman with blonde hair listening to music.
  Fourth: the other blonde woman on the left watching her.
  Fifth: the other woman at the back looking at the photographer.

Audioscript [2.12]

Reinier Gerritson is one of my favourite photographers. He's from the Netherlands but you can often see his photos around the world, in magazines and sometimes in galleries. I've got some books by him as well. His photos are very interesting. They often show people in their everyday life. This one is on the New York subway. It's early morning so I think most of the people are travelling to work. They're all standing close together but they aren't talking to each other. Well, on the right, the man and woman are talking but the others aren't. The woman in the middle is reading her book. And in front of her the woman with blonde hair is listening to music. Then the other blonde woman on the left is watching her. I'm not sure what she's thinking but she looks a bit sad. Oh and look at the other woman at the back. She's looking straight at the photographer. I take the train to work every day but I never think about the other people. I like it because I don't normally look at people very closely. But Gerritson does.

4 [2.12] Ask students to listen to the recording again and match the sentence beginnings (1–10) with the endings (a–j). Give them some time to look at the sentences first. In strong classes, you might want to ask students to match the sentences first, then listen to check their answers. In weaker classes, get students to listen to the recording first, pausing after each sentence. Check answers.

ANSWERS

1 b	3 j	5 f	7 d	9 i
2 a	4 c	6 h	8 e	10 g

Pronunciation silent letters

5 [2.13] Ask students to look at the words from the recording. Explain that all these words have silent letters and that a silent letter is a letter we don't pronounce. Remind the students that they already know some words with silent letters, e.g. *knee*. Ask: *Which letter is silent?* and elicit the answer *k*.

Ask students to listen and cross out the silent letters in the words from the box as they listen. Get them to check answers in pairs. Check answers as a class. Note that in *listening* there are two silent letters. Play the recording again for students to listen and repeat.

ANSWERS

interesting
sometimes
everyday
listening
blonde
closely

---

6 Look at the box of useful expressions for talking about pictures and photos with the class. Check that they understand all the language. Point out the different prepositions used for position: *on the left / right*, *in the middle*, and *at the front / back*. Ask students to go to page 156 and look at another photo by Reinier Gerritsen. They should work in pairs to describe the different aspects of the picture, using the expressions from the box. Check the answers in feedback.

SAMPLE ANSWER

The subject of the photo is a crowd of people. They are in the subway at rush hour, waiting for a train. They look expectant, as if the train is about to come into the station. Several of them are looking at the photographer. One man is reading a book, some of the others might be reading but you can't see the books. One woman is wearing a yellow hat and scarf and she looks cold. The man near the front is wearing a black and white shirt and a green and black tie, with bold patterns.

Background notes

This photo is another one in the 'Wall Street Stop' series of photographs by Reinier Gerritsen, who, in 2009, after the financial crash, decided to take photographs of subway passengers as they came into and left the Wall Street station in New York. Wall Street is one of the world's largest financial centres.

7 Ask students to bring into class a picture or photo they like, show it to their partner and talk about it. They should use the expressions in the box to talk about different aspects of the picture. If students have not brought in photos, ask them to prepare a description of a photo for homework, which they then bring to the next lesson.

Extra activity

Ask students to go through the earlier units and choose a photo or a picture they like and describe it to their partner. Alternatively, if you used a set of photos for the lead-in activity, you could distribute those pictures for students to describe.

Homework

At home, students write a description of their favourite photo, or an interesting photo they have found online.

8e How R U? ☺ tks

Lead-in

Test before you teach: emoticons

Write the following symbols on the board: :-) :-(>:-|
Ask students: *Which one is happy / angry / sad?* and pre-teach *emoticons*. Ask: *Where can you see them?* and elicit, in text messages, on the Internet, etc. Ask: *Why do we use them?* Elicit that we use them to show how we feel. Ask students to come to the board and draw and explain any other emoticons they know.

Speaking and reading

1 Ask students to read the text about emoticons then discuss the questions in pairs. Check the answers in whole-class feedback.

> ANSWERS
>
> 1 In eastern hemisphere countries, the eyes are very important in emoticons, but with western emoticons, the mouth is more important and you turn your head to the left to read them.
> 2 Students' own answers
> 3 Students' own answers

Extra activity

You might ask some of the students to come up to the board and draw the emoticon describing how they are feeling today. The rest of the students must guess the answer by asking: *Are you happy? Are you bored?* etc.

Writing texts and online messages

2 Ask students to read the messages between two people. Then put students in pairs and ask them to discuss how each person feels. Discuss the answers as a class.

> ANSWERS
>
> The first person feels sorry and sad because they have an exam and can't go shopping (Sry; :( ).
> The second person feels great then surprised (Gr8, :-); :0)

Writing skill textspeak

3a Pre-teach *textspeak*. Explain that textspeak uses letters, symbols and numbers to make words shorter, e.g. *gr8 = great*. Ask students to go through the texts in pairs and find the other examples of textspeak, then compare them with the full version in normal English in the second conversation. Check students' answers.

ANSWERS

The texts use the following symbols or abbreviations:

R = are

U = you

Gr8 = Great

4 = for

2 = to

Sry = Sorry

2day = today

After = Afterwards

l8r = later

3b Ask students to go through the text messages again and find the examples. Then get students in pairs to check their answers.

ANSWERS

1 4, 2
2 R, C, U
3 (I am) Shopping 4 clothes. (Do) u wan 2 come? (I have) Got (an) English exam. (I) Didn't know it's 2day.
4 After(wards)
5 Call me after

3c Ask students to look at the sentences and write the full sentences of the textspeak conversation. Do the first sentence as an example. Tell students to pay attention to the grammar.

ANSWERS

1 Are you in town?
2 I am later today.
3 Do you want to meet?
4 OK. At three?

3d Ask students to look at the full sentences and rewrite them using textspeak. Put students in pairs to check their answers. Point out that there isn't just one correct answer, students can use any abbreviations that are clear.

SAMPLE ANSWERS

1 Thx 4 msg
2 meet @ station
3 Sry am l8.
4 c u Mday @ 6.

4 Put students in pairs. Ask students to write a text message to their partner to arrange to meet this week, using textspeak. After they've finished, students swap their messages and write a reply. Ask some of the students about the details of their meeting.

Extra activity

You can do this writing activity as a class game. Ask all the students to write a text message using textspeak. Then collect the messages, shuffle them and hand them out to the students in random order. They must guess what the message is and write a reply using textspeak again. In feedback, ask some of the students to read out their messages.

8f   Festivals and special events

Before you watch

1 Organise the class into pairs to discuss the questions.

2 Students match the words to the pictures.

ANSWERS

1 costume	5 gloves
2 jewellery	6 trumpet
3 mask	7 clown
4 fireworks	

3 Students discuss the questions in pairs or small groups.

While you watch

4 Ask students to watch the video and note which objects in Exercise 2 they see in each photo.

ANSWERS

1 make-up, costume
2 make-up, clown
3 fireworks, trumpet
4 make-up
5 mask, jewellery, gloves

5 Ask students to watch the video again, and answer the questions. Let them compare their answers in pairs.

ANSWERS

1 in Scotland
2 yes
3 the USA
4 He's listening to his national anthem
5 in India
6 loud and happy music
7 in Jaipur
8 yellow, orange, pink, red, purple, light blue and dark blue
9 Venice
10 every year

6 Ask students to look at the sentences from the video and decide whether the underlined words are very positive or very negative. Tell students to practise reading the sentences, stressing the underlined words.

ANSWER

They are all positive.

7 Organise the class into pairs. Then play the video again with NO SOUND. Students take turns to be the narrator.

After you watch

8 Students read the email, and say which event in Exercise 4 the person is writing about.

> **ANSWER**
> Beltane Fire Festival in Scotland

9 & 10 Students choose another festival and write an email to a friend to describe it. Put the class into pairs to exchange emails and guess the festival.

Videoscript

Today I'm looking at photos of special events and festivals from around the world.

This first photo shows a festival in Scotland.

It's called the Beltane Fire Festival.

The man on the left has a white mask on, I think.

And the woman on the right has white make-up on and she's wearing an amazing costume.

00.33 Here's another man with make-up on. But he's a clown in the USA.

Normally he makes the audience laugh at a rodeo with horses, but in this photo he's listening to the national anthem before the performance begins.

00.52 There's also music in this photo, but it's very different.

It's a wedding in India, so here are the musicians playing some loud, happy music.

Look at the man in the middle. He's playing that trumpet really loudly!

And in the background, you can see some fantastic fireworks.

I'd like to go to a wedding like this!

01.22 Here's another one from India.

It's at the Elephant Festival in Jaipur.

The colours of the make-up and cloth on the elephant's head and body are incredible!

There's yellow, orange, pink, red, purple, light blue and dark blue.

01.48 This is the last photo. It's from Venice in Italy.

I love the woman's mask and her jewellery.

And those gloves are wonderful.

She looks like a woman from the past, but in fact the Venice Carnival is every year and you can see lots of people in colourful costumes like this.

I'd love to go there.

UNIT 8 Review

Grammar

1 Ask students to complete the sentences with the correct form of *have got*.

> **ANSWERS**
> 1 has got / 's got   5 have not got / haven't got
> 2 have not got / haven't got   6 has got / 's got
> 3 have got   7 Have … got
> 4 has not got / hasn't got   8 Has … got

2 Ask students to complete the sentences with the present simple or continuous form of the verbs in brackets.

> **ANSWERS**
> 1 are working / 're working   5 are living
> 2 always starts   6 Do you like
> 3 are you doing   7 are you wearing
> 4 is writing / 's writing   8 are driving / 're driving

Vocabulary

3 Students decide which word does not belong in each group.

> **ANSWERS**
> 2 ugly   3 tall   4 lips   5 neck   6 chest

4 Ask students to match the parts of the body with the clothing.

> **ANSWERS**
> 1 e   2 b   3 d   4 a   5 c

5 Ask students to write sentences about the people in the photo, using words from Exercise 3 and the phrases below the photo.

Real life

6 Ask students to choose the correct option to complete the sentences.

> **ANSWERS**
> 1 shows   4 T-shirt   7 like
> 2 in the middle   5 hair   8 interesting
> 3 looks   6 hats

7 Students work in pairs to practise describing people from pictures.

Speaking

8 Students work in pairs to describe members of their family.

Unit 9 Film and the arts

Lead-in

Using words: films and cinemas
Write the following on the board:

My favourite film

My favourite actor

My favourite director

My favourite cinema

Ask students to talk about the subjects in pairs for one minute. In feedback, ask students to tell the class what they heard from their partner.

1 Ask students to look at the photo. Discuss the questions as a class.

> **ANSWERS**
>
> The woman is sleeping. She's in a film which is being shown in Sydney Harbour, projected onto a huge screen.

Background notes

Sydney is Australia's largest city. In the photo, you can see Sydney Harbour Bridge and the famous Sydney Opera House.

2 🔘 [2.14] Play the recording. Students listen and choose the best answers.

> **ANSWERS**
>
> 1 b   2 b   3 a / b

Audioscript 🔘 [2.14]

For a visitor to the city of Sydney, it's a strange sight. You are driving past the harbour with its fantastic view of the Opera House, when you suddenly see the huge face of a sleeping woman. But for local people, this outdoor cinema is popular during the long hot summer evenings. The screen is the same size as a large building and it's above the water. The audience can sit on the beach or in their cars as they watch their favourite actors in the latest film.

3 Ask students to complete the sentences before discussing them in pairs. Point out the language box at the bottom of the page and go through it with students.

Extra activity

Make this a mingle. Ask students to walk round the class, talk to people, and note their answers. Then put them in pairs to compare answers and to tell the class what differences and similarities they found between different class members.

9a All roads film festival

Lead-in

Introducing the theme: types of films
This lead-in makes demands on your acting ability. Tell students that they are going to watch you watching a film. They must watch and make notes on what type of film it is and what happens in the film. Sit down and pretend to open a DVD box, look at the film title, put in on, and watch, start by smiling and laughing at the film, then look tense for a bit, then surprised, then scared, then end by looking a bit relieved.

Tell students in pairs or small groups to discuss what they witnessed. At the end, ask them what type of film it was (elicit *horror* or *thriller*), what happens, and ask students what title the film might have.

Vocabulary types of film

1 Ask students to look at the pictures. Ask: *What types of films are they?* Elicit answers and find out what words students know.

Ask students to match the types of films to the pictures. Let them compare their answers in pairs.

> **ANSWERS**
>
> a horror film   e romantic comedy
> b comedy   f action film
> c documentary   g animation
> d science-fiction film

2 Elicit example films for each of the different categories, then ask students which type of films they like and which they never watch.

Extra activity

Bring in copies of a page from a magazine or website which shows current cinema listings (ideally in English, but it's OK if it's in the students' L1). Ask students to say what type of films are on at the moment.

Reading

3 Ask students to look at the photos and the titles. Ask: *What type of films are they? What do you think happens in the films?*

Students read the first paragraph and answer the question.

> **ANSWERS**
>
> All types of film (including comedies, documentaries and animation, but possibly others too)

4 Ask students to read the rest of the article and decide if the statements are true or false. Let students check their answers in pairs before discussing as a class.

Extra activity

Ask students to correct the false sentences.

5 Discuss the questions as a class. Ask students to give reasons for their answers (e.g. I would like to see *My Wedding and Other Secrets* because I love romantic films).

Extra activity

Ask students in pairs to choose one of the films and imagine what happens in the film and at the end of the film. Ask some pairs to tell the class their ideas.

Background notes

The *National Geographic's All roads film festival* aims to give indigenous and under-represented minority cultures the funds to produce film and photography so that they can share their stories. The festival takes place in various US cities, notably Washington DC, where the *National Geographic's* headquarters is located.

The Tundra Book is about the Chukchi people, who inhabit a remote Russian peninsula in the Arctic Circle. The film tells of the daily struggle of a nomadic reindeer herder called Vukvukai as he lives a traditional life.

Listening

6 [2.15] Give students a moment to read the questions. Then play the recording. Let students compare their answers in pairs.

ANSWERS

1 My wedding and other secrets
2 to a Japanese restaurant
3 no

7 [2.15] Play the recording again. Students listen and write in the missing verbs.

ANSWERS

1 buy   2 see   3 doing   4 have   5 stay

Audioscript [2.15]

C = Charles, B = Beata

C: Hey! Beata. Stop!

B: Hi Charles. Sorry, but I'm going to buy a ticket for the next film. It starts in five minutes. It's called *My Wedding and Other Secrets*. Are you going to see it too?

C: No, I'm not, but what are you doing afterwards? Didier, Monica and I are going to have dinner at a Japanese restaurant. Do you want to come?

B: Sorry, but I'm not going to stay out late tonight. I'm tired.

C: Sure.

B: Oh, I must go. Bye.

C: Bye. See you later.

Extra activity

Ask students to practise reading the conversation in pairs.

Grammar *going to* (for plans)

8 Ask students to look at the conversation, underline the examples with *going to* and the present continuous, and discuss the questions in pairs. In feedback, elicit and label the future forms. Read the grammar box with the students, and check the answers to the questions. Refer students to the information and practice on page 166.

ANSWERS

I'm going to buy a ticket
Are you going to see it too?
I'm not going to stay out late
Monica and I are going to have dinner at a Japanese restaurant
... what are you doing afterwards? (present continuous)
1 future
2 negative: subject + *be* + *not* + *going to*
question: *be* + subject + *going to*
(see also below)

Grammar notes

We use *going to* + infinitive to talk about plans or intentions which have been made before the moment of speaking. It is possible to use the forms *going to go* and *going to come*, but native speakers tend to abbreviate them to just *going to*, like the present continuous form, e.g. *We're going to a Japanese restaurant.*

The contrast in the use of the present continuous for fixed arrangements and *going to* + infinitive for planned intentions is actually quite subtle. They're often interchangeable. For example, you might say: *We're having dinner later* (emphasises the arrangement), or *We're going to have dinner later* (emphasises the intention).

Note that the auxiliary verb *be* is used (and does all the hard work) when forming negatives and questions with the *going to* form:

I'm / They're	going to see a film.
I'm not / We aren't	going to see a film.
Are you / Is he	going to see a film?

9 Ask students to make sentences from the prompts. Do the first sentence together as an example. Let students work in pairs, or work separately then compare their answers in pairs. In feedback, elicit some answers, and make sure students are using the forms correctly. Students can check their answers when they listen to the recording in Exercise 10.

Pronunciation /tə/

10 💿 [2.16] Play the recording. Ask students to listen first, paying attention to the pronunciation and the weak vowel sound in *to*. Then play the recording again so that students can repeat.

Audioscript and key 💿 [2.16]

1 We're going to see a film at the new cinema.
2 I'm not going to watch this DVD.
3 Are you going to buy the tickets online or at the cinema?
4 What time are they going to the cinema?
5 I'm not going to sit at the front of the cinema.
6 Where are you going to sit?
7 Are they going to meet us after the film?
8 I'm never going to watch a film by that director again.

Pronunciation notes

Students should attempt the very weak, barely pronounced /tə/ sound, and should not attempt to give the word its full /tu:/ sound.

Speaking

11 Introduce the activity by choosing a film yourself and telling the class which one you are going to see.

Tell students to prepare to speak by choosing their films.

12 Organise the class into groups of four to six students to discuss their plans. Model the activity by asking a reliable student one or two questions with *What are you going to … ?*. Then ask students to take turns to ask and answer questions about the films they have selected. In feedback, ask students to tell the class which films they are going to see and why.

Homework

Ask students to write about their plans for the weekend.

9b People in film and the arts

Lead-in

Introducing the theme: people in film and the arts
Write the following on the board:

an artist, a writer, a director, an actor, a film-maker, a musician.

Ask students to choose a famous example of one of these people. Tell students that, for the activity, they are that person. Divide the class into groups of four. Students must ask *yes / no* questions to find out who each person in their group is. Students can only answer *yes* or *no*, e.g. *Are you a musician? (No!) Are you an artist? (Yes!) Are you American? (No!) Are you Spanish? (Yes!) Are you dead? (Yes!) Are you Picasso? (Yes!)*

Vocabulary art and entertainment

1 Ask students to number the activities in the order of their preference. Then ask them to compare their order with a partner. In feedback, build up a list of the most popular activities in the class.

2 Students complete the table. Let them compare their answers in pairs.

ANSWERS		
What?	**Where?**	**Who?**
film	at a cinema	directors, actors, actresses
a play or a musical	at the theatre	directors, actors, actresses
art and paintings	in an art gallery	artist or painter
novel	in a book	writer
music	at a concert hall	musician

3 Organise the class into pairs or small groups to discuss the questions. In feedback, find out which people are popular with the class as a whole.

Read through the *Wordbuilding* box with the class. Refer students to page 75 of the Workbook for further information and practice.

Grammar notes

Note that we can also use the suffix *-ist* (*pianist, scientist*) when describing jobs.

The suffixes *-or, -er* and *-ian* are all pronounced with a weak /ə/ sound.

Reading

4 Ask students to look at the photo. Ask: *What can you see? What's his job? What does he do in his job?* Ask students to read the text quickly and answer these questions without worrying about the gaps.

Students read the text again and choose the correct words to complete the text. Let them compare their answers in pairs.

> **ANSWERS**
> 1 b   2 a   3 c   4 a   5 b   6 c   7 b   8 c

Background notes

Dr Seymour is a wildlife ecologist who combines his scientific research with documentary film-making, in order to document the complex pressures that threaten both wildlife and local communities. His recent studies have focused on the ecology of rainforest carnivores, including the Malay civet in Indonesia.

Jacques Cousteau (1910–1997) was an explorer and film-maker who pioneered the aqua-lung and scuba diving, and was very involved in marine conservation. His films and books were instrumental in showing what life was like in the sea to a TV audience for the first time.

Extra activity

Ask students to think of and write down three questions to ask about the text about Adrian Seymour. Tell them to close their books and ask their partner their questions. Find out if the partners can answer the questions.

Listening

5 [2.17] Ask students to predict what questions the interviewer will ask Adrian. Build up a list of questions on the board. In feedback after the first listening, ask students to say which questions were asked.

Play the recording. Students listen and number the topics. Let them check their answers in pairs.

> **ANSWERS**
> 1 a   2 c   3 b

Audioscript [2.17]

I = interviewer, **A** = Adrian Seymour

I: Doctor Adrian Seymour is a film director and a wildlife biologist. He travels to different parts of the world to film animals in the wild. You can see his films on television and on the Internet. Today, I'm talking to Adrian about his films. So, Adrian, how do you plan a film?

A: At the beginning, there is a lot of planning for the journey. You have heavy camera equipment so it's expensive to travel. And you often need special visas to film in some countries.

I: How many people work on a film?

A: It depends on the film. But there's always a director and a camera person. On bigger films you need more people.

I: And how long does it take to make a film?

A: Well, I'm planning a film at the moment and we're going to film it in the summer. Then I'm going to edit it in the autumn. So in total, it takes about a year.

I: So tell us about your next film project. Where are you going?

A: To Malaysia.

I: Why are you going there?

A: I'm going to Malaysia to make a film for television. It's about a man called Alfred Russell Wallace. He was a famous explorer in the nineteenth century. After that, I'm going to Indonesia for three weeks.

I: Why are you going there?

A: To have a holiday!

6 [2.17] Play the recording again. Students listen and write the correct answers. Let them check their answers in pairs.

> **ANSWERS**
> 1 Y   3 Y   5 Y   7 Y   9 Y
> 2 DS   4 N   6 N   8 DS

7 Discuss the questions as a class.

Extra activity

Write the following words from the listening on the board: *travel, edit, heavy, project, explorer.* Check the words then ask students to say how they connect to the listening.

Grammar infinitive of purpose

8 Students look at the sentence and answer the questions. Let them compare their answers in pairs. Read the grammar box with the students. Refer students to the information and practice on page 166.

> **ANSWERS**
> 1 part 1   2 part 2

Grammar notes

English uses the infinitive to express purpose. Common errors students make include trying to use *for* or *for to* instead of just *to*. In formal English, *in order to* or *so as to* are also used to express purpose.

9 Do the first sentence as an example to get students started. Then ask them to write the rest of the sentences in pairs.

ANSWERS
1 a I'm going to buy this book about Martin Scorsese to read about his life.
2 d I'm going to art school to study painting.
3 b I'm going to play this computer game again to reach level five.
4 c I'm going to the theatre to see a play by Shakespeare.

10 Talk about one or two plans that you have for the coming week to get students started. Then give students a couple of minutes to think about how to express their plans.

When students are ready, organise them into pairs or small groups to share their plans. Monitor and note errors for an error feedback on *going to* and the infinitive of purpose after the activity.

Speaking

11 Students write their own plans. Elicit one or two examples to get them started. Monitor and help with ideas.

Start the activity by acting out a conversation with a reliable student.

Organise the class into pairs. Tell students to take turns to discuss plans. Monitor and prompt and note any errors for a correction feedback at the end.

Homework

Ask students to write about their plans for the next few months.

9c Nature in art

Lead-in

Introducing the theme: nature in art

Bring in a large picture of a painting or photograph that shows nature and is interesting or dramatic (or project one on an OHT or interactive whiteboard).

Ask students to look at the picture and write down all the words they can think of that they could use to describe the picture. Students compare their ideas in pairs. Then brainstorm words and write any suggestions on the board, then decide as a class which words are the best ones.

Vocabulary nature

1 Ask students to look at the photos. Ask: *What are they? What is the connection between the pictures? What can you see in the pictures?*

Organise the class into pairs or small groups to discuss the photos. In feedback, check that students understand all the words in the box.

2 Discuss the questions as a class.

Reading

3 Write the names of the five artists on the board and find out if the class know anything about them.

Ask students to read the texts and match artists to pictures.

ANSWERS	
Stanislaw Witkiewicz	2
Ginger Riley Munduwalawala	3
Ando Hiroshige	4
Damien Hirst	5
Vincent Van Gogh	1

4 Ask students to read the article again and tick the sentences that are true for each artist. Let them compare their answers in pairs.

ANSWERS
Stanislaw Witkiewicz 1, 5
Ginger Riley Munduwalawala 1, 7
Andō Hiroshige 1, 6
Damien Hirst 2, 5, 8
Vincent Van Gogh 1, 3, 4, 6

Extra activity

Ask students to find and underline words connected with art in the text: *paintings, paint, artists, art critic, art gallery, lanscape, paper, wood, print.* Check the words with students.

Critical thinking the writer's preferences

5 Read through the sentences with the class then ask students to answer the question.

> ANSWER
>
> *Prefer* means 'to like one thing more than another'.

Grammar notes

We say *I prefer* + noun. When comparing two things, we use *to*, e.g. *I prefer his paintings to his drawings.*

6 Students read the text again and find more preferences. Let them compare their answers in pairs.

> ANSWERS
>
> 1 Stanislaw Witkiewicz, Vincent Van Gogh and Damien Hirst
> 2 She prefers Stanislaw Witkiewicz's landscapes and other nature paintings, Van Gogh's other paintings (not his sunflowers), and Damien Hirst's early paintings.

Speaking

7 Ask students to look at the paintings, and decide which ones they prefer in each pair, and why.

Organise students into pairs to express their preferences.

Extra activity

Ask students to express other art preferences. Write the following pairs on the board for students to express preferences about:

paintings / sculpture

Modern art / Impressionist paintings

Picasso / Van Gogh

9d Making arrangements

Lead-in

Introducing the theme: musicals and *Phantom of the Opera*

Find and download a picture or poster of *Phantom of the Opera*, or just write the name on the board. Ask students what they know about the writer, the music and the story of the musical. Ask if they have seen it or would like to see it.

Listening

1 Ask students to look at the photo. Ask: *What can you see? What do you know about Broadway?* Organise the class into pairs or small groups to discuss the questions. In feedback, revise key words such as *plays, musicals, shows, theatre, actors, singers, directors*. Make sure that you mention the names of some of the shows in the photo (see below).

Background notes

The photo shows advertisements for a number of musicals, notably *Phantom of the Opera, Jersey Boys, the Addams Family, Priscilla Queen of the Desert,* and *Chicago.*

The Phantom of the Opera is a musical by Andrew Lloyd Webber which was first performed on London's West End in 1986, and on Broadway in 1988. It is the longest-running show on Broadway, and the most financially successful theatrical show in history with box-office receipts of over $5 billion. It is based on a French novel of 1910, and was made into a film in 2004.

Broadway is the main thoroughfare that runs from north to south through the whole of Manhattan, New York. On Broadway, in the midtown area of the city, there are numerous theatres, cinemas and restaurants.

2 🔊 [2.18] Give students a moment to read the questions and predict what the speakers might say. Then play the recording. Students listen and answer the questions.

> ANSWERS
>
> 1 Phantom of the Opera
> 2 tonight
> 3 She's working late.
> 4 Yes
> 5 7.30
> 6 7

Audioscript 🔊 [2.18]

R = Rachel, **A** = Adriana

Conversation 1

R: Hi Adriana. It's Rachel.

A: Hi. Sorry but I'm at work. I can't talk now.

R: I know but I'm going to the theatre tonight. I've got two tickets for *Phantom of the Opera*. My friend works at the theatre and sometimes he gets free tickets.

A: Great.

R: So would you like to come?

A: Thanks, I'd love to. When is it?

R: Tonight!

A: Tonight?

R: Yes, are you free?

A: I'm sorry, but I'm working late tonight.

R: Oh, can't you ask your manager?

A: I can try.

R: OK. Bye.

Conversation 2

R: Hello?

A: Hi Rachel. It's me again. Do you still have the extra ticket?

R: Yes, why? Do you want to go?

A: Yes, my manager said I can finish early. What time does it start?

R: At seven thirty so let's meet at seven outside the theatre.

A: That's great. See you at seven.

Real life inviting and making arrangements

3 🔊 [2.18] Ask students to complete the expressions. Do the first as an example to get them started.

Play the recording. Students listen and check. Let students compare their answers in pairs before discussing as a class.

> ANSWERS
>
> | | | |
> |---|---|---|
> | 1 like | 4 'd love | 7 time |
> | 2 free | 5 'm sorry | 8 meet |
> | 3 want | 6 great | 9 See |

Grammar notes

Note the use of *would like* when inviting. Using this conditional form is more polite and tentative than using *want*. So, in polite or neutral situations, it is better for students to say *Would you like to …? Yes, I'd love to.*

Pronunciation showing enthusiasm

4 🔊 [2.19] Play the recording. Students listen and underline the stressed words. Then they listen and repeat.

> ANSWERS
>
> 1 I'd <u>love</u> to.
> 2 I'd <u>really</u> like to.
> 3 That's <u>great</u>!
> 4 That sounds <u>fantastic</u>!

Extra activity

Provide some open-class practice by inviting individuals to different events and encouraging them to respond using the expressions in Exercise 4, e.g. *Would you like to go to the cinema?* Student responds, *Yes, I'd love to!* or *I'm sorry, I'm working late tonight,* etc.

Grammar present continuous for future reference

5 Ask students to look at the sentences. Discuss the questions as a class. Refer students to page 166 of the Student's Book for further information.

> ANSWERS
>
> It's the present continuous. It's talking about the future.

Grammar notes

We use the present continuous to talk about personal arrangements that have already been made for the future. It is often described as the 'diary' future – we use it to talk about things that we could write in a diary.

6 Organise the class into pairs. Ask students to take turns to invite each other to the two musicals.

Monitor carefully and make sure they are showing enthusiasm in their conversations.

Extra activity

Extend this activity with other events. You could bring in pages from 'what's on' listings showing events in a major city which your students know. Alternatively, write the following list on the board:

The Addams Family	7 p.m.
Priscilla Queen of the Desert	7.30 p.m.
Chicago	8.30 p.m.
Cats	8 p.m.
We Will Rock You	7 p.m.

Homework

Ask students to write a dialogue for an event that they are planning to go to in the next week or two.

9e It looks amazing!

Lead-in

Introducing the theme: reviews and comments

Copy the following on to a sheet of A4 paper:

Life Elementary is an exciting new English course book. We think it has great pictures, interesting topics and texts, and a lot of useful grammar and vocabulary. But what do other people think?

Pass the piece of paper around the class before the lesson or during the lesson. Ask students to write their own reviews then pass it on. At the end of the lesson, read out some of the interesting comments, or put it on the class noticeboard for students to read.

Writing reviews and comments

1 Discuss the questions as a class.

2 Students match the extracts 1–5 to the categories in the box. Let them compare their answers in pairs before discussing as a class.

> ANSWERS
> 1 music 4 a film
> 2 a restaurant 5 perfume
> 3 an art exhibition

Extra activity

Ask students which words helped them work out the answers. Use the opportunity to check vocabulary connected with each category.

1 music: *album* (CD with a set of songs), *track* (individual song on a CD)
2 a restaurant: *meal, starter, tasted, main course*
3 an art exhibition: *gallery* (building or room with paintings), *paintings, artist*
4 a film: *scared, funny, laughed for two hours*
5 perfume: *bought, smells*

3 Discuss the questions as a class.

> ANSWERS
> 2 to 4 are generally positive.
> 1 and 5 are negative.

Writing skill giving your opinion with sense verbs

4a Students read the reviews again and find the sense verbs and adjectives. Let them discuss their answers in pairs before discussing as a class.

> ANSWERS
> 1 it sounds very slow
> 2 it tasted great
> 3 They look amazing!
> 4 I felt scared
> 5 it smells awful

4b Divide the class into pairs to discuss which sense verbs to use.

> ANSWERS
> musical: looks, sounds
> book: looks
> fitness centre: looks, smells
> new building: looks
> sports car: looks, feels, sounds
> aftershave: smells
> clothes: look, feel
> chocolate: tastes, smells
> computer game: looks, sounds

4c Students match the verbs to the adjectives in pairs.

> ANSWERS
> angry: look, sound
> beautiful: look, sound
> bored: look, sound, feel
> delicious: look, taste, smell
> loud: sound
> interesting: look, sound, smell, taste
> nice: look, sound, smell, taste, feel
> soft: feel
> terrible: look, sound, smell, taste, feel
> tired: look, sound, feel

5 Lead in by asking students for examples of things they could write about under each of the topics in 4b. Then ask students to choose two topics and write about them.

6 Organise the class into pairs. Students exchange their reviews, read them, and comment on them.

Extra activity

Write the names of different well-known things on the top of various sheets of A4 paper, e.g. write the name of a popular TV show on the top of one, a well-known drink or chocolate bar on another. Write things of interest to your students. Divide the class into pairs and give each pair a sheet of paper. They must write a quick comment about the product then pass the paper to another pair. Continue until all the pairs have written something about each product. Then put the pieces of paper on the classroom walls for students to read.

Homework

Ask students to write a review of something they are interested in (a film, TV show, etc.).

9f **Camera traps**

Before you watch

1 Students discuss the question in groups of four or five.

2 Ask students to read the text and answer the questions.

> **ANSWERS**
> 1 When something moves in front of it, it takes a photograph.
> 2 Because they can take photos of animals that are difficult to see.
> 3 When a plant moves in the wind, the camera sometimes takes photos with no animals.
> 4 You need to put them where animals eat and spend time.

3 Discuss the questions as a class.

While you watch

4 Ask students to number the actions in the order they see them while they watch the video without sound.

> **ANSWERS**
> 1 c   3 d   5 g   7 e   9 h
> 2 i   4 a   6 b   8 f

5 Ask students to watch the video again WITH SOUND, and choose the correct answer.

> **ANSWERS**
> 1 c   2 b   3 a   4 c   5 b / c   6 a, b, d

After you watch

6 Organise the class into pairs. Ask students to decide on their roles and to prepare them. When students are ready, tell them to act out the conversation. You could get some pairs to come to the front of the class to act out their roleplays.

Videoscript

This is the rainforest in Honduras.

Thousands of animals live here, but we rarely see them.

That's because they live in the trees and they don't often come out in the daytime.

00.16 This is Adrian Seymour and his team.

Adrian is a film-maker. He's working in the Honduran rainforest.

Adrian wants to film the animals that humans never see at night.

00.29 Adrian is going to use camera traps to film the animals.

He climbs up into the trees and puts camera traps in different places.

When the animal moves, the camera films it.

Adrian and the team put six camera traps around different parts of the rainforest.

00.50 Now Adrian has to wait …

and wait …

and wait …

and wait.

01.04 Four weeks later, Adrian returns to the trees and collects his camera traps.

He hopes they filmed some good pictures of the animals.

Back in his office and in front of the camera, Adrian starts to study the film from the camera.

All the camera traps filmed something.

But in a lot of the pictures, Adrian can't see any animals.

01.30 He doesn't know if there is a problem with the cameras or if there is something out there.

Then suddenly he sees something in a picture.

It's a kinkajou.

In fact, there are two kinkajous.

01.45 Kinkajous only live in rainforests.

They eat meat and fruit.

These two are looking for fruit and one of them found the camera!

Adrian's camera traps worked, so he's going to use them in the future to film a lot of other species of animals.

UNIT 9 Review

Grammar

1 Ask students to complete the sentences with the *going to* form of the verbs in the box.

> **ANSWERS**
> 1 are going to watch
> 2 are going to play
> 3 am going to meet
> 4 aren't going to drive
> 5 Are ... going to have a
> 6 is going to buy
> 7 isn't going to write
> 8 Is ... going to play

2 Ask students to write five sentences with *going to* and the infinitive of purpose, using the phrases in the box.

> **SAMPLE ANSWERS**
> I'm going to the theatre to see a musical.
> I'm going to a concert hall to listen to music.
> I'm going to an art gallery to look at paintings.
> I'm going to a café to have a drink.
> I'm going to the shops to buy clothes.

3 Ask students to read the sentences and say whether each one is talking about the present or the future.

> **ANSWERS**
> 1 P   2 F   3 P   4 F   5 F   6 F

Vocabulary

4 Students match the type of film with the comments.

> **ANSWERS**
> 1 science fiction   4 horror
> 2 comedy   5 action film
> 3 documentary   6 animation

5 Ask students to read the sentences and complete the missing words.

> **ANSWERS**
> 1 theatre   4 musicians
> 2 art gallery   5 director
> 3 novels   6 concert hall

6 Students write the words from the box in the correct place in the table.

> **ANSWERS**
> landscape: mountains, sea, sky, trees
> plants: flowers, grass, trees
> animals: kangaroos, birds, butterflies

Real life

7 Students read the conversation and number the lines in the correct order.

> **ANSWERS**
> 1 Would you like to come to the cinema?
> 4 Sorry, but I'm working late.
> 2 When are you going?
> 6 OK. I'd love to come at nine.
> 5 The film is also on at nine.
> 7 Great. Let's meet outside the cinema at quarter to nine.
> 3 At six.
> 8 Right. See you there. Bye.

8 Ask students to work in pairs to roleplay a conversation to arrange to meet. They should then change partners and do it again.

Speaking

9 Students work in groups to talk about their favourite musician, writer, etc.

Unit 10 Science

Lead-in

Test before you teach: Science and scientists

Write -*ology* on the the board and ask students to think of as many sciences as they can that end with -*ology* (*biology, technology, ecology, zoology*, etc.).

1 Ask students to look at the photo and pre-teach *a human brain*. Put students in pairs to discuss the question and explain their reasons. Take feedback from the whole class and check their answers.

2 Go through the list with the students and pre-teach *chemicals, fix, shut down* (see Vocabulary notes below). Give students some time to go through the sentences and mark the sentences B (a human brain) or C (a computer) or B, C for both. Do the first sentence as an example. Let students compare their answers in pairs. Get class feedback, but don't give students the answers yet.

Vocabulary notes

chemicals = substances that interact with one another, e.g. H_2O, H_2SO_4

fix = mend, repair, solve a problem

shut down = stop working

3 💿 [2.20] Ask students to listen to the recording of a neuroscientist (a scientist who studies the brain). Play the recording. Students listen and check their answers from Exercise 2.

ANSWERS
2 B   3 B, C   4 C   5 B   6 C

Audioscript 💿 [2.20]

People often compare the brain with a computer. And it's true, there are similarities. For example, both of them need energy. But both use different types of energy. A computer needs electrical energy but the brain uses chemicals and chemical energy. Another similarity is they both store information. One big difference is that computers are easy to fix. OK, so sometimes you have problems with your laptop. Maybe it gets a virus and you can't fix it but the man at the computer shop knows how. With the brain, it's generally more difficult to fix a brain because doctors don't know everything about it. In fact, there's more we DON'T know about the brain than what we do know. The other difference is that a computer can shut down but a brain never stops. Even when you are sleeping, your brain is working.

4 Students match the sciences to the science topics. Let them check their answers with their partner. In feedback, model and drill the words, pointing out the stress and pronunciation.

ANSWERS
1 c   2 f   3 a   4 e   5 d   6 b

Pronunciation notes

Note the stress: *astronomy, zoology, physics, chemistry, biology, technology.*

5 Organise the class into pairs or small groups to talk about their school experience of science, and their current preferences. Monitor and note errors for an error feedback at the end.

Extra activity

Ask students to think of famous scientists who worked in the areas of science in Exercise 4.

10a Technology has changed our lives

Lead-in

Test before you teach: technology
Use mime to elicit some of the words in the vocabulary section, e.g. mime reading a book, writing a letter, reading an ebook, playing a video. Elicit the words from the class and write them on the board.

Vocabulary everyday technology

1 Ask students to look at the photo. Ask: *What can you see? What is the boy doing?* Elicit ideas. Organise students into pairs to discuss the questions. Take feedback from the whole class.

> **ANSWERS**
> The boy is using a public telephone, probably coin operated. Most people rarely use public telephones now because they use their own mobile phones instead.

2 Read through the pairs of words with the class and pre-teach and drill the new vocabulary. Ask students to say which word in each pair is 'old' and which is 'new' technology. Put students in pairs to discuss the questions. Get class feedback.

Vocabulary notes

download = (noun) any file taken from the Internet, e.g. songs, photos, etc. It can also be used as a verb (e.g. *download a file from the Internet*).

ebook = an electronic 'book' that can be read on an electronic device, or a device designed to read electronic books

sat nav / GPS = an electronic gadget, often used in a car, to help you find your way from one place to another

podcast = news items, articles or programmes that can be downloaded to a computer

search engine = a program that finds the information you need from the Internet

3 Ask students to look at the age groups and ask: *How old are they?* Elicit age ranges for each group. Put students in pairs to discuss the questions in relation to the different age groups. Get class feedback.

Background notes

In European culture, teenagers are considered to be people between the ages of 13 and 19, young adults are people between the ages of 19 and 24, and middle-aged people are usually considered to be approximately between the ages of 40 and 60.

Reading and listening

4 Ask students to look at the photo and the title. Ask: *Do you agree with the title? Why?* and elicit ideas.

Students read the text and answer the questions. Let them compare their answers in pairs.

> **ANSWERS**
> 1 T   2 T   3 F   4 F

5 Discuss the questions as a class and write the results of the survey on the board.

6 💿 [2.21] Ask students to look again at the list of 15 activities in the text. Then play the recording. Students listen to the extract and tick the six activities that the speaker asks about. Let students compare their answers in pairs.

> **ANSWERS**
> 2 booked a holiday at a travel agent
> 6 bought a CD
> 9 used a map
> 11 paid for something by cheque
> 12 watched a programme at the time it's on TV
> 14 sent a letter in an envelope

Audioscript 💿 [2.21]

A: Hello, I'd like to ask you a few questions about how technology has changed your life.

B: OK. Go ahead.

A: So, have you ever booked a holiday at a travel agent?

B: Yes, I have but it was a long time ago. Nowadays I always book online.

A: Right. Thanks. Here's the next question. Have you ever bought a CD?

B: Actually, yes, I have bought a CD. Normally I download music but last week I bought a CD for my father. It was his birthday and he doesn't know how to download music.

A: I see. And before a car journey, have you ever used a map?

B: Yes, I have. Well, I did in the past but now I use a sat nav, you know, a GPS, because I drive a lot for my job.

A: OK. And what about money? Have you ever paid for something by cheque?

B: No, because I've never had a cheque book. I pay for everything with a credit card. Oh, and I also bank online.

A: Right. And TV. Have you ever watched a programme at the time it's on TV?

B: Yes, of course. I do that every night.

A: So you never watch TV programmes online?

B: Oh, I see what you mean. Err, well I have watched videos on YouTube.

A: OK. And finally, have you ever sent a letter in an envelope?

B: Err. I'm not sure. Let me think. Err. No, I haven't because I send emails or texts.

7 🔊 [2.21] Give students some time to go through the questions first. Then play the recording again. Students listen and choose the correct ending for the sentences. Note that sometimes more than one option is possible. Let students compare their answers in pairs.

ANSWERS

1 b   2 b, c   3 a   4 a, c   5 a   6 a, c

Teaching notes

You might want to ask stronger classes to go through the options first and do the task before they listen, then listen to the recording to check and complete their answers.

Grammar present perfect

8 Ask students to look at the question and answer from the interview, then read the questions and choose the correct options. Let them compare their answers in pairs. Read the grammar box with the students, and check the answers. Refer students to the information and practice on page 167.

ANSWERS

1 They are talking about an experience in the past.
2 No

Grammar notes

The present perfect is formed with the auxiliary verb *have / has* and the past participle form of the verb.

We choose to use the present perfect when the past experience is important and the past time is unknown or unimportant and not mentioned.

9 🔊 [2.21] Do the first two sentences as examples to get students started. Then ask them to complete the rest of the sentences. Ask students to compare their sentences in pairs before discussing as a class. Students can check their answers by listening again to the recording from Exercise 7.

ANSWERS

1 have bought / 've bought
2 have
3 have never had / 've never had
4 have watched / 've watched
5 have you ever sent
6 haven't

Pronunciation 've / 's

10 🔊 [2.22] Ask students to listen and choose the correct options. Play the first sentence of the recording and elicit the correct form from the class as an example. Students then listen and notice the difference between the full and the contracted form of *have / has* in the rest of the sentences. Let students compare their answers in pairs.

ANSWERS

| 1 have | 3 haven't | 5 've | 7 haven't |
| 2 has | 4 hasn't | 6 's | 8 hasn't |

Audioscript 🔊 [2.22]

1 Have you ever sent a letter?
2 Yes, he has.
3 I haven't telephoned from a public telephone.
4 No, she hasn't!
5 We've never written letters by hand.
6 She's bought a CD.
7 No, I haven't.
8 The computer hasn't printed your photo.

Pronunciation notes

Note the pronunciation: *haven't* /'hævənt/, hasn't /'hæzənt/

Extra activity

Ask students to open their books at page 173 and find audioscript 2.22. Play the recording again. Students listen and repeat.

Speaking

11 Model the activity first. Ask students to look at the 15 activities in the interview again. Ask questions of individual students, e.g. *Anna, have you ever telephoned a cinema for the times of the films?* Then put students in pairs or groups of three or four to take turns to ask and answer the questions.

In feedback, ask students what they have in common with their partner(s).

12 Ask students to say as many new technology words as they can remember. Write the words on the board. Then put students in pairs and ask them to interview each other, using the new words. In feedback, ask what their partner has done or hasn't done.

Extra activity

Play *Find someone who … ?* Ask students in pairs to write down five questions with *Have you ever…?*. Then tell students to stand up, walk round, and ask people in the class their questions.

10b How well can you remember?

Lead-in

Introducing the theme: memory
Write twenty words that students have learnt during this course at random on the board. Choose interesting words and / or words you want your students to have learnt. For example (from Unit 9), *paintings, documentary, flowers*. Tell students to look at the words for one minute and try to remember them (without writing them down). After one minute, rub the words off the board (make sure you've made your own copy of them!) and ask students to write down all the words they remember. At the end, find out which student remembered most words accurately, and ask if any student used a memory technique to remember the words.

Speaking and reading

1 Discuss the questions as a class or in small groups.

2 Divide the class into groups of three. Tell students to decide who is A, B and C, then find and read their paragraph about memorising on pages 154, 155 and 156 of the Student's Book, respectively. After they have memorised the information, students turn back to page 120 and make notes in the table.

3 When students are ready, ask them to take turns talking about what they've read while the others complete the table. In feedback, ask students: *Do you think these techniques are useful?*

ANSWERS

Student A
Topic: memorising names and faces
Techniques: listen to the people and repeat their names, look at their faces and the clothes they're wearing, write down their names and where you met them.

Student B
Topic: memorising numbers
Techniques: try to 'see' the number in your head, repeat it a few times and learn numbers in groups, make it personal.

Student C
Topic: memorising directions and addresses
Techniques: try to 'see' the map, repeat the directions a few times or draw the directions in different colours.

4 Give students some time to read all three articles and compare their notes. Organise students into pairs to discuss these questions. Get class feedback.

Vocabulary memory and learning

5 Ask students to look at the groups of words and choose the odd word out in each group. Do the first as an example with the class. Let students compare their answers in pairs. Read the *Wordbuilding* box with the students. Refer students to the information and practice on page 83 of the Workbook.

ANSWERS

1 teach   2 test   3 forget   4 relax

Extra activity

Ask (or write on the board) the following questions to check the meaning of the words in Exercise 5:

1 *What do you do if you want to pass your university exams? (study)*
2 *What do teachers do if they want to know you've learnt something? (test)*
3 *What do you do if someone tells you their phone number and you can't write it down? (memorise it)*
4 *What do sports people do if they want to be good? (train, practise)*
5 *What's the opposite of remember? (forget)*

6 Organise the class into pairs. Give students some time to read through the questions. When students are ready, ask them to take turns asking and answering their questions. Monitor and prompt and note any errors for a correction feedback at the end.

With weaker classes you could get students to prepare and write their answers first.

Listening

7 Ask students to look at the photos and the headline and discuss the questions as a class.

ANSWERS

1 His name is Nelson Dellis.
2 He has won the USA Memory Championship. Yes, he has. (Because he won it 'again')

8 [2.23] Give students time to read through the topics, then play the recording. Students listen and number the topics in the order the reporter mentions them. Let students compare their answers in pairs.

ANSWERS

1 b   2 a   3 c

Audioscript 🔊 [2.23]

Do you always forget names and faces? All the time? And how many numbers such as telephone numbers can you remember? Not many? Well, meet Nelson Dellis. Nelson can listen to 99 names and look at their faces. Then he can memorise every one of them. He can also hear 300 different numbers and then repeat them.

Because of his special memory, Nelson has won the USA Memory Championship twice. He won the competition in 2011 and again in 2012. The USA Memory Championships are like the Olympic Games but the athletes train their brains and they take different memory tests.

So how does Nelson do it? He says he doesn't have a special memory. Like normal people, he's forgotten names, dates and numbers, but in 2010 he studied memory techniques and he practised for hours and hours and hours every day. Since then, he's won competitions and he's taught his techniques to people all over the USA.

9 🔊 [2.23] Play the recording again. Ask students to listen and answer the questions. Let students compare their answers in pairs. In stronger classes, ask students to answer the questions from memory first, then listen to the recording again and check.

> **ANSWERS**
> 1 99
> 2 300
> 3 2011 and 2012
> 4 the Olympic Games
> 5 memory techniques
> 6 for hours and hours and hours every day.
> 7 people all over the USA.

Extra activity

Write these key words on the board: *numbers, remember, names, championships, special memory, hours.*

Ask students in pairs to remember how these words are used in the listening.

Grammar present perfect and past simple

10 Ask students to look at the sentences and answer the questions. Let students compare their answers in pairs. Read the grammar box with the students, and check the answers to the questions from Exercise 10. Refer students to the information and practice on page 167.

> **ANSWERS**
> 1 present perfect, past simple
> 2 past simple
> 3 present perfect

11 Start the activity by acting out the first conversation with a reliable student.

Organise the class into pairs. Give students some time to prepare, then ask them to act out the conversations from the prompts, using the present perfect then the past simple. Monitor and note any errors for a correction feedback at the end.

> **ANSWERS**
> 1 Have you ever taken an English exam? When did you take it?
> 2 Have you ever studied science? Where did you study?
> 3 Have you ever taught a subject? What did you teach?
> 4 Have you ever learnt a musical instrument? What did you learn?

Speaking

12 Organise the class into pairs or small groups to talk about their learning experiences. Give students some time to prepare their questions.

In feedback, ask individual students what they found out about their partner and check errors.

Extra activity

Write the following answers from a conversation on the board:

...	Yes, I have.
...	Two years ago.
...	In London.
...	Oh, no! No, I haven't.

Ask students in pairs to write their own conversation, filling in the blanks with questions. Ask a few pairs to read out their dialogues for the class.

10c Why haven't scientists invented it?

Lead-in

Introducing the theme: inventions

Write the following inventions on the board: *the computer, the plane, the TV, the telephone, the car.*

Ask students to put these inventions from the last one hundred and fifty years in order, from the most to the least important. Divide the class into groups to discuss their order and come up with a group list.

Vocabulary science and invention

1 Go through the word box with students and check that they know all the words. Use mime or drawings to check the meanings.

Ask students to categorise the words individually. Then discuss the answers as a class.

Reading

2 Ask students to look at the diagrams of new inventions and match them with the section titles in the article. Let students compare the answers in pairs first, then get class feedback.

ANSWERS
1 A   2 B   3 D   4 C

3 Students read the text and answer the questions. Let them compare their answers in pairs.

ANSWERS
1 Invisible objects, teleporting
2 Flying cars, robot servants

4 Ask students to match the words with the definitions. Let students compare their answers in pairs.

ANSWERS
1 b   2 c   3 e   4 d   5 a

5 Go through the glossary on page 123 with students and help with any difficult vocabulary. Ask students to read the article again and mark the sentences true (T) or false (F). Let them compare their answers in pairs. Get class feedback.

ANSWERS
1 T
2 F (the wheels were not invisible)
3 F (cars are heavy and difficult to fly, and there are other problems with flying cars)
4 T
5 T
6 T (not specifically in the text)
7 T
8 T

6 Divide the class into pairs or small groups to discuss the question. Monitor and note errors for an error feedback at the end.

Critical thinking the main argument and supporting information

7 Read through the example sentences with the class and make sure students are clear how to identify the main argument and the supporting information. Point out that if they can identify the main argument for each point the writer makes, then any other sentences on this topic are likely to be supporting information. Ask students to mark the sentences M (main argument) or S (supporting information). Let students compare their answers in pairs. Discuss the answers as a whole class.

ANSWERS
1 M   2 S   3 S   4 M   5 S   6 M   7 S

Writing

8 Put students in small groups. Students read the questions and choose one to discuss as a group. Tell them to think of reasons together and make notes. Monitor and help with ideas and vocabulary at this stage.

When students are ready, ask them to write a paragraph individually. You could collect this in and mark it.

Extra activity

Once students have written their paragraphs, tell them to pass them round to other members of their group. Students write comments and suggestions and mark errors. Students then revise and rewrite their paragraphs. Collect the paragraphs and put them on the classroom wall for students to read.

10d Problems with technology

Lead-in

Test before you teach: telephone numbers
Dictate the following telephone numbers to the class:

01925 708996
0107 655432
44 1864 657880

Ask students to check in pairs to see if they wrote the numbers down correctly. Ask students to practise saying the numbers in pairs.

Listening

1 Ask students to look at the photo and discuss the questions as a class. Get class feedback.

2 🔘 [2.24] Give students some time to read through the questions. Play the recording. Students listen and answer the questions. Let students compare their answers in pairs.

> **ANSWERS**
> 1 in Kuala Lumpa (at the Ancasa hotel)
> 2 it's three o'clock in the afternoon
> 3 Omar's mobile
> 4 the Ancasa Hotel
> 5 603 2169 2266
> 6 on the company website

Audioscript 🔘 [2.24]

R = Richard, **O** = Omar

R: Hello, Omarox Engineering.

O: Hello, Richard. This is Omar.

R: Hello Omar. Where are you now?

O: I'm in Kuala Lumpa.

R: Great. What time is it there?

O: Err, it's three o'clock.

R: Is that three in the morning?

O: No, in the afternoon. I've just arrived but my mobile isn't working. I'm calling from a telephone at the hotel.

R: I see.

O: So I want to give you the name of my hotel for the next two days. It's the Ancasa Hotel …

R: One moment. I need a pen. OK. Sorry, was that the Encasa Hotel?

O: No, the Ancasa Hotel. A for apple.

R: Oh sorry. Ancasa.

O: And the number is six oh three, two one six nine, double two double six.

R: So that's six zero three, two one six nine, two two, six six.

O: That's right.

R: Is there anything else?

O: Yes, one thing. Have you called our colleagues about tomorrow?

R: Yes, I have. They can meet you at three.

O: Good. And have you emailed me all the designs?

R: No, I haven't because your email wasn't working. The email came back three times this morning.

O: That's because my mobile isn't receiving emails. Ermm, can you put them on the company website and I can download them?

R: Yes, I've done that.

O: Oh, great. Thanks. Bye for now.

Real life checking and clarifying

3 🔘 [2.24] Ask students to read through the expressions and match them to the clarifying responses. Then play the recording again for students to listen and check. Let students compare their answers in pairs.

> **ANSWERS**
> 1 b   2 e   3 a   4 d   5 c   6 f

Pronunciation contrastive stress

4 🔘 [2.25] Let students read the sentences first, then play the recording and ask students to underline the stressed word in the responses. Let them compare their answers in pairs.

Play the recording again. Students listen and repeat.

Audioscript and key 🔘 [2.25]

1 Is that three in the <u>morning?</u>
 No, in the <u>afternoon.</u>
2 Was that the <u>Encasa</u> hotel?
 No, the <u>Ancasa</u> hotel.
3 Is that <u>E</u> for <u>England?</u>
 No, it's <u>A</u> for <u>Apple.</u>

5 Organise the class into pairs. Tell students to decide who is A, and who is B, then tell them to read the information and think of what they are going to say. Monitor and help with vocabulary and question forming.

When students are ready, ask students to take turns role-playing the conversations. Monitor and note errors for an error feedback at the end.

10e Please leave a message after the tone

Lead-in

Using words: Internet and gadgets

Ask students: *If you're far away from your friends or family, how can you contact them?* Elicit all possible ways of making contact, e.g. *letters, postcards, mobile phones, emails, social networks, websites, blogs, forums, chat,* etc. Ask: *What way of communicating do you prefer?* and elicit answers.

Vocabulary email addresses and websites

1 [2.26] Ask students to say the email addresses and websites in pairs. Play the recording. Students listen and check.

Audioscript and key [2.26]

1 j underscore jones at hotmail dot co dot uk

2 www dot ancasa dot com

3 charity help dot org slash b dash 2

Vocabulary notes

In English, the computer symbols are called the following:

/ is 'slash'

// is 'double slash'

– is a 'dash'

_ is an 'underscore'

@ is 'at'

. is 'dot'

: is 'colon'

e.g. *info_12@mail.net* is 'info, underscore, 12, at, mail, dot, net'.

2 Organise the class into pairs to say their email address and a website address for their partner to write down. Monitor and note errors for an error feedback at the end.

Extra activity

Ask students to dictate the addresses of more of their favourite websites to each other.

Writing a telephone message

3 [2.27] Ask students to look at the message, and pre-teach *a voicemail message*. Ask: *What kind of information is it?* and elicit that it is important or urgent information. Ask: *Why are voicemail messages useful? When do people leave voicemail messages?* Play the recording. Students listen and correct the four mistakes. Let students compare their answers in pairs.

Audioscript [2.27]

V = voicemail, **R** = Richard

V: Hello. This is the Ancasa Hotel. Please leave a message after the tone.

R: Hello. This is Richard Sanger calling. That's S-A-N-G-E-R. This is a message for Doctor Omar Al Harbia. Please tell him I can't email the designs so they are on a website. He can download them from this address. It's omarox – that's O-M-A-R-O-X – dot com slash e dash one, once again that's omarox dot com slash e dash one. And can he call me back on my mobile number? That's 0770 234 3785. Or email me at r_sanger@omarox.com. Please give him this message before he leaves this morning. It's urgent.

ANSWERS

1 Name of caller: Richard Sanger
2 omarox.com/e-1 (not a-1)
3 Call him back on his **mobile** number
4 0770 234 3785
5 r_sanger@omarox.com (underline, not dash)

Writing skill imperatives

4a Ask students to look at the example. Ask: *In what way are the two sentences different? Which sentence can we use when we write a message?*

Grammar notes

The imperative form in English is the same as the base infinitive. It is simple and direct, and it is used to give instructions or inform in a functional way when politeness is not important.

4b [2.28] Ask students to listen to five sentences on voicemails and rewrite them as imperatives. Play the first sentence of the recording and change it into the imperative as an example. Then play the rest of the recording, pausing after each sentence to let students write down their answers. In weaker classes, play the whole of the recording first and help with any difficulties (first names, etc.), then play it again for students to write down their answers. Alternatively, refer students to the audioscript on page 174. Let them compare their answers in class.

ANSWERS

2 Email the date of the meeting.
3 Meet Mrs Rivers at the airport.
4 Book a room for two nights at the hotel.
5 Buy two new mobile phones.

Audioscript [2.28]

1 Can you call Jim back this evening?

2 I'd like you to email the date of the meeting.

3 Can you meet Mrs Rivers at the airport?

4 Would you book a room for two nights at the hotel?

5 Can you buy two new mobile phones?

5 Ask students to read through the details and give them some time to prepare their messages. Monitor and help with ideas or vocabulary. If necessary, play the recording from Exercise 3 again and ask students to note down how the man introduces each piece of information (i.e. *this is* + name, *this is a message for* + colleague's name, *can he call me on* + phone / mobile number, *or email me at* + email address).

6 When students are ready, ask students to take turns reading their voicemail messages to their partner, who must write down the most important information.

7 Ask students to check the information their partner noted down. In feedback, ask: *Is everything correct* (e.g. the spelling, phone numbers, the email address)?

Extra activity

Ask students to think of a message to pass on to another classmate, e.g. *Don't forget to do your homework tonight* or *Remember that there is a party on tomorrow night.* Give students time to think of, and write down, a message.

When students are ready, divide them into groups of six to eight, depending on the size of your class. Ask them to sit in a circle. Nominate one student in each group to whisper their message into the ear of the student to their right. That student listens then whispers the message into the next student's ear. Students continue until the message reaches the ear of the student who started the 'Chinese whispers'. Find out if the message remained intact or got changed during the whispering.

Play the game again with a different student's message.

10f Memory and language learning

Before you watch

1 Ask students to look at the photo. Ask: *What can you see? What are the girls doing?* Elicit ideas. Put students in pairs to discuss the questions.

While you watch

2 Ask students to watch the video and write the questions that the people answer. Let them compare their ideas in pairs.

ANSWERS

1 Which language are you learning at the moment?
2 What do you find difficult about learning a language?
3 When you hear or see a new word in the language, how do you memorise it?
4 What is your advice for someone who wants to learn a new language?

---

3 Ask students to watch the video again. Tell them to take notes about the answers to the questions. Let them compare their ideas in pairs.

4 Divide the class into groups of four students. Tell them to compare notes and write answers in more detail. Play the recording again for students to check.

ANSWERS

Speaker 1
1 English
2 so many new words to learn; it's difficult to understand every word
3 write words and definitions down
4 have fun, but work hard; study every day and practise

Speaker 2
1 French
2 remembering vocabulary; ends of verbs, particularly the irregular ones
3 think about whether it looks or sounds like something you already know
4 make it fun; read a newspaper, listen to a podcast, make it more like a hobby

Speaker 3
1 English
2 new words; pronunciation
3 write the meaning of the word; draw a picture
4 use every chance to speak the language; watch the news and look at the Internet in English

Speaker 4
1 Chinese
3 repeat new words over and over again

After you watch

5 Organise the class into pairs. Ask them to say which answers are true for them. Take feedback from the class.

6 Organise the class into groups of four. Ask them to discuss the questions and plan a list of advice. It is a good idea to get students to think of other useful questions first which might prompt them to think of good advice.

Ask students to make their posters and put the posters on the classroom walls. Ask two people from each group to walk round and look at the posters while the other two stay with their poster to describe it.

Videoscript

Which language are you learning at the moment?

00.10 I'm learning English in England because I need it for my job. Also because I enjoy learning languages.

00.20 At the moment, I'm learning French. I use it mostly for holidays, but from time to time I use it for business.

00.28 I'm from Mumbai. I'm learning to speak English to take my exam in it because I need it for work.

00.35 I'm learning Chinese at the moment because there are so many businesses in China. I feel that in the future it will help me with my work.

What do you find difficult about learning a language?

00.54 Well, there are so many new words to learn and I forget them. So if I listen to the radio in English, it's difficult to understand every word.

01.04 Sometimes I find it hard to remember lots of vocabulary and also ends of verbs, particularly the irregular ones.

01.13 With English, there are a lot of new words to learn and sometimes I forget them. And also the pronunciation is sometimes very difficult. Like when I'm watching the news, I don't always know what they are saying.

When you hear or see a new word in the language, how do you memorise it?

01.36 I've got a book and every time I learn a new word I write it down and I also write the definition so I can go back to it and memorise it.

01.48 I use different techniques. I might think: 'Does it sound like something I know? Does it look like something I know?' For example, 'un plat' is 'a plate' and I think: 'It's like "a plate" but without the e.'

02.04 Sometimes I write the meaning of the word or draw a picture of it on a card and then I carry these cards with me so I can learn them when I'm on the bus on the way to work.

02.14 Well, when I hear a word, I repeat that word over and over again.

What is your advice for someone who wants to learn a new language?

02.30 Well, I think you should have fun, but also you need to work hard. I think you need to study every day and practise.

02.40 I think my best advice is to make it fun. Buy the newspaper in the language. Download a podcast. Draw stuff. Above all, make it more like a hobby, not like you're trying to learn.

02.56 Every chance I can, I use to speak English. So when I am in England, I will speak English all the time. But also when I am at home, I will watch the news and look at the Internet in English also.

UNIT 10 Review

Grammar

1 Ask students to write the questions.

> **ANSWERS**
> 2 Have you ever ridden a motorbike?
> 3 Have you ever learnt / learned a musical instrument?
> 4 Have you ever met a famous person?
> 5 Have you ever made a film?

2 Ask students to match the answers with the questions in Exercise 1.

> **ANSWERS**
> a 5   b 2   c 4   d 1   e 3

3 Ask students to take turns to ask and answer the questions in Exercise 1, giving true answers.

4 Students complete the conversation with the present perfect or past simple form of the verbs.

> **ANSWERS**
> 1 Have you ever visited   4 did you
> 2 did you study   5 Did you learn
> 3 worked   6 have spoken / 've spoken

Vocabulary

5 Ask students to replace the words in bold in the sentences with a word for new technology from the box.

> **ANSWERS**
> 2 text message   4 podcast   6 download
> 3 GPS   5 search engine

6 Students choose the correct options.

> **ANSWERS**
> 1 study   3 forget   5 test
> 2 remember   4 practise

7 Students complete the sentence so it is true for them, then compare their answer with a partner.

Real life

8 Students make sentences from the prompts.

> **ANSWERS**
> 1 Is that A as in Amsterdam?
> 2 Was that thirty or thirteen?
> 3 Is the number 675 6475?
> 4 Is there anything else?
> 5 Have you sent the email?

9 Students discuss the questions in pairs.

Unit 11 Tourism

Lead-in

Using words: holidays

Tell students that they are going on holiday and that they have to pack their backpack. Put them in pairs and tell them to think of ten things that they have to put in their backpack – apart from clothes. After a few minutes, ask pairs to work with another pair to share their ideas. Finally, elicit and write up a class list of the ten most important items.

A possible list: *passport, camera, mobile phone, sunglasses, travel guide, ipod or mp3 player, good book to read, umbrella, driving licence.*

1 Ask students to look at the photo. Discuss the question as a class.

2 💿 [2.29] Students listen to the recording and check their answer to the question in Exercise 1. Discuss the answers as a whole class.

> **ANSWERS**
>
> The speaker met some Bedouins who lived in tents in the desert. They put the table outside and made tea. They drank tea together and watched the sun go down.

Audioscript 💿 [2.29]

When I was nineteen, I took a gap year between school and university. I saved some money and then I went backpacking around the world. My favourite memory is when I was travelling in the desert in Jordan and I met some local people. They were called Bedouin and they lived in tents in the desert. They were very friendly and invited me for tea. It was a hot afternoon but they put the table outside and made hot tea. We all sat in the middle of the desert, drank tea and watched the sun go down. It was wonderful!

Background notes

Jordan is an Arab kingdom in the Middle East. Over half the country is covered by the Arabian Desert, which includes one of the largest areas of sand in the world.

3 Students read the types of holiday in the box and say which holiday the man in Exercise 2 took. Check the language for the other types of holiday with the class (see vocabulary notes below).

> **ANSWER**
>
> backpacking around the world

Vocabulary notes

camping = staying in a tent (usually on campsites)

backpacking = travelling cheaply, with a 'backpack' (bag that you carry on your back)

sightseeing = visiting tourist places, e.g. museums, castles, monuments

package holiday = a holiday which is all organised for you, usually including travel, hotel accommodation and some sightseeing trips

hiking = walking long distances in the countryside, often in mountains

4 Organise students into groups to discuss the questions about their own holiday preferences. In feedback, find out which type of holiday is most popular in the class as a whole.

Extra activity

As students do Exercise 4, take notes about how well they manipulate the different tenses. In feedback, comment on good examples of tense use and put some incorrect sentences on the board for students to correct as a class. This is a good opportunity to see how well students can manipulate past, present and future tenses.

11a Going on holiday

Lead-in

Introducing the theme: going on holiday
Write the following on the board:
the beach, the mountains, the jungle, the Arctic.

Ask students in pairs to say which of these places they would like to go to on holiday and why. To test students' use of *should* and *take* before the lesson, ask them what they should take to the holiday destination they choose.

Reading and vocabulary tourism

1 Ask students to look at the quiz. Ask: *What can you see? How many questions are there? Which picture looks more like you when you are on holiday?* Elicit answers.

Ask students to match the definitions to words from the quiz. Let them compare their answers in pairs.

> **ANSWERS**
> 2 single
> 3 carry-on bag
> 4 book the hotel in advance
> 5 souvenirs
> 6 check in
> 7 sightseeing

2 Organise the class into pairs to do the quiz. Tell students to compare their answers with their partner. Then have a class discussion. Read through the *Wordbuilding* box with the class. Refer students to page 91 of the Workbook for further information and practice.

Extra activity

Write *travel, backpack* and *holiday* on the board. Ask students to use their dictionaries to find other forms based on these words (e.g. *traveller, travelling, travel guide, travel book, backpacker, backpacking, holidaymaker, holiday resort,* etc.).

Listening

3 Ask students to look at the website on page 131 of the Student's Book. Discuss the questions as a class.

> **ANSWERS**
> It is for independent tourists who like to travel alone.
> Jan Lanting gives advice for independent travellers, in particular suggestions for good places to visit.

4 🔊 [2.30] Play the recording. Students listen and number the places in the order Jan mentions them. Let students check their answers in pairs before discussing as a class.

> **ANSWERS**
> 1 Thurlestone
> 2 Malaysia
> 3 The Arctic

Audioscript 🔊 [2.30]

I = interviewer, J = Jan

I: Hello and welcome to your weekly podcast from indietravelinfo dot com. With me today is travel writer Jan Lanting with some more suggestions on holidays for the independent traveller. So Jan, today I want to start with your advice for travellers this month. We're sitting in London and it's the end of March. Can you give me some suggestions for good places to visit?

J: Well actually, you don't have to leave England. There are some nice places to visit. Last week I was in a place called Thurlestone. It's in the south-west of England and it's a beautiful part of the country.

I: What's the best way to travel there?

J: Good question. You can buy a return ticket on the train but actually I think you should rent a car. Then you can drive along the coast.

I: And what's the weather like at this time of year?

J: Sometimes it rains, so you should take a coat.

I: OK. So after England, let's travel somewhere warmer.

J: OK. Well, Malaysia is good for this time of year. It's very hot.

I: Great, maybe I should take a holiday there. What about the language? Do people speak English?

J: Yes, a lot of people speak some English. But of course, when you travel you should take a phrase book and learn a few phrases in the local language as well.

I: And what about hotels?

J: In the big cities, hotels are often busy so you should book in advance. But in the countryside it's no problem. You can always find a room. I also recommend a tour into the jungle.

I: The jungle?!

J: That's right. You can go walking through the jungle and see lots of amazing animals and plants.

I: Should I go on my own or with a tour guide?

J: You shouldn't go into the jungle on your own. Always go with a local guide because it can be dangerous.

I: Sure. Now for our final destination. The Arctic?

J: That's right. The Arctic.

I: But it's very cold.

J: Yes, you shouldn't go in the winter because it's very cold and very dark. At the end of March it's sunny and the days are longer so you should go then.

I: Yes, but how do you get there?! Should I go on my own or with a tour?

J: It's very difficult on your own but you can take a ship with a lot of travel companies now. They offer special tours. So it is possible. If you want more details, there are links on my blog at www…

5 🔊 [2.30] Play the recording again. Students listen and answer the questions. Let students check their answers in pairs before discussing as a class.

ANSWERS
1 They are in London, it's March.
2 renting a car
3 a coat
4 It's very hot
5 No, but a lot of people do.
6 It can be dangerous.
7 At the end of March it's sunny and the days are longer so you should go then.
8 You can take a ship with a lot of travel companies now. They offer special tours.

6 Discuss the question as a class.

Extra activity

Ask students in pairs to think of three places that are good to go to on holiday in March, and why. Ask some pairs to tell the class their ideas.

Background notes

Thurlestone is a village, a bay and a beach on the coast of south Devon. The village takes its name from the Thurlestone Rock, which is an arch-shaped rock formation off the coast.

Malaysia is in Southeast Asia, south of Thailand.

Word focus *take*

7 Ask students to match the words to the examples of how *take* is used. Let students compare their answers in pairs.

ANSWERS
1 an umbrella
2 a lunch break
3 a taxi

Grammar notes

Take is one of those verbs with many meanings and collocations. Its most basic meaning is to move or carry someone or something from one place to another. However, it can also be synonymous with *accept, steal, study, use* or *win*.

8 Students read through audioscript 2.30 at the back of their book and find other examples of *take* + noun. Let students compare their answers in pairs.

ANSWERS
take a coat, take a holiday, take a phrase book, take a ship

Extra activity

Ask students to think of other phrases they know with *take* and build up a list on the board. Alternatively, ask students to research the verb in learner dictionaries and find useful examples.

Possible answers: *take a shower or bath, take an exam, take an aspirin, take English at university, take sugar in your coffee, take money from somebody, take a rest, take a photograph, take the bus, train or tram, take your temperature*

Grammar: *should / shouldn't*

9 Ask students to look at the sentences and discuss the questions in pairs. In feedback, elicit and label the forms. Read the grammar box with the students, and check the answers to the questions. Refer students to the information and practice on page 168.

ANSWERS
1 the infinitive (without *to*)
2 You invert *should* and the subject. You don't use *do* or *does*.

Grammar and pronunciation notes

Should is a modal auxiliary verb. We make the negative form by adding *n't* or *not*, and we make the question form by inverting the verb with the subject. *Should* is used to express a mild obligation or strong advice or a strong recommendation.

Notice its pronunciation: *should* /ʃʊd/, *shouldn't* /ˈʃʊdənt/

Extra activity

Take the opportunity to do some prompt drilling here to practise pronunciation. Write the prompts from the table in Exercise 10 (*take a holiday, go sightseeing,* etc.) on the board before doing the exercise. Then say: *I'm so tired.* Elicit: *You should take a holiday* from the class and ask them to repeat it chorally and individually. Continue with all the prompts, making sure students get plenty of repetition practice. At the end, ask students to do Exercise 10 in the Student's Book. Their pronunciation and accuracy will be much better for the drilling practice.

10 Ask students to read the sentences and then make sentences to give advice for each situation, using the prompts in the table. Do the first as an example. Let students work in pairs, or work separately then compare their answers in pairs. In feedback, elicit some answers, and make sure students are using and pronouncing the forms correctly.

ANSWERS
1 You should take a holiday.
2 You should wear sun cream. You shouldn't go sightseeing.
3 You should learn some words.
4 You shouldn't take the bus.
5 You shouldn't buy your souvenirs here.
6 You should go sightseeing.

Extra activity

Fast finishers can write other holiday problems. At the end, ask them to read out the problems. The rest of the class must offer advice with *should* or *shouldn't*.

Speaking

11 Introduce the activity by eliciting a few examples of advice for visitors to your country (or another country), using the topics listed. Then organise the class into pairs. Ask them to choose a country they know well and prepare advice for tourists. Monitor and help with ideas and vocabulary.

12 Organise the class into pairs. Then model the activity by offering advice to a reliable student and eliciting responses. Ask students to work in their pairs to take turns to give advice and ask questions. In feedback, ask students to tell the class which good pieces of advice they received.

Homework

Ask students to write a short advice leaflet for a tourist who is visiting their city.

11b Planning a holiday

Lead-in

Introducing the theme: Australia and Canada
Write *Australia* and *Canada* on the board. Ask students in pairs to write down as many facts and opinions as they can about the two countries in two minutes. At the end of that time, brainstorm ideas and write them on the board. For information, see the Background notes below.

Reading

1 Divide the class into groups of four or five to discuss the questions. In feedback, ask different students to tell the class about the others in his or her group.

2 Ask students to look at the photo and the title. Ask: *What can you see? What's the text about?* Ask students to read the information quickly and match the sub-headings to the sections. Let them compare their answers in pairs.

> ANSWERS
> 1 Visas and immigration
> 2 Money and currency
> 3 Language
> 4 Weather
> 5 Safety and emergencies
> 6 Road travel

3 Ask students to read the comments and decide if the people writing them have read the information in the leaflet or not. Explain that if the comments agree with the information in the leaflet, students should put a tick. If the people have not followed the advice, they should put a cross.

> ANSWER
> Students should tick b and e

Background notes

Australia is the sixth largest country in the world and the twelfth largest economy. It was inhabited for 40,000 years by aborigines before Dutch settlers arrived in the early seventeenth century. It was claimed by the UK in 1770. It has a population of about 23 million. Its capital is Canberra but its largest cities are Sydney and Melbourne. It's famous for the Great Barrier Reef, the Sydney Opera House, its unique wildlife which includes koalas and kangaroos, and its sports traditions, which include successful cricket, rugby and Australian rules football teams.

Vocabulary in another country

4 Ask students to look at the words in the box. Ask what they refer to. Then ask students to read and complete the text. Let students compare their answers in pairs.

ANSWERS

1 visa	4 multicultural	7 licence
2 currency	5 climate	8 illegal
3 time zones	6 hand side	

5 Discuss similarities between the two sets of information as a class.

Background notes

Canada is the world's second-largest country and its border with the USA is the world's longest land border. British and French colonists started settling in Canada from the early seventeenth century. In 1763, France ceded all its Canadian territories to Britain, but the former French colony of Quebec and the cities of Montreal and Quebec City have retained their French character and language. Today, Canada is made up of ten provinces and three territories. Its capital is Ottawa but its largest city is Toronto. It has a population of 35 million. Ice hockey is the national sport.

6 Divide the class into groups. Give students a moment to read through the questions first before sharing information with other people in their groups. In feedback, find out if any students' countries have interesting or unusual rules.

Grammar *have to / don't have to, can / can't*

7 Students look at the sentences and match the highlighted verbs to the words in the box. Let them compare their answers in pairs. Read the grammar box with the students. Point out that *cannot* is the formal and emphatic full form of *can't*. Refer students to the information and practice on page 168.

ANSWERS

1 necessary
2 possible
3 not possible
4 not necessary

Grammar notes

English uses the semi-modal *have to* to express an obligation, and *don't have to* to express a lack of obligation. It behaves like a modal in terms of meaning, but uses the auxiliary *do* to form questions and negatives (e.g. *Do you have to … ?*).

The modal verb *can* is used here to express permission, and *can't* (or the more formal full form *cannot*) is used to express prohibition.

8 Complete the first sentence with the class as an example to get students started. Then ask them to make sentences in pairs by choosing the correct verb.

ANSWERS

1 have to	4 don't have to	7 don't have to
2 cannot	5 can	8 can
3 have to	6 cannot	

Pronunciation /hæftə/

9 [2.31] Play the recording. Students listen and note the pronunciation. Play the recording again. Students listen and repeat.

Audioscript [2.31]

1 You have to drive on the left-hand side.
3 Guests have to leave their room before 11 a.m. or they pay a fee.
4 Airline passengers with an online boarding card don't have to go to the check-in desk.
7 Business class passengers don't have to wait.

Pronunciation notes

Note that the weak pronunciation of *have* in this structure has an /f/ sound, and that *to* has a very weak /ə/ sound.

Writing and speaking

10 Organise the class into pairs. Students choose a situation and prepare their sentences. Elicit one or two examples to get them started. Monitor and help with ideas.

Start the activity by acting out a conversation with a reliable student.

11 Organise students into pairs. Tell them to take turns to read their sentences. Their partner must guess which situation they are describing. Monitor and prompt and note any errors for a correction feedback at the end.

Homework

Ask students to write about rules for visiting their country.

11c Should I go there?

Lead-in

Using words: holidays

Ask students to look at the two pictures on these two pages of the Student's Book.

Ask: *Which of these two places would you rather visit on a holiday? Why?* Ask students to discuss the question with a partner, explaining their reasons. Take feedback from the class and help students with any language they need (e.g. *I don't like cold / hot places, I like to look at museums / art galleries / wildlife, I don't like places that have a lot of tourists, I (don't) like places that are quiet / relaxing / noisy / busy / beautiful,* etc.).

Reading

1 Ask students to look at the photo on page 135. Ask: *What do you know about Antarctica?* Elicit ideas and discuss the questions as a class.

2 Ask students to read the article and match the questions to the paragraphs. Let them compare their answers in pairs.

> ANSWERS
>
> 1 c   2 b   3 a   4 e   5 d

3 Ask students to read the article again and answer the questions. Let them compare their answers in pairs.

> ANSWERS
>
> 1 He wants to do something exciting.
> 2 backpacking over the Andes, going on a safari, swimming with dolphins
> 3 other tourists – he doesn't want to see them everywhere

Background notes

The aim of the IAATO is to make sure that travel to Antarctica is safe and causes the mimimum impact on wildlife and the environment. The organisation supports science and research in the region, and promotes public awareness of conservation issues.

Several different countries have claimed that they own territory in Antarctica, but no claims have been internationally recognised, which means that no country is responsible for the region and its conservation and preservation. It is important therefore that the tourist industry takes responsibility itself for avoiding damage to the region.

4 Discuss the questions as a class or ask students to discuss them in small groups.

Extra activity

Use the text to revise types of holiday. Ask students to read the text to find: a beach holiday, a backpacking holiday, a sightseeing holiday, a safari, a cruise, an adventure holiday (dolphins). Ask students to say which type of holiday they prefer and why.

Critical thinking arguments for and against

5 Ask students to read the text and find arguments for and against a holiday in Antarctica. Elicit one or two reasons as a class first to get students started.

6 Students discuss their lists in pairs. In feedback, ask students if they think going to Antarctica is a good idea.

> ANSWERS
>
> **For:** he doesn't like holidays with hotels, beaches and swimming pools; he doesn't want to go somewhere with a lot of tourists; Antarctica is huge and beautiful; nobody lives there; there's no pollution or traffic; it has lots of nature and wildlife
>
> **Against:** you can't stay overnight; there are increasing numbers of tourists and decreasing numbers of animals and birds

Grammar *everywhere, somewhere, nowhere, anywhere*

7 Ask students to look at the sentences. Discuss the questions as a class. Refer students to page 169 of the Student's Book for further information and practice.

> ANSWERS
>
> everywhere / anywhere = places; nobody = people; something = an event or object

Grammar notes

These words can be used as pronouns and sometimes as adverbs (e.g. *We looked everywhere*).

everybody = all people
somebody = one person (but we don't know who)
nobody = no people
everywhere = all places
somewhere = one place (but we don't know where)
nowhere = no place
We often use *any* when we mean to say that it doesn't matter who or where (e.g. *Anywhere near here is great for a picnic*).

We use singular verbs after these words, e.g. *everywhere was silent.*

8 Ask students to read the text about Florence very quickly first, and find one fact that they find interesting.

Students then read the text again and choose the correct words to complete the text. Let them check their answers in pairs before discussing as a class.

Background notes

Florence (or *Firenze* in Italian) is the capital city of the region of Tuscany in central Italy. It is considered the birthplace of the Renaissance (or *Risorgimento*). In the fifteenth century, Michelangelo, Leonardo da Vinci and Botticelli worked in the city and left great works of art. It is one of the world's most visited cities.

Writing

9 Ask students to work in pairs to write their paragraph about their chosen tourist destination. Tell them first to make brief notes to gather ideas, and to use the text about Florence as a model.

10 Collect the paragraphs and put them on the classroom walls. Students walk round, and read the paragraphs. Once students have sat down again, have a whole-class discussion and decide which destinations seem most attractive.

Extra activity

While the students are reading the paragraphs on the wall, use the opportunity to go round yourself and note errors. At the end, write up some incorrect sentences on the board and ask the class to correct them. Then return the paragraphs to the pairs and ask them to look again and see if they made errors.

Homework

Ask students to research and write about a capital city that they would like to visit. Tell them to write a text encouraging people to visit, using *everywhere*, *somebody*, etc.

11d A holiday in South America

Lead-in

Introducing the theme: South America
Ask students in pairs to list as many countries in South America as they can. In feedback, list the countries on the board and find out which pair knew the most. Elicit one fact or association for each country, e.g. *Brazil – carnival*.

South American countries: Argentina, Bolivia, Brazil, Chile, Colombia, Ecuador, Guyana, Paraguay, Peru, Suriname, Uruguay, Venezuela, and French Guiana (an overseas region of France)

Listening

1 Ask students to look at the photo. Ask: *What can you see? Where is this place and what's happening?* Elicit ideas. Organise the class into pairs or small groups to discuss the questions about choosing a holiday.

Vocabulary notes

A *holiday brochure* (pronounced /ˈbrəʊʃə/ in British English, but /ˈbrəʊʃjʊə/ in American English) is a glossy magazine produced by holiday companies to advertise and provide information about the holidays they offer.

2 💿 [2.32] Give students a moment to read the questions and predict what the speakers might say. Then play the recording. Students listen and answer the questions.

ANSWERS
1 a holiday brochure
2 Brazil, Argentina, Chile
3 a tour followed by two weeks of travelling at the end

Audioscript 💿 [2.32]

A: That's looks interesting.

B: Yes, it's a holiday brochure.

A: Oh really?

B: Yes, I've got a month in South America so I'm looking at places to go.

A: I went there last year. It's an amazing part of the world. I went on a cruise all the way from Brazil to Argentina. You should go on that.

B: Yes, but I'm interested in the wildlife.

A: How about visiting the Andes? That was part of my bus tour in Chile.

B: But the disadvantage is that there are lots of other people with a bus tour. I like travelling on my own.

A: But the advantage is that you see more with a tour guide. And you visit places other tourists don't normally go to.

B: Hmm. Maybe you're right …

A: Can I make a suggestion? If you have a month, why don't you go on a tour for two weeks AND then you could travel on your own afterwards.

B: Actually, that's a really good idea.

Real life making suggestions

3 🔊 [2.32] Organise the class into pairs. Ask students to decide who is A, and who is B. Then ask them to think about how they might match the two halves of the sentences to complete the expressions. Do one as an example to get them started.

Play the recording. Students listen and match. Let students compare their answers in pairs before discussing as a class.

ANSWERS
1 You should go on that.
2 How about visiting the Andes?
3 Can I make a suggestion?
4 Why don't you go on a tour?
5 You could travel on your own.
6 Yes, but I'm interested in the wildlife.
7 But the disadvantage is that there are lots of other people with a bus tour.
8 But the advantage is that you see more with a tour guide.
9 Maybe you're right.
10 That's a really good idea.

Grammar notes

You should … makes a strong suggestion or recommendation whereas *You could …* , *How about …* ? and *Why don't you …* ? make suggestions which the speaker expects the listener to take or leave.

You should … , *You could …* , and *Why don't you …* ? are followed by the infinitive without *to*. *How about …* ? is followed by *-ing*.

Alternative phrases include *You ought to …* , *You might …* , *Have you thought of …* (+ *-ing*)? and *What about …* (+ *-ing*)?

Pronunciation /ʌ/, /ʊ/ or /uː/

4a 🔊 [2.33] Play the recording. Students listen to the three sounds and look at the symbols. Play the recording a few times until students are familiar with the sounds and the symbols. If necessary, point to the symbols on the board as the sounds are spoken.

4b 🔊 [2.34] Ask students in pairs to match the sounds to the words. Play the recording so that students can check their answers. Play the recording again so that students can listen and repeat.

ANSWERS
/ʌ/: bus, but, love
/ʊ/: could, should, book
/uː/: cruise, you, food

Extra activity

Write some other words students know on the board for students to put into categories (or ask them to find words in the text on page 135):

/ʌ/: *doesn't, number, somewhere*

/ʊ/: *look, cook*

/uː/: *pool, do, huge, choose*

5 Ask students to read the situations. Ask: *What does Gary like doing? What's Nigella's problem? What advantages do Dorothy and Frank have?*

Organise the class into pairs to discuss what type of holiday is best for each person.

6 Organise the class into pairs. Ask students to take turns choosing a person from Exercise 5 and suggesting holidays.

Monitor carefully and make sure they are using phrases for suggesting and responding in their conversations.

SAMPLE ANSWERS
1 hiking in the mountains, a bus tour
2 backpacking round a region of the world or round her own country
3 a cruise, a sightseeing tour of different cities

Extra activity

Ask students to write down three things they like doing on holiday and two things they don't like, in note form on a piece of paper.

Organise the class into groups of four to six. Tell students to pool their pieces of paper in a pile. Tell the group to read out what is on the first piece of paper and to discuss what sort of holiday they would suggest to that student. The groups continue until they have made suggestions for each student.

11e Your feedback

Lead-in

Introducing the theme: feedback
Brainstorm situations in which students give feedback (restaurants, courses, sports centres). Build up a list on the board. Ask: *When did you last give feedback? What did you give feedback about? What did you write?*

Speaking

1 Read through the list with the class and check any unknown words. Then ask students to put the list in order.

2 Ask students to compare their list in groups of four or five before discussing as a class.

Extra activity

Ask students to make a list individually, then discuss with a partner and agree on a new list. Then ask each pair to work with another pair to agree on a new list. Finally, elicit an agreed class list.

Writing a feedback form

3 Students read the form and answer the questions. Discuss the answers as a class.

> **ANSWERS**
> 2 the bedroom, the gym, the restaurant
> 3 It was so-so – positive about the facilities, but negative about the staff

Writing skill closed and open questions

4a Read through the information with the class, and elicit an example of an open and a closed question. Tell students to decide whether the questions are open or closed, then discuss their answers in pairs.

> **ANSWERS**
> 3 C   4 C   5 O   6 C   7 C   8 O

4b Discuss the question as a class.

> **ANSWER**
> It says: 'please comment'

5 Elicit examples of feedback questions for each situation. Students then write a feedback form for one situation.

6 Ask students to exchange their forms and comment on them.

Homework

Ask students to design and write a feedback form for a hotel or restaurant they have recently visited.

11f Mecca and the Hajj

Before you watch

1 Ask students to look at the photo. Ask: *What can you see? Where are the people?* Elicit ideas. Explain that the photograph was taken using time lapse photography, so the moving people show as a blur. Put students in pairs to discuss the questions.

> **ANSWERS**
> 1 Muslim
> 2 around the Kaaba in Mecca

2 Students match the people to the holidays. Let students compare their answers in pairs.

> **ANSWERS**
> 1 c   2 a   3 b

3 Discuss the questions as a class. If you have students of other religions in your class, ask them to say what holidays are important for them.

While you watch

4 Students complete the sentences with words from the box.

> **ANSWERS**
> 1 Mecca   3 Masjid-al-Haram   5 Mina
> 2 the Hajj   4 Kaaba   6 Arafat

5 Give students a moment to read through the questions and answer any they can. Then play the video again. Let students compare their answers in pairs before discussing as a class.

> **ANSWERS**
> 1 a   2 a   3 a   4 b   5 a   6 c   7 b

After you watch

6 Ask students to read the text quickly. Ask: *Where is the pilgrimage to?* (Santiago); *What type of religious people go there?* (Christians).

Then ask students to complete the text with the missing words. Let them check their answers in pairs.

> **ANSWERS**
> 1 religious   3 pray   5 pilgrims
> 2 cathedral   4 Christianity 6 pilgrimage

7 Divide the class into groups of four. Ask them to discuss and plan the documentary film.

8 Students present their documentary plans to the class.

Videoscript

All around the world, every day of the year, Muslims pray in the direction of the city of Mecca.

Mecca is in Saudi Arabia.

In the centre of the city, there is a mosque called Masjid al-Haram and in the centre of the mosque there is the Kaaba.

00.25   All Muslims visit the Kaaba once in their life for the Hajj.

The Hajj is a special religious festival.

It's a religious journey, or pilgrimage, that lasts four days.

00.45   About two million Muslims come for the Hajj and on their first day, they walk around the Kaaba.

For a lot of Muslims, the first day is very emotional.

01.05   After the Kaaba, the pilgrims travel to Mina.

During the year, no one lives in Mina, but at Hajj there are around two million white tents in Mina and the pilgrims sleep here.

01.21   The next day, people get up early.

Two million people go to Arafat. It's about eight miles east of Mina.

Around 50,000 vehicles travel there.

01.46   People spend the day in prayer and silence at Arafat.

And finally, when the sun goes down, the two million people return to Mina.

02.25   On the last day of the Hajj, pilgrims return to Mecca.

At the end of their spiritual journey, each pilgrim receives a special name.

The men are called 'Hajji'. The women are called 'Hajjah'.

UNIT 11 Review

Grammar

1 Students circle the correct option. Let them compare their answers in pairs before discussing as a class.

ANSWERS			
1 shouldn't	2 should	3 shouldn't	4 should

2 Students complete the sentences with *have to, don't have to, can* or *can't*.

ANSWERS	
1 don't have to	3 can
2 can't	4 have to

3 Students write their own sentences using the verbs given.

4 Ask students to read the text about space tourism and complete the words.

ANSWERS		
1 somewhere	2 something	3 someone

Vocabulary

5 Students organise the words in the box into the different holiday categories.

ANSWERS
1 camping, hiking, sightseeing
2 single, return
3 souvenir
4 tourist, tour guide

6 Students complete the sentences with collocations using a word from each box.

ANSWERS	
1 time zones	3 hand side
2 work visa	4 driving licence

Real life

7 Students match the suggestions to the responses.

ANSWERS			
1 b	2 c	3 d	4 a

Speaking

8 Ask students to talk with a partner about their last holiday, giving the information to answer the questions. Their partner can ask the questions to prompt them.

Unit 12 The Earth

Lead-in

Introducing the theme: the Earth

Bring in a globe, a map of the world, or a map or picture that shows the Earth. Ask students to imagine they are in space and to describe what they can see of the Earth from there. Elicit key words for this unit: *northern and southern hemisphere, equator, oceans, continents, North and South Pole, Arctic and Antarctic.* Ask students what adjectives describe the view of Earth from space.

1 Ask students to look at the photo. Ask: *What can you see? Where is the person? What picture is he holding?* Then ask students to compare the photos in pairs.

> **SAMPLE ANSWERS**
>
> The main photo shows an Inuit man in the Arctic Circle with his dogs (huskies) and sledge. The place is flat, dry, very cold and covered in snow. The man is holding a large photo of a tropical, equatorial landscape which shows a mangrove swamp with lots of trees. It is wet, green, hot and humid.

2 [2.35] Give students a moment to read through the sentences and gaps. Then play the recording. Ask students to listen and complete the sentences. Let them compare their answers in pairs.

> **ANSWERS**
>
> | | | | |
> |---|---|---|---|
> | 1 | 2,500 | 4 | 25 |
> | 2 | 2,500 | 5 | -10 |
> | 3 | 56 | | |

Audioscript [2.35]

Ira Block took this photo of an Inuit man near his home in the Arctic Circle. He lives on Baffin Island in Canada. That's about two and half thousand kilometres from the North Pole. The Inuit man is also holding another photo by Ira Block. Ira took this photo in the US state of South Carolina which is about two and half thousand kilometres from the equator. Ira took the two photos because about fifty-six million years ago, the Arctic Circle probably looked like South Carolina today. The temperature at the Arctic Circle was around twenty-five degrees Celsius. Nowadays, the average temperature in the Arctic is around minus ten degrees.

Background notes

Ira Block was born in New York in 1949. He has been a *National Geographic* photographer since the 1970s.

The word *Inuit* is used to describe culturally similar indigenous people who inhabit Arctic regions of Greenland, Canada, the US and eastern Siberia.

3 Divide the class into groups of four or five to discuss the questions. If you have a range of nationalities in your class, mix students from different parts of the world. In feedback, ask a few students to tell the class about the countries of others in their group.

Extra activity

Write the following capital cities on the board: *London, Paris, Washington, Buenos Aires, Brasilia, New Delhi, Beijing, Bangkok* and *Tokyo.* Ask students to discuss which one they think is closest to the North Pole, South Pole and the equator. Tell students to research their answers on the Internet.

Answers: London (North Pole), Buenos Aires (South Pole), Bangkok (equator)

12a Climate change

Lead-in

Test before you teach: weight, size and temperature

Place something quite heavy on a table in front of the class. It could be your school bag or a plastic bag full of your shopping.

Ask: *How big is it? How wide is it? How heavy is it? How warm is it?* Elicit guesses from students. Let them lift it to guess the weight and touch it to guess the temperature. Find out how well they can use measurements. You could weigh and measure your bag before the lesson so that you can correct or confirm the students' guesses.

Vocabulary measurements

1 Ask students to match the abbreviations to the measurements. Do the first line together as an example. Let students check their answers with a partner before discussing as a class.

```
ANSWERS
2  °C     degrees Celcius     temperature
3  km     kilometres          distance
4  l      litres              quantity of water (or liquid)
5  m²     square metres       area
6  kg     kilograms           weight
```

Background notes

Celcius is also known as 'centigrade'. It is named after the Swedish astronomer Anders Celcius (1701–1744).

2 Ask students to read and complete the fact file using the abbreviations from Exercise 1. Let them compare their answers in pairs. In feedback, ask students which facts they found surprising.

```
ANSWERS
1  °C      4  m²
2  km      5  kg, kg
3  %       6  l
```

3 Give students some time to think of answers. Let them check their answers with a partner before discussing as a class. Read through the *Wordbuilding* box as a class. Refer students to page 99 of the Workbook for further information and practice.

```
ANSWERS
juice: litres
weather: degrees Celcius
journey: kilometres
fruit or vegetables: kilograms
tax: percentage
house: square metres
```

Pronunciation notes

Note the irregularity and difficult pronunciation of these nouns: *length* /lɛŋθ/, *height* /haɪt/, *weight* /weɪt/.

Extra activity

Get students to guess or measure the weight, height and length of different things in the classroom.

Reading

4 Discuss the questions as a class. In a mixed nationality class, get students to make brief presentations about their country to the class. Pre-teach the key words *increase* (go up) and *decrease* (go down).

5 Ask students to look at the maps. Ask: *What can you see?* Tell them to discuss the three questions quickly in pairs, then take feedback from the whole class. Ask if they are surprised by any of the information. Students then read the text to confirm their answers.

```
ANSWERS
Map 1
1  It shows the change in temperature.
2  30 years
3  By different colours for the different levels of change.

Map 2
1  It shows the change in rainfall.
2  30 years
3  By different colours for the different levels of change.
```

6 Ask students to look at the maps again and discuss in pairs whether the statements are true or false.

```
ANSWERS
1  F      2  T      3  T      4  T      5  T      6  T
```

7 Discuss the questions in groups or as a class.

Grammar will / won't

8 Ask students to look at the sentences and choose the correct option to complete the rules. Tell them to find further examples and discuss them with a partner. Read through the grammar box with the class. Refer students to the information and practice on page 169.

```
ANSWERS
1  future      2  don't add      3  is
```

Grammar notes

We use *will* to make predictions about the future which are based on our knowledge or personal opinions. Note that we use *going to* when the prediction is based on evidence.

In spoken English (and written English except when it's very formal) we abbreviate *will* to *'ll* and *will not* to *won't*.

9 Ask students to reorder the words to make sentences about the future, then check their answers in pairs.

ANSWERS

1 It'll be hotter in my country in the future.
2 The temperature in this country won't increase in the future.
3 I think I'll visit Antarctica one day.
4 There will be more ice in the Arctic Circle.
5 The percentage of people living in cities will decrease.
6 Everyone will speak English.
7 People won't buy cars.
8 I don't think the number of dry deserts will increase.

---

10 Organise the class into pairs to make questions from the sentences in Exercise 9, then ask them to take turns asking and answering the questions.

Extra activity

Extend any questions that the students find very interesting into a class discussion.

Alternatively, ask fast finishers to write their own *will* or *won't* questions and discuss them as a class at the end.

Pronunciation *'ll*

11a [2.36] Point out the weak pronunciation of abbreviated *'ll*. Then play the recording. Students listen and note which word they hear.

Audioscript [2.36]

1 It'll rain here tonight.
2 I will visit space in my lifetime.
3 I think I'll learn Spanish.
4 Will you visit me one day?
5 The percentage of people in the countryside will decrease.
6 I don't think there'll be more snow this winter.

11b [2.36] Students check their answers in the audioscript on page 174.

ANSWERS

1 'll   2 will   3 'll   4 Will   5 will   6 'll

Pronunciation notes

Saying *'ll* after pronouns can be very tricky. Point out the following: *I'll* /ail/, *she'll* /ʃiːl/, *we'll* /wiːl/.

Extra activity

Use a drill to practise the way that pronouns combine with *'ll* in sentences.

Writing and speaking

12 Elicit some examples to get students started, then give them a minute to prepare sentences about their partner. Monitor and help with ideas and vocabulary.

13 In pairs, students take turns to read out their sentences to each other and comment on them. In feedback, ask students to say how good or accurate they think their partners' sentences were.

Homework

Ask students to write predictions about their own life. Tell them to imagine where they'll be and what their life will be like ten years from now.

12b Exploring the Earth

Lead-in

Using words: the Earth

Write the following words on the board:

Pacific, Amazon, Everest, Sahara, Antarctic.

Ask students in pairs to choose one of the words and write as many words as they can think of that connect to the word, e.g. they could choose *Amazon* and write the words *river, forest, hot, humid, Brazil, trees, jaguar, piranha, deep, wet, huge, dangerous*, etc.

At the end, ask different pairs to read out their lists. Write any new or interesting words on the board.

Reading and vocabulary land and water

1 Discuss the questions as a class.

2 Ask students to look at the picture. Ask: *What can you see? What is special about this place?* Elicit ideas. Ask students to read the text and answer the questions. Let them compare their answers in pairs.

> **ANSWERS**
> 1 The Black Hole of Andros
> 2 Mount Dinpernalason, Merume Mountains, the Foja Mountains

3 Ask students to read the text again and find the words. Let them check their answers in pairs.

> **ANSWERS**
>
> | areas of water | areas of land |
> | --- | --- |
> | sea | desert |
> | ocean | island |
> | lake | forest |
> | river | mountain |

Extra activity

Check *glacier* (an area of ice that stays frozen all through the year) and *tropical* (very hot and wet and near the equator). Ask students if they know any other words to describe areas of land or water (*canal, hill, plain*, etc.).

4 Organise the class into pairs to discuss the questions.

Grammar definite *the* or no article + names

5 Ask students to read the article and find examples of *the* + place names. Let them compare their answers in pairs.

> **ANSWERS**
> 2 the Atlantic Ocean
> 3 the Himalayan mountains
> 4 the Mazaruni River

6 Ask students to scan the article again and find examples of no article + place name. Let them compare their answers in pairs. Read through the grammar box with the class. Refer students to page 169 for further information and practice.

> **ANSWERS**
> 1 Mount Dinpernalason, Mount Everest
> 2 Lake Vostok
> 3 Guyana, Papua New Guinea
> 4 Antarctica

Grammar notes

The way places are named in English may be counter-intuitive to many students – why say *Lake Vostok* but *the Black Sea*, for example? Why not *Vostok Lake* or *Sea Black*? It is a good idea to get students to think about differences and similarities between their language and English.

Note that we generally use *the* with other names of unique places: *the Amazon rainforest, the Bermuda Triangle, the Panama Canal*.

Note also that *the Earth, the world, the Sun* and *the Moon* take *the*, but the other planets don't: *Jupiter, Saturn, Mars*, etc.

7 Divide the class into groups of four or five to think of new examples. If your students have access to the Internet, they could do this as a research task.

> **SAMPLE ANSWERS**
>
> The United Arab Emirates, the Seychelles, the Pacific Ocean, the Indian Ocean, the Pyrenees, the Andes, the Rocky Mountains, the Thames, the Nile, the Rhine, Mount Fuji, Mount Etna, Lake Baikal, Ecuador, Asia, etc.

Extra activity

Play a team game. Keep students in the same groups as for Exercise 7. Say: *mountains.* Team 1 says the name of a mountain or group of mountains. Team 2 says a different name and so on round the class until a team can't think of any more mountains. They're out. Continue until there is a winner. Then say a different category.

8 Ask students to look at the title and the photo and predict what the text is about. Tell them to read it quickly to confirm their prediction.

Ask students to complete the text with *the* or no article. Let them compare their answers in pairs.

> **ANSWERS**
> 2 the   3 the   4 Ø   5 the   6 the   7 Ø

Listening

9 🔊 [2.37] Ask students to read through the topics. Play the recording. Students listen and number the topics in the order they are mentioned. Let students check their answers in pairs before discussing as a class.

ANSWERS

1 b   2 a   3 d   4 c   5 e

Audioscript 💿 [2.37]

A = interviewer, B = Jenny Walters

A: It's the deepest place on the Earth and before now, nobody has ever been to the bottom. But the film director and *National Geographic* Explorer, James Cameron, has travelled down to the bottom of the Mariana Trench. With me in the studio is our science expert Jenny Walters to tell us how he did it.

B: Good evening.

A: So Jenny. First of all, how deep is the Mariana Trench?

B: It's eleven kilometres to the bottom. That's a long way down.

A: Indeed, and how long did the journey take?

B: James Cameron took over two hours to get to the bottom and then he spent about four hours down there.

A: And how did he travel there? In some kind of submarine?

B: That's right. It was a special one-man submarine.

A: I see. How big is it exactly?

B: It's seven metres long but it has a big engine so there isn't much space for a human.

A: So you're in a small space and it's dark down there. I couldn't do it. How well could he see?

B: It's very dark but the submarine has lights of course. So Cameron could see small sea creatures. He described it as a 'desert'. He also had film cameras on the submarine and he plans to make a 3D film about the adventure.

A: And of course he isn't the first explorer, is he? How many other explorers have been there?

B: There was one other. Don Walsh went down in 1960 but he didn't go to the bottom. In fact he was on the ship when Cameron went down.

A: Wow. How old is he now?

B: I think he's in his eighties.

A: That's amazing. And I have one last question that everyone wants to know the answer to. How much did James Cameron spend on this? Thousands? Millions?

B: I'm afraid I don't know, but films like *Titanic* and *Avatar* made a lot of money at the cinema so I think he could afford it.

10 💿 [2.37] Play the recording again. Students listen and answer the questions. Let students check their answers in pairs before discussing as a class.

ANSWERS

1 eleven
2 two hours
3 seven metres long
4 the submarine had lights
5 a 3D film
6 the first explorer of the Mariana Trench
7 on the ship
8 He made a lot of money from his films.

Extra activity

Divide the class into pairs to roleplay the interview on the recording. Student A asks the questions in Exercise 10, using *you* / *your* instead of *he* / *his*. Student B plays the interviewee, using their answers to reply to the questions.

Background notes

James Cameron was born in Canada in 1954. His films include *The Terminator* (1984), *Aliens* (1986), *The Abyss* (1989), *Terminator 2: Judgment Day* (1991), *True Lies* (1994), *Titanic* (1997), *Dark Angel* (2000–02), and *Avatar* (2009). He became the first person to reach the bottom of the Mariana Trench in a solo descent on March 26th 2012. He has estimated earnings of over $250 million.

Word focus *how*

11 Ask students to look at the questions and match them to the uses.

ANSWERS

1 f   2 c   3 d   4 b   5 a   6 e

Vocabulary notes

How is a question word which is used to ask about the way that something happens or is done (*How do you open this?*).

It combines with adjectives and adverbs to ask about quantity or degree (*How old is it? How far is it? How much is it?*).

Extra activity

Ask students to write their own sentences beginning *How big … ?*, *How well … ?*, *How old … ?*, etc. Divide them into pairs to ask and answer their questions.

Speaking

12 Ask students to write the names of famous places they have visited. Provide an example.

13 Organise the class into pairs. Students take turns to ask questions to guess their partner's place.

Homework

Students write a description of the most interesting place on Earth that they have visited.

12c Looking for a new Earth

Lead-in

Introducing the theme: planets
Revise the planets. Elicit their names and write them on the board, then ask students to put them in order from closest to furthest from the Sun: *Sun, Mercury, Venus, Earth, Mars, Saturn, Jupiter, Uranus, Neptune.*

Ask students which planet they would like to visit and why.

Speaking

1 Organise the class into groups of four or five to talk about the places and discuss how likely it is that people will live there, using the three phrases given. Have a whole-class discussion in feedback and elicit reasons for students' views.

2 Ask students in their groups to discuss any other places that they think humans might live. Take feedback from the class.

Reading

3 Ask students to look at the picture and title. Ask: *What do you think the article is about?* Elicit ideas.

Ask students to read the article quickly to check their ideas. Then ask them to work out which sentence goes at the end of which paragraph. Let students compare their answers in pairs before discussing as a class.

> ANSWERS
> Paragraph 1: c
> Paragraph 2: a
> Paragraph 3: d
> Paragraph 4: b

Extra activity

Ask some follow-up questions to check comprehension, e.g. *What do astronomers look for first?* (a star) *What three things do astronomers think a planet needs to support life?* (water, air, rock) *What is the name of the planet that is similar to Earth?* (Gliese 581 g).

Vocabulary the Earth and other planets

4 Students match the words to the definitions. Let them compare their answers in pairs.

> ANSWERS
> 1 a explorers; b astronomers
> 2 a star; b planet
> 3 a to orbit; b to travel
> 4 a surface; b rock

Critical thinking structuring an argument

5 Ask students to read the whole of the article again and find the phrases that are used to structure the arguments, then match them to their purpose. Let them compare their answers in pairs or in small groups.

> ANSWERS
> Paragraph 1: <u>First of all</u>, astronomers look for a star.
> <u>More importantly</u>, it is the correct distance from the Sun …
> <u>Unfortunately</u>, many of these planets are either too near to the star or too far away.
> Paragraph 2: <u>However</u>, if the planet is in a good position, …
> <u>That's because</u> there is often water under the rocks.
> 1 d   2 a   3 b   4 e   5 c

Speaking

6 Ask students to complete the sentences with their opinions about finding a new Earth. Then ask them to share their opinions with a partner.

7 Ask students to write a short paragraph about their opinions, using the phrases from Exercise 5 to structure their arguments.

12d Earth Day

Lead-in

Introducing the theme: presentations
Make a brief presentation about a special day in your country to the class, using some of the expressions in this section. At the end, ask students what the presentation was about and what they learnt.

Reading

1 Ask students to look at the photo and guess what Earth Day is and what people do on that day.

Then ask students to read the text and answer the questions. Let them compare their answers in pairs.

> ANSWERS
> 1 They help the Earth – they clean parks, pick up rubbish or plant trees.
> 2 April 22nd 1970 in the USA
> 3 They wanted to help the Earth and the environment.

Extra activity

Ask students if they think Earth Day is a good idea and why. Ask what other things people could do on Earth Day. Build up a list of activities on the board.

Real life making a presentation

2 🔘 [2.38] Give students a moment to read through the sentences. Then play the recording. Students listen and choose the correct endings. Let students compare their answers in pairs.

> ANSWERS
> 1 a   3 b   5 a
> 2 a and b   4 a and b

Audioscript 🔘 [2.38]

Good morning, and thank you for coming. My name's Davi and I'm from Brazil. Today, I'd like to talk about an important day in my year called Earth Day.

First of all, Earth Day began on April 22nd in 1970. Over 20 million people went to Earth Day in different cities across the USA. There were politicians, teachers, artists and musicians. Since that day in 1970, Earth Day has become famous all over the world.

Nowadays, more than 175 countries have an Earth Day. Lots of people do different things. Last year, people in China planted 600,000 new trees. In New Orleans in the USA, they put 300,000 energy efficient bulbs into houses. And finally, in my country lots of people picked up rubbish in the cities and in the countryside.

In conclusion, I really think Earth Day is important. Next year, I hope you will do something on Earth Day. Thank you very much for listening.

3 🔘 [2.38] Ask students to listen again and complete the sentences. Let them compare their answers in pairs before discussing as a class.

> ANSWERS
> 1 thank you   5 Nowadays
> 2 I'm from   6 finally
> 3 I'd like to   7 In conclusion
> 4 First of   8 for listening

Extra activity

Ask students to listen and repeat the phrases. You could do this by playing and pausing the recording, or by reading out the sentences yourself, and asking students to repeat.

Pronunciation pausing on commas

4a 🔘 [2.39] Play the recording. Ask students to listen and notice the pausing. You could play it again, and ask students to repeat.

Audioscript 🔘 [2.39]

1 Today, I'd like to talk about my company.

2 First of all, we started the company in 1999.

3 In conclusion, I think it's very important.

4b Ask students to work in pairs. Tell them to practise reading out the sentences in Exercise 3, practising pausing on the commas.

5 Ask students to choose a topic and prepare their presentation. Tell them to use Davi's talk as a model, and to include expressions from the box. Remind them to be careful with the structure, following the numbered points given. Monitor and help with vocabulary.

6 Organise the class into groups of four or five. Students take turns to make their presentations to the group.

Extra activity

Ask students in groups to research one of the following British or American festivals: Bonfire Night, Shrove Tuesday, Martin Luther King Day, Thanksgiving. Tell them to organise the information they find into a short presentation and to give their presentation to the class.

Homework

Ask students to research a festival or special day from their own country or another country and prepare a presentation.

12e Planning an event

Materials

Bring in sheets of A3 paper and a variety of different-coloured pens for students to use when designing their posters.

Lead-in

Introducing the theme: posters
Bring in some real posters and put them on the classroom walls before the lesson. Ask students to walk round and read the posters. In feedback, ask: *What are the posters advertising? What do you find out about the events?*

Writing a poster

1 Ask students to look at the poster. Discuss the answers to the questions as a class.

> **SAMPLE ANSWERS**
> Normal places include notice boards, walls in entrance halls or corridors where a lot of people walk, or outside places that a lot of people visit in the community (e.g. village halls, shops and supermarkets, bus stops, etc.).

2 Students look at the poster and find answers to the questions. Let them compare their answers in pairs.

> **ANSWERS**
> It answers all of the questions except 5 and 7. The answer to 9 is implied (to help the environment).

Extra activity

Ask students to answer the questions.
Answers
1 Newmarket Environmental and Conservation Group
2 Earth Day celebration
3 April 22
4 planting trees, theatre, music, art, environmental presentations
5 (not given)
6 Newmarket Park
7 (not given)
8 free
9 to celebrate and help protect the Earth's environment
10 environmentally-friendly products
11 Yes – hot and cold food
12 on the website

Writing skill important words and information

3a Read the information and discuss the questions as a class.

> **ANSWERS**
> Writer uses key words – nouns, verbs, numbers, times
> Writer doesn't use grammatical words which carry little meaning – prepositions, auxiliary verbs, pronouns, possessives, articles, etc.

3b Ask students to go through the sentences and underline key words. Let students check their answers in pairs, comparing their ideas with the poster before discussing as a class.

> **ANSWERS**
> 1 There will be presentations about how to help the environment.
> 2 You can watch theatre, listen to music and look at art by local performers and artists.
> 3 Shops are going to be selling environmentally-friendly products.
> 4 You can also buy hot and cold food.
> 5 Entrance to the event is free.
> 6 Visit our website at NECG.org / earthday for more information.

4 Organise the class into groups of four or five to design a poster. Ask them first to discuss the different activities and choose the one they think is best for their poster.

5 Hand out the sheets of A3 paper and coloured pens and ask students to design their posters. Monitor and help with ideas. Make sure students are using short sentences with only the most important words.

6 Put the posters on the classroom wall. Ask students to walk round and comment on each other's posters.

Extra activity

Ask students to design a poster for the end-of-course party!

12f Volcanoes

Before you watch

1 Ask students to look at the photo. Ask: *What can you see?* Put students in pairs to write three words to describe it, then ask them to compare their words with another pair. Take feedback from the whole class.

2 Discuss the questions as a class.

While you watch

3 Ask students to watch the video and put the things in order. Let them compare their ideas in pairs.

ANSWERS

1 d	2 b	3 a	4 f	5 c	6 e	7 g

4 Ask students to watch the video again. Tell them to match the names and words to the descriptions. Let them compare their ideas in pairs.

ANSWERS

1 b	2 c	3 a	4 f	5 h	6 d	7 e	8 g

5 Students watch the video again and decide if the sentences are true or false.

ANSWERS

1 T	2 T	3 T	4 F	5 T	6 F

6 Divide the class into groups of four students to make a list of reasons. Have whole-class feedback.

ANSWERS

Volcanoes have created 80% of the world's surface. Humans, animals and plants can live on the ground created by volcanoes.

After you watch

7 Ask students to read the text quickly. Ask: *Will Mount Vesuvius erupt again?* (no one knows). Then ask students to complete the text with the missing words. Let them check their answers in pairs.

ANSWERS

1 volcano	4 eruption
2 tectonic plates	5 lava
3 active	6 magma

8 Organise the class into groups of four. Ask them to discuss the information points and plan their presentation. Tell them to brainstorm ideas from the video and their own general knowledge before using the Internet.

9 Ask groups to work with another group and take turns to read out their presentations.

Videoscript

In the past, people thought volcanoes were mountains of fire. Nowadays, we know they are openings in the surface of the Earth.

00.17 There are about 1,500 active volcanoes around the world. Most of these are in an area called the Ring of Fire. It's around the Pacific Ocean.

00.36 The surface of the Earth is made of large plates of rock. These are called tectonic plates. These tectonic plates are moving all the time and volcanoes usually come up where these plates meet. In these places, the rock becomes very hot and melts. This is called magma.

01.05 When magma comes to the surface, it's called lava. The lava can run like water. But over time, it builds up into a volcano.

01.34 One of the world's most active volcanoes is Kilauea in Hawaii. It's a popular destination for many tourists. You can stand close to the Kilauea and feel its heat.

02.07 But some volcanoes are more dangerous. Mount Vesuvius is one the most famous volcanoes in history. It buried the city of Pompeii two thousand years ago. Two thousand people died under the lava, gas and hot ash.

02.34 But volcanoes don't always destroy life. Volcanoes have also created 80 per cent of the Earth's surface, which means that humans and animals can live, and plants can grow, on the ground created by volcanoes.

UNIT 12 Review

Grammar

1 Students complete the conversations with *'ll, will* or *won't*.

ANSWERS

1 'll	5 won't
2 won't	6 Will
3 Will	7 will
4 will	

2 Ask students to decide if the place names are used with *the* or no article.

ANSWERS

1 The	5 Ø	9 The
2 Ø	6 The	10 The
3 The	7 Ø	11 Ø
4 The	8 The	12 The

3 Ask students to think of places they would like to visit in the future, and list their top three places. They should then compare their choices with a partner and give their reasons.

Vocabulary

4 Ask students to complete the text with the abbreviations for measurements.

ANSWERS

1 km²   2 °C   3 kg   4 m   5 %

5 Ask students to complete the questions with words from the box, then find the answers in the text.

ANSWERS

1 big, 163 km²
2 warm, 20 °C
3 tall, 9.8 m
4 many, 3,790 people

6 Ask students to choose the correct options to complete the sentences.

ANSWERS

1 Sea   2 River   3 island   4 deserts

7 Students discuss with a partner which areas of land and water from Exercise 6 they have in their own country.

Real life

8 Ask students to read the sentences and delete one word which is not needed in each sentence.

ANSWERS

2 the   3 am   4 has   5 to   6 your

Speaking

9 Organise the students into groups of about four students. Ask each group to look back through the book and write one question about the information in each unit, to produce a quiz about the whole coursebook. Tell them to focus on the information they found most interesting in the book.

10 Ask groups to work with another group to ask and answer their quiz questions. Alternatively, groups can present their quiz as a whole-class activity.

Grammar summary: answer key

Unit 1

1

1 'm not, 's
2 Are, are, 'm, is
3 Is, is
4 is, 's
5 Are, are
6 Is, isn't, 's
7 is, 'm
8 is, isn't, 's

2

2 … wife's name …
3 Louise's son …
4 … Ranulph's stepson …
5 Ranulph's daughter …
6 Ranulph's distant cousins

3

1 Her
2 his
3 your
4 our
5 my
6 their

UNIT 2

1

2 plants
3 families
4 addresses
5 brothers
6 cities
7 boxes
8 gloves

2

2 these
3 This
4 These
5 this

3

1 that
2 Those
3 those
4 that
5 Those

4

1 's
2 Is, isn't, 's
3 Are, are, 's
4 Is, isn't
5 Are, aren't, 's

5

2 of
3 in
4 opposite
5 on
6 on
7 between
8 to

UNIT 3

1

2 work
3 don't have
4 live, have
5 don't like
6 meet

2

2 Where do your parents live?
3 What time do the shops close?
4 Do you go to work by bus?
5 What do people do in the evenings?
6 Where do you meet your friends?

3

2 He doesn't have children.
3 Does your husband work in an office?
4 Sarah studies archaeology at university.
5 Murad doesn't teach Arabic.
6 Does the bus stop on this street?

4

2 goes
3 finishes
4 Does, live
5 does, do
6 doesn't speak

UNIT 4

1

2 going
3 dancing
4 studying
5 climbing
6 travelling
7 doing
8 swimming

2

1 On holiday Karla always reads books.
2 Luke doesn't often play computer games.
3 We often go to the theatre.
4 My life is never boring.
5 I usually have a snack in the afternoon.
6 He always watches TV after work.
7 We usually go for a walk on Sundays.
8 I sometimes go to art galleries in my lunch break.

3

2 can't speak
3 Can, play
4 can drive
5 can't see it
6 can write
7 can't sleep
8 can take

UNIT 5

1

2 a
3 some
4 any
5 an
6 any
7 any
8 some

2

2 a lot of
3 many
4 a lot of
5 much
6 much
7 much
8 many

UNIT 6

1

2 was
3 was
4 were
5 wasn't
6 was
7 weren't
8 were
9 were

2

2 had
3 went
4 became
5 lived
6 worked
7 discovered
8 made

UNIT 7

1

1 did
2 did, didn't
3 Did, did
4 did, didn't
5 did, didn't
6 Did, did
7 Did, didn't, didn't
8 Did, did

2

2 My car is older than your car.
3 Trains are more expensive than buses.
4 A bike is slower than a car.
5 Geese are faster than small birds.
6 Learning a language is more difficult than learning a musical instrument.
7 Male elephants are bigger than females.
8 My journey to work is longer than your journey to work.

3

2 the oldest
3 smallest
4 the best
5 the most famous
6 the most expensive
7 the most amazing
8 busiest

UNIT 8

1

2 I haven't got any climbing boots.
3 Has Lily got curly hair?
4 Her parents have got a furniture business.
5 Has your car got air-conditioning?
6 Have you got a new phone?
7 Rob and Helen haven't got children.
8 Our house has got two bathrooms.

2

2 'm reading
3 isn't working
4 Do you usually have
5 are you waiting
6 doesn't like
7 'm making
8 are staying

UNIT 9

1

2 are, going to see
3 Is, going to come
4 's going to write
5 Are, going to visit
6 'm not going to have
7 's going to study
8 'm not going to pay

2

2 To learn
3 To change
4 To get
5 To invite
6 To make
7 To see
8 To drive

UNIT 10

1

2 's travelled
3 has never used
4 've been
5 haven't written
6 Have, cooked
7 hasn't read
8 has never bought

2

1 Have you ever been, have, worked
2 've forgotten, was
3 Did you see, did, saw
4 did you do, came
5 did you learn, taught
6 Have you ever studied, I have, learned
7 's visited, have you ever travelled
8 Did you win, didn't, had

UNIT 11

1

2 should wear
3 should watch
4 should learn
5 shouldn't eat
6 should get
7 shouldn't stay
8 shouldn't go

2

1 c   2 a   3 b   4 b   5 c   6 a   7 c   8 c

3

2 thing
3 body
4 body
5 every
6 some
7 no
8 any

UNIT 12

1

2 'll
3 will
4 won't
5 won't
6 'll
7 won't
8 'll

2

1 We went to **the** Andes when we were in Argentina.
2 ✓
3 **The** Mississippi is the longest river in **the** United States.
4 Montblanc is the highest mountain in **the** Alps.
5 Would you like to go to Lanzarote in **the** Canary Islands?
6 Have you ever swum in **the** Atlantic Ocean?
7 I'd love to visit **the** Atacama Desert.

Photocopiable tests

Unit 1 Test

Grammar

1 Complete the sentences with *'m* or *'re*.

1 Hi! I _____ Mia.
2 They _____ explorers.
3 I _____ married.
4 We _____ from Canada.
5 I _____ thirty-two.

(5 points)

2 Complete the sentences with *'m* or *'re* or *'s*.

1 I _____ from Italy.
2 He _____ single.
3 We _____ married.
4 You _____ from the USA.
5 She _____ a teacher.

(5 points)

3 Complete the sentences. Use contractions if possible.

1 _____ they from China?
2 _____ he a student?
3 Are they from Great Britain? No, they _____.
4 I _____ Russian. I'm from Moscow.
5 'Is Mary an explorer?' 'Yes, she _____.'

(5 points)

4 Underline the possessive *'s* and circle the contracted verb *'s*.

1 It's my mother's bag.
2 Erick's from Canada.
3 My friend's from Mexico.
4 That's Erin's house.
5 Tim's my sister's husband.

(5 points)

5 Circle the correct word.

1 I'm Spanish. *I / My* family is from Madrid.
2 They're Italian. *Their / They* names are Aldo and Clara.
3 What's *your / you* name?
4 *We / Our* are from America.
5 This is my friend. *His / He* name is John.

(10 points)

Vocabulary

6 Match the information 1–7 to a–g.

1 First name ____   a married
2 Surname ____   b wife
3 Age ____   c the UK
4 Job / Occupation ____ d photographer
5 Country ____   e Johnson
6 Marital status ____ f Alex
7 Relationship ____   g thirty-one

(7 points)

7 Complete the family words.

1 m _ th _ r
2 f _ th _ r
3 s _ st _ r
4 n _ _ ce
5 br _ th _ r
6 h _ sb _ nd

(6 points)

8 Write the family words.

1 your aunt's son   _____
2 your sister's son   _____
3 your mother's sister   _____
4 your aunt's husband   _____
5 your mother's mother and father _____

(5 points)

9 Match the letters that have the same sound.

D	Y	M	U	A

1 I, ____
2 F, S, L, ____
3 J, K, H, ____
4 B, P, C, ____
5 W, Q, ____

(5 points)

10 Complete the description with these words.

talk	travel	live	speak	work	have	use

My name is Amber. I ¹ _____ in France. I
² _____ French, English and a little Italian. I
³ _____ a big family. I ⁴ _____ in an office.
At work, I ⁵ _____ the computer and
⁶ _____ to clients. In the summer, my family and I
⁷ _____ to Spain together.

(7 points)

Functions

11 Complete the parts of the conversation with the words from the box. Then order them 1–5.

introduce	meet	too	later	Bye!

a Nice to _____ you, Anna.
b _____.
c Nice to meet you _____
d Well, see you _____. Goodbye.
e I'd like to _____ you to Anna.
    1 ____ 2 ____ 3 ____ 4 ____ 5 ____

(10 points)

Writing

12 Join the sentences with *and* or *but*.

1 I'm 21. My sister is 21. <u>I'm 21 and my sister is 21.</u>

2 I'm 35. My husband is 36.

3 I'm from Argentina. I work in Spain.

4 We are students. We are at school.

5 I'm Chinese. My husband is Chinese, too.

6 My family is in the USA. I live in England.

(5 points)

13 Write your personal profile. Answer the questions.

What's your name?

What's your surname?

How old are you?

Where are you from?

Are you married?

What's your job?

Personal profile
_____
_____
_____
_____
_____
_____

(15 points)

Speaking

14 Work in pairs. Introduce yourself. Ask and answer the questions from 12b.

(10 points)

Unit 2 Test

Grammar

1 Circle the correct word.

1 These are *bus / buses*.

2 My daughters are here with their two *babys / babies*.

3 These are the new *shelves / shelfs*.

4 These *persons / people* are Chinese.

5 These students are from different *countries / countrys*.

(5 points)

2 Put the words in order to make questions. Then match the questions (1–5) with the answers (a–e).

1 What / that / is / ? _____

2 your / gloves / Are / these / ? _____

3 laptop / this / Is / your / ? _____

4 What / those / are / ? _____

5 this / What / is / ? _____

____ **a** My climbing boots.

____ **b** That's a map.

____ **c** Yes, it is.

____ **d** No, they aren't.

____ **e** That is my hat.

(10 points)

3 Complete the sentences with the correct positive (+) or negative (−) form of *be*.

1 There _____ a window in the room. (+)

2 There _____ any blinds on the window. (−)

3 There _____ any curtains. (−)

4 _____ there a kitchen? Yes, there _____. (?)(+)

(5 points)

4 Choose the correct option to complete the description.

There is a sofa on [1] *the left / the right*. There is a television [2] *on the left / on the right*. There is a plant [3] *next to / opposite* the sofa. There is an armchair [4] *behind / opposite* the television. There is a cupboard [5] *in front of / behind* the sofa. There is a table [6] *in the middle of / next to* the room. There is a carpet [7] *on / in* the floor. The carpet is [8] *behind / under* the table. There are many pictures [9] *in / on* the room. There is a mirror [10] *behind / between* two pictures.

(10 points)

Vocabulary

5 Write the words.

1
2

3
4
5

6
7
8

1 b _____
2 a k _____
3 a t _____
4 g _____

5 f _____ -a _____ k _____
6 a m _____ p _____
7 a c _____
8 a c _____

(8 points)

6 Write the nationalities.

1 Sally is from Australia. She's <u>Australian.</u>
2 Dai is from Vietnam. He's _____.
3 Erin is from Canada. She's _____.
4 Alberto is from Brazil. He's _____.
5 Adèle is from France. She's _____.
6 Misha is from Russia. He's _____.

(10 points)

7 Write the opposites.

1 big   <u>small</u>
2 fast   _____
3 modern   _____

4 useful   _____
5 good   _____
6 cheap   _____

(5 points)

8 Add the missing letters to the furniture words.

1 cmptr _____
2 rmchr _____
3 tlvsn _____
4 cpbrd _____

5 crpt _____
6 mrrr _____
7 drwrs _____

(7 points)

Functions

9 Complete the parts of the conversation with the words from the box. Then order them 1–5.

help	Large	one	coffee	much

a How _____ is it?
b Can I _____ you?
c _____ or small?
d I'd like a _____, please.
e A small _____, please.

1 __ 2 __ 3 __ 4 __ 5 __

(10 points)

Writing

10 Rewrite the sentences.

1 The desk is modern. <u>It's a modern desk.</u>
2 The house is old. _____
3 The curtains are white. _____
4 The rucksack is big. _____
5 The book is cheap. _____
6 The roller blades are Japanese.

_____

(10 points)

11 Write the adjectives in the correct order to make sentences.

1 It's a German / new / fast car.
   <u>It's a fast, new, German car.</u>
2 It's a brown / small / nice table.

_____

3 A small / English / red / car for sale.

_____

4 There are two modern / lovely / grey / blinds for sale.

_____

5 For sale. A white / new / Japanese laptop.

_____

6 It's a black / old / big house.

_____

(10 points)

Speaking

12 Describe your room. Talk about five different things.

(10 points)

Unit 3 Test

Grammar

1 Put the words in order to write sentences.

1 city / centre / the / They / live / in /.
2 We / work / in / don't / the / hospital /.
3 go / I / to/ car / by / work /.
4 shopping / on / They / like / Saturdays /.
5 the / meet / I / don't / friends / in / afternoon /.
(5 points)

2 Write questions from the prompts.

1 you / have / a / car / ?

_____

2 you / like / pizza / ?

_____

3 your parents / live / in /a / big / house / ?

_____

4 they / finish / work / late / ?

_____

5 you / work / in /an /office / ?

_____

(10 points)

3 Complete the text with the correct negative (−) or affirmative (+) form of the verb in brackets.

My friend's day.

My friend Jessica [1] _____ (study) in a university. She [2] _____ (live) with two students but she [3] _____ (see) them very often. She [4] _____ (get) up at seven o'clock and she [5] _____ (have) a sandwich and a cup of coffee for breakfast. She [6] _____ (go) to the university at eight o'clock. She [7] _____ (finish) late. At home, she [8] _____ (read) books but she [9] _____ (watch) TV. She [10] _____ (go) to bed late.
(10 points)

4 Choose the correct option to complete the sentences.

1 _____ they live in Poland?
  a Do   **b** Does   **c** Are
2 _____ you work in a hospital?
  a Does   **b** Are   **c** Do
3 How old _____ your sister?
  a does   **b** do   **c** is
4 _____ you American?
  a Do   **b** Are   **c** Does
5 _____ your father work in an office?
  a Does   **b** Do   **c** Are
(5 points)

Vocabulary

5 Write the opposites.

1 fast	slow		4 expensive	_____
2 dirty	_____		5 quiet	_____
3 beautiful	_____		6 small	_____

(5 points)

6 Write the places.

1 I'm a nurse. I work in a h_____ .
2 I'm a teacher. I work in a c_____ .
3 I'm a student. I study at u_____ .
4 I'm a manager. I work in an o_____ .
5 I'm a waiter. I work in a r_____ .
(5 points)

7 Write the numbers.

1 629   _____
2 6,000   _____
3 750,000   _____
4 2,000,000 _____
5 50%   _____
(5 points)

8 Complete the table.

1 six	sixth	6 three	_____
2 one	_____	7 _____	second
3 _____	fifth	8 twelve	_____
4 _____	twentieth	9 _____	twenty-fourth
5 _____	eighth		

(8 points)

9 Write the places in the city.

1 You park the car at a car p_____ .
2 You see a play or a musical at a th_____ .
3 You go shopping in a s_____ a_____ .
4 You stay the night at a h_____ .
5 You get tourist information at a v_____ c_____ .
6 You read a book in a l_____ .
7 You meet clients and colleagues in the b_____ d_____ .
(7 points)

Functions

10 Put the words in the correct order to make sentences.

1 the / where / me / museum / is / Excuse / ?
2 about / It's / away / minutes / ten /.
3 park / the / past / Go /.
4 right / the / the / street / Take / on / first /.
5 It's / hospital / the / opposite /.
(10 points)

Writing

11 Rewrite the sentences. Use correct punctuation and capital letters.

1 my names alex. _____

2 i live in london in england. _____

3 i m australian. _____

4 i work on saturdays and sundays. _____

5 my birthday is on the first of december.

_____

(5 points)

12 Write a letter to your friend telling them about your favourite city. Use the questions to help you.

What is the name of the city?

What are good places to visit?

What is a good way to travel around the city?

What is a good month or season to visit? Why?

> *Hi Jack!*
>
> *How are you? I'd like to tell you about my favourite city. It's*
>
> _____
>
> _____
>
> _____
>
> _____
>
> *All the best,*
>
> _____

(15 points)

Speaking

13 Talk about your job.

1 What do you do?

2 When do you get up?

3 When do you start and finish work?

4 What do you do at work?

5 What do you do after work?

(10 points)

Unit 4 Test
Grammar

1 Complete the text with the *-ing* form of these verbs.

listen	watch	do	cycle	read	meet	go	play

I live in a flat with my best friend, Katie. We are very different. I love [1] _____ books, but Katie likes [2] _____ films on DVD. I like [3] _____ the guitar, but Katie doesn't like [4] _____ to my music! I like [5] _____ yoga, but Katie loves [6] _____ on her bike. We both like [7] _____ shopping and [8] _____ our friends!

(8 points)

2 Put the words in order to complete the sentences.

1 often / in / have / I / office / lunch / the /.

_____

2 tired / work / usually / She / after / is /.

_____

3 always / at / starts / Anna / work / o'clock / ten /.

_____

4 work / am / I / late / for / never /.

_____

5 evening / We / watch / sometimes / in / TV / the /.

_____

(10 points)

3 Replace the underlined words in the sentences with an expression of frequency.

1 I go to the gym on Tuesdays, Thursdays and Saturdays. *three times a week.*

2 I call my mother in the evening. _____

3 We usually go on holiday in the summer. _____

4 We have exams in September and in May.

_____

5 The shop is closed on the first day of the month. _____

6 I drink a cup of tea at 8 a.m. and at 9 p.m. _____

(5 points)

4 Look at the table. Write *can* or *can't*.

	Swim well	Speak French	Play tennis	Play the piano	Play the guitar
Mike	✗	✓	✓	✗	✓
Gina	✗	✗	✓	✓	✓

1 Mike _____ speak French.

2 Gina _____ speak French.

3 Mike and Gina _____ swim well.

4 Mike and Gina _____ play tennis.

5 Gina _____ play the piano.

6 Mike _____ play the piano.

7 Mike and Gina _____ play the guitar.

(7 points)

Vocabulary

5 Match the verbs (1–8) to the nouns (a–h).

1 do	___	**a** the gym
2 go	___	**b** yoga
3 listen to	___	**c** friends
4 read	___	**d** cycling
5 play	___	**e** TV
6 go to	___	**f** a magazine
7 meet	___	**g** the radio
8 watch	___	**h** tennis

(8 points)

6 Reorder the letters in each word to find eight sports.

1 eic ohceky	5 ilgaisn
2 sinkig	6 snenti
3 bektsablla	7 ringunn
4 wigmimns	8 ckrecit

(8 points)

7 Add two words to each category.

1 winter sports: skiing, _____, _____

2 countries: Canada, _____, _____

3 ball games: tennis, _____, _____

4 family: sister, _____, _____

5 water sports: surfing, _____, _____

6 everyday objects: a mobile phone, _____,

_____

7 furniture: a bed, _____, _____

8 free-time activities: reading, _____, _____

(8 points)

8 Choose the correct adjective.

1 I don't like golf. It's *boring / exciting*.

2 Watching boxing in real life is very *relaxing / exciting*.

3 A Ferrari is a *fast / slow* car.

4 Listening to classical music is *dangerous / relaxing*.

5 I think that motorbikes are *slow / dangerous*.

6 My car is very old and *slow / fast*.

(6 points)

Functions

9 Write the questions and match them with the responses.

1 animals / Do / like / you / ?

2 can / well / drive / How / you / ?

3 English / well / How / do / speak / you / ?

4 year / you / for / Can / stay / a / ?

5 at / you / teaching / Are / good / ?

___ **a** I speak English a bit. ___ **d** I love them!

___ **b** No, I can't. ___ **e** I can drive very well.

___ **c** I'm very good at it.

(10 points)

Writing

10 Replace the underlined words with the words from the box.

it	here	one	her	them

1 I like pasta. Can we have <u>pasta</u> for lunch? _____

2 I'm at work. You can call me <u>at work</u>. _____

3 I don't like this bag. Can I look at that <u>bag</u>? _____

4 Our friends live next door. We often visit <u>our friends</u>.

_____

5 I often call my grandmother. Sometimes I visit <u>my grandmother</u>. _____

(5 points)

11 Write a short email to your friend. Invite him / her to a café / restaurant / cinema, etc. Use reference words (it, one, here, etc.) to avoid repetition.

Dear ...

_____

_____

_____

_____

_____

Regards

_____

(15 points)

Speaking

12 Talk about what you can and can't do.

What sports can you play? How well?

What languages do you speak? How well?

What other things can you do? How well?

(10 points)

Unit 5 Test

Grammar

1 Complete the table with the words from the box.

lemons	tomato	banana	sandwich
egg	orange	apple	nuts

a	an	–

(8 points)

2 Complete the sentences with *a, an, some,* or *any.*

1 You can't have _____ sandwich.
2 We need _____ milk for breakfast.
3 There are _____ potatoes in that bag.
4 Can I have _____ apple, please?
5 You can put _____ lemon juice on your salad.
6 There isn't _____ cheese.
7 I'd like _____ bottle of water, please.

(7 points)

3 Underline the correct word or phrase in each sentence.

1 There are *a lot of / much* potatoes.
2 There isn't *many / much* milk in the fridge.
3 I don't drink *much / many* tea for breakfast.
4 Chris doesn't eat *a lot of / many* chocolate.
5 Do you eat *a lot of / much* eggs? No, *not many / not much.*
6 Do you drink *much / many* coffee? No, *not much / not many.*

(8 points)

4 Complete the dialogue with one word.

A: I'd like ¹ _____ pasta, please.
B: Sure. How ² _____ packets do you want?
A: One, please. Oh, and ³ _____ sauce, please.
B: How ⁴ _____ bottles do you want?
A: Two bottles, please. Oh, I'd also like ⁵ _____ onion and
   ⁶ _____ rice, please.
B: How ⁷ _____ rice do you want?
A: A packet, please.

(7 points)

Vocabulary

5 Match 1–6 to the food words a–f.

1 a bottle of ____   a bread
2 a piece of ____   b oil
3 a slice of ____   c sweets
4 a glass of ____   d tuna
5 a tin of ____   e chocolate
6 a bag of ____   f water

(6 points)

6 Write the words from the box in the correct column.

lemons	tea	apples	onions	juice
coffee	peppers	milk	potatoes	oranges

Fruit	Vegetables	Drinks

(10 points)

7 Reorder the letters in brackets to complete the sentences.

1 I'd like a tomato and prawn _____, please. (ladas)
2 You can have some _____ after your meal. (cie remca)
3 Cola, tea, and water are _____. (sinkdr)
4 People eat _____ at the beginning of their meal. (setstarr)
5 People eat _____ at the end of their meal. (sterdess)
6 I'd like _____ of the day, please. (puso)
7 The list of food in a restaurant is a _____. (nume)

(7 points)

8 Write *of* in these sentences.

1 There are many types <u>of</u> seeds.
2 I'd like a tin tuna, please.
3 A lot people have lunch at work.
4 I drink a cup of tea in the middle the day.
5 A friend mine is a photographer.
6 I'd like a cup coffee, please.
7 New York is in the United States America.
8 We sell three varieties potato.

(7 points)

Functions

9 Complete the sentences with the words from the box. Then order the sentences 1–5.

have	order	bill	glass	delicious

a Could I have the _____, please?
b I'd also like a _____ of water.
c That was _____.
d I'll _____ a seafood special.
e Are you ready to _____?

1 ___ 2 ___ 3 ___ 4 ___ 5 ___

(10 points)

Writing

10 Punctuate the text.

To make this easy delicious apple cake you need the following apples flour two eggs and sugar First take some apples Cut them into pieces After you mix the flour eggs sugar and apples pour the mixture onto a tray

(10 points)

11 Write instructions to make your favourite cake, sandwich or salad. Check the punctuation.

_____ (the name of the dish)

You need the following:_____

_____

First of all, _____

_____

_____

After you _____

_____

(10 points)

Speaking

12 Talk about your food habits.

1 What do you eat for breakfast?

2 What do you eat for dessert?

3 What is your favourite food?

4 What is your favourite drink?

(10 points)

Unit 6 Test

Grammar

1 Complete the sentences about famous Japanese people. Use *was* or *were*.

1 Ichiyō Higuchi _____ a Japanese writer.

2 She _____ born in 1872.

3 Murasaki Shikibu _____ a Japanese poet.

4 She _____ born in 973.

5 Takahashi Korekiyo and Itō Hirobumi _____ Prime Ministers.

6 Their faces _____ on Japanese money.

(6 points)

2 Choose the best option.

1 Where *was / were* you yesterday?

2 *Was / Were* you born in 1977?

3 Yesterday *was / were* Monday.

4 I *was / were* in Moscow last summer.

5 *Was / Were* Anna and Liz at work yesterday?

6 They *wasn't / weren't* explorers.

7 What *was / were* they famous for?

(7 points)

3 Write the past simple form of the verbs.

1 have	_____		5 discover	_____
2 work	_____		6 phone	_____
3 come	_____		7 study	_____
4 make	_____			

(7 points)

4 Complete the text with the past simple form of these verbs.

live	die	be (x3)	meet
visit	go	become	travel

Sir Francis Drake [1] _____ born in about 1540. There [2] _____ 12 children in the family. They [3] _____ in England. At the age of 12, Francis Drake [4] _____ a sailor and [5] _____ abroad. As an explorer, Drake [6] _____ Cape Horn, Magado, Cape Blanko, and many other places. He [7] _____ his wife, Mary Newman, in 1569. Sir Francis Drake [8] _____ the first Englishman who [9] _____ round the world. He [10] _____ in 1596.

(10 points)

Vocabulary

5 Choose the correct option.

1 *In / on* his mid-twenties, he became a photographer.

2 I visited Mexico *in / on* 1930.

3 The head of the Emperor was *in / on* the money.

4 My birthday is *in / on* the 14th of May.

5 *In / On* the thirteenth century, he travelled to China.

6 Nicola was born *in / on* Italy.

(6 points)

6 Complete the sentences with one word.

Me, 29   Terry, 2   Tim, 33   Susan, 59   Alex, 62

This is my family album. In this photo, I am 29 [1] _____ old. My husband Tim is [2] _____, too: he is in his early [3] _____. Our son Terry is just two years [4] _____! Tim's mother Susan is in her late [5] _____, and her husband Alex is in his [6] _____ sixties.

Maggie, 35   Dan, 41   Peter, 10   Alice, 4

This is my sister's family album. Peter is ten [7] _____ old in this picture. Alice, his sister, is only four years [8] _____. Maggie is in her [9] _____-thirties, and Dan is in his early [10] _____ here.

(10 points)

7 Choose the correct alternative.

1 It was a very *tired / tiring* film. It lasted for three hours.

2 Jerry is *interested / interesting* in ancient coins.

3 He left the cinema because the film was *bored / boring*.

4 She was very *tired / tiring* after a long day at work.

5 He was so *excited / exciting* to know he passed the test.

6 I was *bored / boring* with watching TV.

7 The book was so *interested / interesting* that he read it all night.

8 Our holiday in Mexico was very *excited / exciting*!

(8 points)

8 Reorder the letters in brackets to complete the sentences.

1 The Queen's face was on the Canadian twenty-dollar _____. (tone)

2 Jack found an old silver _____. (noci)

3 I keep all my money in the _____. (kanb)

4 When I travel to the USA, I _____ pounds to dollars. (caghen)

5 In this shop you can only pay by _____. (sach)

6 You can pay with a _____. (retcid darc)

(6 points)

Functions

9 Complete the parts of the conversation with the words from the box. Then order them (1–5).

certainly	much	us	welcome	charity

____ **a** Yes, _____. Here you are.

____ **b** Thanks very _____.

____ **c** Could you give _____ something?

____ **d** You're _____.

____ **e** Hi! I'm collecting for a _____.

(10 points)

Writing

10 Complete the expressions with the words from the box.

forward	regards	Yours	next	soon

1 See you _____!

2 See you again _____ year.

3 Best _____,

4 I look _____ to hearing from you.

5 _____ sincerely,

(5 points)

11 You studied English for a month in London. It was a fantastic experience. Write a 'thank you' email to the school director.

_____

_____

_____

_____

_____

_____

_____

(15 points)

Speaking

12 Talk about a famous person from the past.

Who was he or she?

Why was he or she famous or important?

(10 points)

Unit 7 test

Grammar

1 Write the negative form of the underlined verbs.

1 Karen <u>went</u> on holiday last year. _didn't go_

2 He <u>flew</u> to Africa last month. _____

3 Dave <u>studied</u> German at school. _____

4 I <u>worked</u> from 9 to 5 yesterday. _____

5 Sam <u>left</u> the party early. _____

6 Martin <u>had</u> a map in his bag. _____

(5 points)

2 Write the questions and match them to the responses.

1 open / did / window / you / Why / the / ? ____

2 come / time / What / you / did / home / ? ____

3 the / Did / go / you / at / shopping / weekend / ? ____

4 they / yesterday / Were / home / at / ? ____

5 she / you / phone / week / Did / last / ? ____

   a No, they weren't.   **d** At 9.

   b Yes, she did.   **e** Because it was hot.

   c No, I didn't.

(10 points)

3 Complete the sentences. Use the comparative form of the adjectives in the box.

cold	hot	expensive	dangerous	cheap

1 Bears are _____ than giraffes.

2 Antarctica is _____ than Europe.

3 A new Ferrari is _____ than an old Ford.

4 The weather in Thailand is _____ than in Norway.

5 A magazine is _____ than a book.

(5 points)

4 Complete the sentences. Use the superlative form of the adjectives in the box.

dangerous	high	deep	expensive	cold

1 Everest is the _____ mountain in the world.

2 Neptune is the _____ planet of the solar system.

3 Rolex makes the _____ watches in the world.

4 Lake Baikal is the _____ lake in the world.

5 The Black Mamba is the _____ snake in Africa.

(5 points)

5 Complete the sentences with one word.

1 A plane is faster _____ a car.

2 The tickets _____ cheaper in winter than in summer.

3 This building is _____ highest in the town.

4 Antarctica is the coldest place _____ the world.

5 This was the _____ dangerous trip in my life.

(5 points)

Vocabulary

6 Choose the correct option.

1 This test is very ____. You can do it without any help.

   a interesting   **b** easy   **c** dangerous

2 Hurry up! Don't be so ____.

   a long   **b** short   **c** slow

3 I can't do this exercise. It's very _____.

   a dangerous   **b** difficult   **c** different

4 This car is very ____. It can go 300 km p/h.

   a fast   **b** slow   **c** safe

5 This bank is very ____. I put all my money here.

   a safe   **b** fast   **c** expensive

6 This animal is ____. Don't go near it.

   a expensive   **b** dangerous   **c** slow

7 Our trip was very ____. We only walked for an hour.

   a big   **b** safe   **c** short

(7 points)

7 Complete the extract from a blog with these words.

tiring	journey	travel	terrible
trip	interesting	delicious	

[1] _____ is great because you learn a lot of new things. Last year I went on a long [2] _____ into the forests of Russia. All the food was [3] _____. I loved it. I lived with a nice family. One day, we went on a short one-day [4] _____ to the city and we visited many [5] _____ places.

Of course, there were days when the weather was [6] _____: it rained a lot. The journey home was very long: it was really [7] _____!

(7 points)

8 Complete the text. Use one word in each space.

uploads	homepage	online	blogger
blogs	comments	posts	website

Katie is a [1] _____ on an archaeologists' [2] _____. She travels to different cities. Every day she [3] _____ about her work. She writes [4] _____ from different countries. She is often [5] _____ at night! She [6] _____ photographs of fantastic places. Readers leave Katie lots of [7] _____ on her articles. Her [8] _____ is http://katierniss.blogspot.com

(16 points)

Functions

9 Complete the questions with the words from the box. Then match the questions and the responses.

comfortable	trip	food	like	What

1 How was your _____? _____

2 Did you try the local _____? _____

3 What was the hotel _____? _____

4 Was it _____? _____

5 _____ was the weather like? _____

    a Terrible! There wasn't a TV in the room.

    b Very interesting.

    c It rained all day.

    d Yes, it was. I had a good night's sleep.

    e Yes, I did. It was delicious.

(10 points)

Writing

10 Join the sentences. Use *so* or *because*.

1 I was at a party last night. I came back late.

_____

2 We travelled to Egypt. We wanted to see the pyramids.

_____

3 We don't like travelling by plane. We booked train tickets. _____

4 I went shopping. I wanted to buy something for lunch.

_____

5 They have a big family. They bought a big car.

_____

(5 points)

11 Write a short travel blog about a journey or a place you visited.

    Where did you go?

    When did you go?

    What did you see?

    Did you like it? Why?

_____

_____

_____

_____

_____

(15 points)

Speaking

12 Talk about your last holiday.

    Where did you go?

    How did you travel there?

    How long did the journey take?

    Did you have any problems?

    Did you have a good time?

(10 points)

Unit 8 Test

Grammar

1 Rewrite the sentences. Use contractions.

1 I have not got a map. *I haven't got a map.*

2 We have not got a car. _____

3 You have got a new mobile. _____

4 Emily has not got a camera. _____

5 He has got two children. _____

6 Jason has not got blue eyes. _____

(5 points)

2 Choose *have got* or *has got* to complete the sentences.

1 I *have got / has got* green eyes.

2 We *have got / has got* many friends.

3 It *have got / has got* a camera.

4 Jenny *have got / has got* two brothers.

5 Martin *have got / has got* a moustache.

(5 points)

3 Rewrite the sentences with a negative form. Use contracted forms.

1 I have got a sister. *I haven't got a sister.*

2 The boy has got brown eyes.

3 They have got a big house.

4 Robert has got dark hair.

5 Your mobile has got a camera.

6 She has got a nice flat.

(5 points)

4 Complete the dialogue. Use the present continuous form of the verbs.

Diana: Hi Mum!

Mum: Hi! What [1] _____ (you / do)?

Diana: We [2] _____ (go) shopping. And you?

Mum: I [3] _____ (cook) lunch. Your father [4] _____ (watch) TV. Is Kevin with you?

Diana: No, he [5] _____ (study) for his test. Gary's here, he [6] _____ (not work) today. Oh, he [7] _____ (say) hello to you!

Mum: Say hello to him, too. Speak to you later!

(7 points)

5 Complete the email. Use the present simple or present continuous form of the verb in brackets.

Hi Jenny, I [1] _____ (write) to you from the hotel room. At the moment, I [2] _____ (travel) in Spain. I usually [3] _____ (travel) in the summer with my boyfriend, but now he [4] _____ (stay) with his parents in England. I [5] _____ (think) Barcelona is a very beautiful city! I usually [6] _____ (not take) many photos, but now I [7] _____ (take) photos of everything. I [8] _____ (send) some photos. Can you see them?

(8 points)

Vocabulary

6 Complete the table with the words from the box.

long	fair	ugly	tall	handsome
green	curly	blonde	straight	blue

General appearance	Height	Eyes	Hair
beautiful	short	brown	dark

(10 points)

7 Reorder the letters to make the clothes words.

1 ite _____
2 kirst _____
3 blet _____
4 resds _____
5 sohes _____
6 tah _____
7 sirth _____
8 rotersus _____
9 ksosc _____
10 pjemur _____

(10 points)

8 Write the words for the parts of the body.

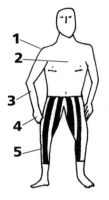 

1 _____
2 _____
3 _____
4 _____
5 _____
6 _____
7 _____
8 _____
9 _____
10 _____

(10 points)

Functions

9 Choose the correct option.

1 The photos often *show / look* people in their everyday life.
2 This girl *looks / shows* a bit sad.
3 Look at the other woman *at / in* the back.
4 I don't normally look at people very *nearly / closely*.
5 *In / At* front of him, the woman is reading a book.
6 *On / At* the right, the man and woman are talking.
7 This photo is *on / at* the Los Angeles subway.
8 He is *wearing / having* a tie.
9 The woman is standing in front *from / of* the picture.
10 The man is *looking / watching* her.

(10 points)

Writing

10 Write the text messages using full sentences.

1 How R U?
2 Don't B L8.
3 C U soon.
4 OK. @ 6?
5 Plz w8 4 me.

(5 points)

11 Write a text message to your friend using textspeak. Invite him / her somewhere. Write about the day, the time and the place to meet.

_____
_____
_____
_____
_____

(15 points)

Speaking

12 Talk about your appearance and what clothes you are wearing today.

(10 points)

Unit 9 Test

Grammar

1 Make sentences with *going to*.

1 We _____ (watch) a new film tonight.

2 I _____ (not / listen) to this album.

3 _____ (you / have) dinner now?

4 What time _____ (we / come) to the party?

5 I _____ (not / play) tennis today.

6 _____ (you / drive) to the beach?

7 Where _____ (they / meet) us after the film?

8 Suzie _____ (buy) a new car next year.

9 When _____ (he / call) me?

(9 points)

2 Complete sentences 1–5 with a–e.

1 I'm going to the shop   **a** to watch a new film.

2 We're going to the cinema   **b** to get some money.

3 Dave is going to the bank   **c** to buy some milk.

4 Jon is going to call Amy   **d** to have a coffee.

5 We're going to the café   **e** to talk to her.

(5 points)

3 Complete the email. Use *going to*, the present continuous or the infinitive of the verb in brackets.

Hi Amy, what ¹ _____ you _____ (do) at the weekend? On Saturday I ² _____ (go) to the Language Club ³ _____ (practise) my English a bit. After classes, Karen and I ⁴ _____ (meet) at the café ⁵ _____ (have) a coffee and ⁶ _____ (talk). ⁷ _____ you _____ (come), too?
On Sunday I ⁸ _____ (go) to the theatre ⁹ _____ (see) a play by Shakespeare. I think it ¹⁰ _____ (be) interesting!

(10 points)

4 Circle the correct form.

1 I *go* / *'m going* to the cinema tonight.

2 I *go* / *'m going* to the cinema every weekend.

3 We *meet* / *'re meeting* our friends once a week.

4 We *meet* / *'re meeting* our friends tomorrow.

5 Tim often *has* / *is having* meetings at work.

6 Tim *has* / *is having* a meeting at four o'clock today.

(6 points)

Vocabulary

5 Write the job words made from these words.

1 write   _____

2 act   _____

3 paint   _____

4 direct   _____

5 music   _____

6 art   _____

(6 points)

6 Write the types of films.

1 _____   4 _____

2 _____   5 _____

3 _____   6 _____

(6 points)

7 Write the places where you see or do these things.

1 film   cinema

2 painting   a_____ g_____

3 music   c_____ h_____

4 story   b_____

5 dinner   r_____

6 play   t_____

(5 points)

8 Circle the word which is different in each group.

1	tree	kangaroo	leaf	grass
2	flower	DVD	mountain	rock
3	rock	mountain	grass	butterfly
4	cow	bird	sheep	horse
5	bird	kangaroo	tree	butterfly
6	painting	novel	music	actor
7	musical	novel	cinema	play

(7 points)

9 Write the verb.

1 _____ at paintings   4 _____ a play

2 _____ to live music   5 _____ a novel

3 _____ TV   6 _____ a film

(6 points)

Functions

10 Write the questions and match them with the responses.

1 you / Would / come / to / like / ?   ____

2 you / free / Are / ?   ____

3 want / go / you / Do / to / ?   ____

4 start / What / does / time / it / ?   ____

5 seven / at / meet / Let's /.   ____

    a At seven.

    b OK. See you at seven.

    c Yes, I do.

    d I'm sorry, but I'm working late tonight.

    e I'd love to.

(10 points)

Writing

11 Choose the correct option.

1 They felt very *interesting / bored* in the lesson.

2 This tomato soup tastes *delicious / interested*.

3 You look *delicious / beautiful* in this dress!

4 I felt *angry / scared* after watching the horror film.

5 This new perfume smells *nice / soft*.

(5 points)

12 Look at the advertisement for chocolate biscuits. Write a review. Use at least three phrases in the box.

SNAPPIES chocolate biscuits

Mmm, they're delicious!

Only 2 euros!

They look … Unfortunately	They taste … so	in general

_____

_____

_____

_____

(15 points)

Speaking

13 Talk about your plans for the weekend.

(10 points)

Unit 10 test

Grammar

1 Write the past participle of the verbs.

1 be	been	6 go	_____
2 buy	_____	7 get	_____
3 come	_____	8 eat	_____
4 pay	_____	9 drink	_____
5 have	_____		

(8 points)

2 Make sentences. Use the present perfect of the verbs.

1 you / ever / travel to Asia? _____

2 I / never / be / to Mongolia. _____

3 I / watch / this film twice. _____

4 he / ever / write / to you? _____

5 We / never / meet / before. _____

6 I / never / have / Japanese food. _____

7 you / ever/ see / this festival? _____

(7 points)

3 Choose the correct alternative.

1 *Have / Did* you ever *be / been* to Canada?

2 I *been / was* in Canada last year.

3 He *hasn't visited / didn't visit* this city in 2001.

4 Has *your brother / your brother's* ever read this book?

5 I *seed / saw* this play last year.

6 I *hasn't / haven't had* breakfast today.

7 I saw this musical two years *last / ago*.

8 I *haven't / have* never *win / won* a lottery.

(8 points)

4 Choose the correct alternative.

A: [1] *Have you ever / Did you ever* run a race?

B: Yes, I [2] *have / ran*. Once, when I [3] *have been / was* at university.

A: [4] *Have you ever / Did you ever* been to China?

B: Yes, I [5] *have travelled / travelled* to China in 2009.

A: [6] *Have you / Did you* go on holiday last year?

B: No, I [7] *haven't / didn't*.

(7 points)

Vocabulary

5 Complete the sentences with the words in the box.

postcard	search engine	email	text message
online video	letter	sat nav (GPS)	

1 On holiday, we buy a _____ to send to friends.

2 In a car, we use _____ to find the road home.

3 We use a _____ to find interesting websites.

4 We write a formal _____ when we apply for a job.

5 We watch an _____ on our computer.

6 We send a _____ on our mobile phone.

7 We write and send an _____ on our computer.

(7 points)

6 Tick (✓) the words that go with the verb.

1 go	**a** home ✓	**b** shopping ✓	**c** TV
2 listen to	**a** a podcast	**b** the radio	**c** an ebook
3 read	**a** a CD	**b** an ebook	**c** a novel
4 download	**a** a podcast	**b** a photo	**c** a library
5 learn	**a** a language	**b** a map	**c** a word
6 write	**a** an email	**b** a GPS	**c** a text message
7 watch	**a** a DVD	**b** a CD	**c** an online video
8 use	**a** a map	**b** GPS	**c** a letter

(7 points)

7 Match the words in the box to the pictures.

a knife	an MP3 player	a wheel	the Internet
fire	a vacuum cleaner	sticky tape	electricity

(8 points)

8 Reorder the letters in brackets to complete the sentences.

1 I _____ five English words a day. (morismee)

2 I work in a school. I _____ children. (techa)

3 I watch TV to _____ after work. (exlar)

4 Try to _____ speaking English with friends. (prisecat)

5 I'm at university. I _____ biology. (sudty)

6 I don't _____ what this word means. (meberrem)

7 I often _____ people's names. (fortge)

8 I don't _____. Please speak slowly! (derstandun)

(8 points)

Functions

9 Write the sentences and match them with the responses.

1 in / three / the / Is / afternoon / that / ?

2 that / James hotel / the / Is / ?

3 number / The / 794 66 54 / is / .

4 anything / there / Is / else / ?

5 colleagues / you / our / called / Have / ?
___ **a** So that's 794 66 54?
___ **b** Yes, I have.
___ **c** No, it's four in the afternoon.
___ **d** No, the John's hotel.
___ **e** Yes, one thing.

(10 points)

Writing

10 Rewrite the sentences. Use imperatives.

1 Can you download the music?
Download the music.
_____

2 Can you book two tickets online?
_____

3 I'd like you to meet me at the station.
_____

4 Can you call me back tomorrow?
_____

5 Would you email the date of the trip?
_____

6 Can you send me a message?
_____

(5 points)

11 Write a message for a hotel voicemail. Include your name, your number, your email. Ask a colleague at the hotel to email you the meeting details.

_____
_____
_____
_____
_____

(15 points)

Speaking

12 Talk about your experiences. Give the information to answer the questions.

Have you ever travelled abroad? Where did you go?

Have you ever seen a horror film? What film did you see?

Have you ever done an extreme sport? Which sport did you do?

(10 points)

Unit 11 test

Grammar

1 Complete the sentences with *should / shouldn't*.

1 You _____ go there in January, it's cold!

2 It's very, late. You _____ go out.

3 A: 'I'm so tired.' B: 'You _____ relax.'

4 It's a beautiful city. You _____ take a tour.

5 It's a long way to the city centre. You _____ take a bus.

6 A: 'I work 10 hours a day.' B: 'You _____ work so hard.'

7 You _____ look a word up if you don't know it.

8 There is snow on the road. You _____ drive fast.

(8 points)

2 Read the information for tourists in South Africa. Choose the correct alternative.

To travel to South Africa on holiday you [1] *have to / can to* get a holiday visa. And you [2] *don't have to / can't* enter the country more than once on this visa. You [3] *have to / don't have to* get a new visa if you want to travel again.

There are 11 official languages in South Africa, but you [4] *have to / don't have to* speak all of them, of course! The only currency in the country is the rand, so you [5] *can / can't* use any foreign money. You [6] *have to / don't have to* change your currency to South African Rands.

(6 points)

3 Complete the sentences with *somebody, something, anything, anywhere, nobody,* or *nothing*.

1 I wanted some information about visas but I couldn't find _____.

2 _____ smells good in the kitchen. What is it?

3 John had to do all the work. _____ helped him.

4 There is _____ at the door. Who is it?

5 I am looking for my map but can't find it _____.

6 I didn't know about it! _____ told me!

7 I'm bored – there's _____ interesting on TV.

8 This is the best café. Don't go _____ else.

(16 points)

Vocabulary

4 Complete the phrases. Use the verbs from the box.

buy	use	meet	go	book	learn	take	find

1 _____ local people

2 _____ a hotel room

3 _____ a tour guide

4 _____ local food

5 _____ sightseeing

6 _____ an umbrella

7 _____ some phrases

8 _____ a nice hotel

(8 points)

5 Choose the correct option to complete the sentences.

1 I'm going to Spain and back, so I booked a ___ ticket.
  a return   b back   c double

2 Don't forget to ___ souvenirs when you go on holiday.
  a take   b buy   c book

3 To go on a plane, you have to ___ bags over 50kg.
  a reserve   b book   c check in

4 If you don't want to travel by bus you can ___ a car.
  a rent   b have   c own

5 I'm going to London, and I'm not planning to come back. I have to buy a ___ ticket.
  a one   b double   c single

6 Before we go on holiday, we have to ___ a hotel.
  a find   b use   c have

7 We always ___ buses because cars are expensive.
  a use   b rent   c go

(7 points)

6 Complete the sentences with the words from the box.

multicultural	climate	licence	visa
left-hand side	currency	time zones	illegal

1 The _____ in the USA is extreme, with snow in winter and hot summers.

2 The euro is the national _____ in Ireland.

3 To work in the US you need a work _____.

4 Taking animals out of the country is _____ in Egypt.

5 Drive on the _____ of the road in England.

6 There are nine _____ in Russia. When it's 5 p.m. in the west, it's 2 a.m. in the east of the country.

7 Dubai is a _____ city. A lot of people from all over the world work and study there.

8 You have to carry your driving _____ when you drive everywhere in the world.

(8 points)

7 Reorder the letters in brackets to complete the sentences.

1 The people are very _____ and nice. (delyfrin)

2 Buy the ticket at the _____. (titaons)

3 _____ and climate is different in different parts of Canada. (mteturepera)

4 Don't sit in the sun with no _____ on. (nus camre)

5 If you get lost, ask for _____. (resodictin)

6 79% of the _____ speak English as a first language. (lapotionpu)

7 _____ can stay for six months. (vistosir)

(7 points)

Functions

8 Put the words in the correct order to make sentences.

1 holiday / going / How / on / about / ?
2 suggestion / I / a / Can / make / ?
3 tour / don't / go / Why / on / a / you / ?
4 is / The / is / that / cold / disadvantage / it / very / .
5 a / really / That / good / 's / idea / .

(10 points)

Writing

9 Write the questions and match them with the responses.

1 advance / you / the / book / Did / tickets / in / ?
_____

2 visit / you / any / places / interesting / Did / ?
_____

3 journey / was / How / your / ?
_____

4 you / this / Would / anybody / hotel / to / recommend / ? _____

5 cities / other / visit / What / you / did / ?
_____

  a It was great!
  b Yes, a lot.
  c Of course I would.
  d Rome, Venice and Milan.
  e Yes, two weeks before I went.
  1 ___ 2 ___ 3 ___ 4 ___ 5 ___

(10 points)

10 Write a feedback form for the museum visitors. Ask at least five questions.

> Thank you for your visit to our museum. We hope you enjoyed it! Please spend a few minutes and complete this form. Your feedback and suggestions are very important to us.
> 1
> 2
> 3
> 4
> 5

(10 points)

Speaking

11 Give a piece of advice for a tourist coming to your city. Talk about these topics.

• weather
• local food
• transport
• language
• interesting places

(10 points)

Unit 12 test
Grammar

1 Complete the sentences with *will* and these verbs.

use	live	speak	study	grow
wear	be	die	travel	buy

In the future, cities [1] _____ bigger. More people [2] _____ in the country. More people [3] _____ food for their families. Children [4] _____. at home. Everybody [5] _____ the same international language. At the weekends people [6] _____ to the Moon and other planets. Men and women [7] _____ similar clothes. They [8] _____ everything from online shops. Everybody [9] _____ mobile phones, even elderly people. Often people [10] _____ at the age of 120 years old.

(10 points)

2 Correct the mistakes and rewrite the sentences.

1 People ~~do~~ buy more cars next year. <u>People will buy more cars next year.</u>
2 In the future, people live longer. _____
3 I don't think Jerry won't call you. _____
4 It will cold tomorrow. _____
5 I will be have a big house in the future.
_____
6 He willn't come to work tomorrow.
_____

(10 points)

3 Choose *the* or no article (–).

1 *The* / – Asia is the world's largest continent.
2 *The* / – Gobi Desert is one of the world's great deserts.
3 *The* / – Lake Baikal is 25 million years old.
4 To travel to *the* / – UK, some visitors have to get a visa.
5 I took a language course in *the* / – Spain last year.
6 We flew over *the* / – Atlantic Ocean to the USA.
7 *The* / – Alps is one of the great mountain ranges in Europe.
8 *The* / – River Nile is the longest in the world.
9 *The* / – Mount Everest is situated in southern Asia.
10 *The* / – Bahamas is a country with lots of islands.

(10 points)

Vocabulary

4 Write the measurements for the abbreviations. Match them with the meaning (a–f).

1 %   p_____ c_____
2 °C   d_____ Celsius
3 m^2 s_____ m_____
4 l   l_____
5 km   k_____
6 kg   k_____

   a It measures an amount out of 100.
   b It measures a quantity of water (or liquid).
   c It measures distance.
   d It measures area.
   e It measures temperature.
   f It measures weight.

   1 ___ 2 ___ 3 ___ 4 ___ 5 ___ 6 ___

(12 points)

5 Match the words in the box to the pictures.

region	lake	continent	desert	river
island	sea	forest	mountain	ocean

(10 points)

6 Reorder the letters in brackets to complete the sentences.

1 Christopher Columbus was a famous _____. (reploxer)

2 Scientists study the air and _____ of the planets. (cork)

3 Pluto is the farthest _____ from the Sun. (taplen)

4 I _____ to different countries every year. (terlav)

5 Sirius is the brightest _____ in the sky. (satr)

6 An _____ is a scientist who studies planets. (aromonster)

7 The _____ of Mars is a very dry and has no water. (fascure)

8 Some planets go round a star. For example, the Earth _____ the Sun. (torbis)

(8 points)

Functions

7 Put the words in correct order to complete the key sentences in the presentation.

1 1990 / company / First / we / of / all, / started / our / in / .

2 more / people / than / company / for / our / 100 / Nowadays, / work / .

3 a / we / new / in / opened / Peru / Finally, / office / .

4 important / In / I / really / is / think / conclusion, / your / work / .

5 much / listening / Thank / you / for / very / .

(10 points)

Writing

8 Rewrite the sentences for a poster, giving only the important information. Leave out *one to three* words.

1 We will be dancing and singing. *Dancing and singing.*

2 The party is on June 10th.

3 Everyone is welcome.

4 There will be dance music.

5 The entrance is free.

6 You can find more information at www.partytime.com

(5 points)

9 Prepare and design a poster for a special event, e.g. your birthday party or a business presentation. Use short sentences.

(15 points)

Speaking

10 Talk about how your life will change in 15 years.

(10 points)

Photocopiable tests: answer key

Unit 1 Test

Grammar

1

1 'm   2 're   3 'm   4 're   5 'm

2

1 'm   2 's   3 're   4 're   5 's

3

1 Are   4 'm
2 Is   5 is
3 aren't

4

1 It's my mother's bag.
2 Erick's from Canada.
3 My friend's from Mexico.
4 That's Erin's house.
5 Tim's my sister's husband.

5

1 My   3 your   5 His
2 Their   4 We

Vocabulary

6

1 f   2 e   3 g   4 d   5 c   6 a   7 b

7

1 mother   3 sister   5 brother
2 father   4 niece   6 husband

8

1 cousin   3 aunt   5 grandparents
2 nephew   4 uncle

9

1 Y   2 M   3 A   4 D   5 U

10

1 live   4 work   7 travel
2 speak   5 use
3 have   6 talk

Functions

11

1 e introduce   3 c too   5 b Bye!
2 a meet   4 d later

Writing

12

2 I'm 35 and my husband is 36.
3 I'm from Argentina but I work in Spain.
4 We are students and we are at school.
5 I'm Chinese and my husband is Chinese, too.
6 My family is in the USA but I live in England.

Unit 2 Test

Grammar

1

1 buses   3 shelves   5 countries
2 babies   4 people

2

1 What is that? b
2 Are these your gloves? d
3 Is this your laptop? c
4 What are those? a
5 What is this? e

3

1 is   3 aren't
2 aren't   4 Is, is

4

1 the left   6 in the middle of
2 on the right   7 on
3 next to   8 under
4 opposite   9 in
5 behind   10 between

Vocabulary

5

1 boots   4 gloves   7 camera
2 knife   5 first-aid kit 8 compass
3 torch   6 mobile phone

6

1 Vietnamese   3 Brazilian   5 Russian
2 Canadian   4 French

7

2 slow   4 useless   6 expensive
3 old   5 bad

8

1 computer   4 cupboard   7 drawers
2 armchair   5 carpet
3 television   6 mirror

Functions

9

a much   c Large   e one
b help   d coffee

1 b   2 d   3 c   4 e   5 a

Writing

10

1 It's an old house.
2 They're white curtains.
3 It's a big rucksack.
4 It's a cheap book.
5 They're Japanese roller blades.

11

1 It's a nice, small, brown table.
2 A small, red, English car for sale.
3 There are two lovely, modern grey blinds for sale.
4 For sale. A new, white Japanese laptop.
5 It's a big, old black house.

Unit 3 Test

Grammar

1
1 They live in the city centre.
2 We don't work in the hospital.
3 I go to work by car.
4 They like shopping on Saturdays.
5 I don't meet friends in the afternoon.

2
1 Do you have a car?
2 Do you like pizza?
3 Do your parents live in a big house?
4 Do they finish work late?
5 Do you work in an office ?

3
1 studies	5 has	9 doesn't watch
2 lives	6 goes	10 goes
3 doesn't see	7 finishes	
4 gets	8 reads	

4
1 a   2 c   3 c   4 b   5 a

Vocabulary

5
2 clean	4 cheap / free	6 big
3 ugly	5 noisy	

6
1 hospital	3 university	5 restaurant
2 classroom	4 office	

7
1 six hundred and twenty-nine
2 six thousand
3 seven hundred and fifty thousand
4 two million
5 fifty per cent

8
2 first	5 eight	8 twelfth
3 five	6 third	9 twenty-four
4 twenty	7 two	

9
1 park	4 hotel	7 business district
2 theatre	5 visitor centre	
3 shopping area	6 library	

Functions

10
1 Excuse me, where is the museum?
2 It's about ten minutes away.
3 Go past the park.
4 Take the first street on the right.
5 It's opposite the hospital.

Writing

11
1 My name's Alex.
2 I live in London, in England.
3 I'm Australian.
4 I work on Saturdays and Sundays.
5 My birthday is on the first of December.

Unit 4 Test

Grammar

1
1 reading	4 listening	7 going
2 watching	5 doing	8 meeting
3 playing	6 cycling	

2
1 I often have lunch in the office.
2 She is usually tired after work.
3 Anna always starts work at ten o'clock.
4 I am never late for work.
5 We sometimes watch TV in the evening.

3
2 every day / once a day	4 twice a year	6 twice a day
3 once a year	5 once a month	

4
1 Mike can speak French.
2 Gina can't speak French.
3 Mike and Gina can't swim well.
4 Mike and Gina can play tennis.
5 Gina can play the piano.
6 Mike can't play the piano.
7 Mike and Gina can play the guitar.

Vocabulary

5
1 b   2 d   3 g   4 f   5 h   6 a   7 c   8 e

6
1 ice hockey	4 swimming	7 running
2 skiing	5 sailing	8 cricket
3 basketball	6 tennis	

7
Students' own answers

8
1 boring	3 fast	5 dangerous
2 exciting	4 relaxing	6 slow

Functions

9
1 Do you like animals? d
2 How well can you drive? e
3 How well do you speak English? a
4 Can you stay for a year? b
5 Are you good at teaching? c

Writing

10
1 it	3 one	5 her
2 here	4 them	

Unit 5 Test

Grammar

1

a   banana, tomato, sandwich
an   apple, orange, egg
–   lemons, nuts

2

1 a	4 an	7 a
2 some	5 some	
3 some	6 any	

3

1 a lot of	4 a lot of
2 much	5 a lot of, not many
3 much	6 much, not much

4

1 some	4 many	7 much
2 many	5 an	
3 some	6 some	

Vocabulary

5

1 b   2 e   3 a   4 f   5 d   6 c

6

Fruit: lemons, apples, oranges
Vegetables: onions, peppers, potatoes
Drinks: tea, juice, coffee, milk

7

1 salad	4 starters	7 menu
2 ice cream	5 desserts	
3 drinks	6 soup	

8

1 There are many types *of* seeds.
2 I'd like a tin *of* tuna, please.
3 A lot *of* people have lunch at work.
4 I drink a cup of tea in the middle *of* the day.
5 A friend *of* mine is a photographer.
6 I'd like a cup *of* coffee, please.
7 New York is in the United States *of* America.
8 We sell three varieties *of* potato.

Functions

9

a bill
b glass
c delicious
d have
e order

1 e   2 d   3 b   4 c   5 a

Writing

10

To make this easy, delicious apple cake, you need the following: apples, flour, two eggs and sugar. First, take some apples. Cut them into pieces. After you mix the flour, eggs, sugar and apples, pour the mixture onto a tray.

Unit 6 Test

Grammar

1

1 was	3 was	5 were
2 was	4 was	6 were

2

1 were	4 was	7 were
2 Were	5 Were	
3 was	6 weren't	

3

1 had	4 made	7 studied
2 worked	5 discovered	
3 came	6 phoned	

4

1 was	5 went	9 travelled
2 were	6 visited	10 died
3 lived	7 met	
4 became	8 was	

Vocabulary

5

1 In	3 on	5 In
2 in	4 on	6 in

6

1 years	5 fifties	9 mid
2 young	6 early	10 forties
3 thirties	7 years	
4 old	8 old	

7

1 tiring	4 tired	7 interesting
2 interested	5 excited	8 exciting
3 boring	6 bored	

8

1 note	3 bank	5 cash
2 coin	4 change	6 credit card

Functions

9

a certainly	c us	e charity
b much	d welcome	

1 e   2 c   3 a   4 b   5 d

Writing

10

1 soon	3 regards	5 Yours
2 next	4 forward	

Unit 7 test

Grammar

1

2 didn't fly
3 didn't study
4 didn't work
5 didn't leave
6 didn't have

2

1 Why did you open the window? e
2 What time did you come home? d
3 Did you go shopping at the weekend? c
4 Were they at home yesterday? a
5 Did she phone you last week? b

3

1 more dangerous
2 colder
3 more expensive
4 hotter
5 cheaper

4

1 highest
2 coldest
3 most expensive
4 deepest
5 most dangerous

5

1 than
2 are
3 the
4 in
5 most

Vocabulary

6

1 b
2 c
3 b
4 a
5 a
6 b
7 c

7

1 Travel
2 journey
3 delicious
4 trip
5 interesting
6 terrible
7 tiring

8

1 blogger
2 website
3 blogs
4 posts
5 online
6 uploads
7 comments
8 homepage

Functions

9

1 trip b
2 food e
3 like a
4 comfortable d
5 What c

Writing

10

1 I was at a party last night <u>so</u> I came back late.
2 We travelled to Egypt <u>because</u> we wanted to see the pyramids.
3 We don't like travelling by plane <u>so</u> we booked train tickets.
4 I went shopping <u>because</u> I wanted to buy something for lunch.
5 They have a big family <u>so</u> they bought a big car.

Unit 8 Test

Grammar

1

2 We haven't got a car.
3 You've got a new mobile.
4 Emily hasn't got a camera.
5 He's got two children.
6 Jason hasn't got blue eyes.

2

1 have got
2 have got
3 has got
4 has got
5 has got

3

2 The boy hasn't got brown eyes.
3 They haven't got a big house.
4 Robert hasn't got dark hair.
5 Your mobile hasn't got a camera.
6 She hasn't got a nice flat.

4

1 are you doing
2 we're going
3 'm cooking
4 's watching
5 's studying
6 isn't working
7 's saying

5

1 'm writing / am writing
2 'm travelling / am travelling
3 travel
4 's staying / is staying
5 think
6 don't take
7 'm taking / am taking
8 'm sending / am sending

Vocabulary

6

General appearance	Height	Eyes	Hair
beautiful ugly handsome	*short* tall	*brown* green blue	*dark* long fair curly blonde straight

7

1 tie
2 skirt
3 belt
4 dress
5 shoes
6 hat
7 shirt
8 trousers
9 socks
10 jumper

8

1 shoulder
2 chest
3 arm
4 hand
5 leg
6 neck
7 back
8 knee
9 ankle
10 foot

Functions

9

1 show	5 In	9 of
2 looks	6 On	10 watching
3 at	7 on	
4 closely	8 wearing	

Writing

10

1 How are you?
2 Don't be late.
3 See you soon.
4 OK. At six o'clock?
5 Please wait for me.

Unit 9 Test

Grammar

1

1 We are going to watch a new film tonight.
2 I am not going to listen to this album.
3 Are you going to have dinner now?
4 What time are we going to come to the party?
5 I am not going to play tennis today.
6 Are you going to drive to the beach?
7 Where are they going to meet us after the film?
8 Suzie is going to buy a new car next year.
9 When is he going to call me?

2

1 c   2 a   3 b   4 e   5 d

3

1 are … doing / going to do
2 I'm going
3 to practise
4 are meeting / going to meet
5 to have
6 to talk
7 Are … coming / going to come
8 I'm going
9 to see
10 's going to be

4

1 'm going	3 meet	5 has
2 go	4 're meeting	6 is having

Vocabulary

5

1 writer	3 painter	5 musician
2 actor / actress	4 director	6 artist

6

1 horror film
2 comedy
3 documentary
4 science fiction
5 romantic comedy
6 action film

7

2 art gallery	4 book	6 theatre
3 concert hall	5 restaurant	

8

1 kangaroo	3 butterfly	5 tree	7 cinema
2 DVD	4 bird	6 actor	

9

1 look	3 watch	5 read / write
2 listen	4 see	6 see / watch

Functions

10

1 Would you like to come? e
2 Are you free? d
3 Do you want to go? c
4 What time does it start? a
5 Let's meet at seven. b

Writing

11

1 bored	3 beautiful	5 nice
2 delicious	4 scared	

Unit 10 test

Grammar

1

2 bought	4 paid	6 gone	8 eaten
3 come	5 had	7 got	9 drunk

2

1 Have you ever travelled to Asia?
2 I've never been to Mongolia.
3 I've watched this film twice.
4 Has he ever written to you?
5 We've never met before.
6 I've never had Japanese food.
7 Have you ever seen this festival?

3

1 Have, been	4 your brother	7 ago
2 was	5 saw	8 have, won
3 didn't visit	6 haven't had	

4

1 Have you ever	5 travelled
2 have	6 Did you
3 was	7 didn't
4 Have you ever	

Vocabulary

5

1 postcard	5 online video
2 sat nav (GPS)	6 text message
3 search engine	7 email
4 letter	

6

2 a, b	4 a, b	6 a, c	8 a, b
3 b, c	5 a, c	7 a, c	

7

1 an MP3 player	5 a knife
2 a wheel	6 fire
3 a vacuum cleaner	7 sticky tape
4 electricity	8 the Internet

8

1 memorise	4 practise	7 forget
2 teach	5 study	8 understand
3 relax	6 remember	

Functions
9

1 Is that three in the afternoon? c
2 Is that the James hotel? d
3 The number is 794 66 54. a
4 Is there anything else? e
5 Have you called our colleagues? b

Writing
10

2 Book two tickets online.
3 Meet me at the station.
4 Call me back tomorrow.
5 Email the date of the trip.
6 Send me a message.

Unit 11 test

Grammar
1

1 shouldn't	4 should	7 should
2 shouldn't	5 should	8 shouldn't
3 should	6 shouldn't	

2

1 have to	3 have to	5 can't
2 can't	4 don't have to	6 have to

3

1 anything	4 somebody	7 nothing
2 Something	5 anywhere	8 anywhere
3 Nobody	6 Nobody	

Vocabulary
4

1 meet	3 use (take)	5 go	7 learn
2 book	4 buy	6 take	8 find

5

1 a   2 b   3 c   4 a   5 c   6 a   7 a

6

1 climate	4 illegal	7 multicultural
2 currency	5 left-hand side	8 licence
3 visa	6 time zones	

7

1 friendly	4 sun cream	7 Visitors
2 station	5 directions	
3 Temperature	6 population	

Functions
8

1 How about going on holiday?
2 Can I make a suggestion?
3 Why don't you go on a tour?
4 The disadvantage is that it is very cold.
5 That's a really good idea.

Writing
9

1 Did you book the tickets in advance? e
2 Did you visit any interesting places? b
3 How was your journey? a
4 Would you recommend this hotel to anybody? c
5 What other cities did you visit? d

Unit 12 test

Grammar
1

1 will be	5 will speak	9 will use
2 will live	6 will travel	10 will die
3 will grow	7 will wear	
4 will study	8 will buy	

2

2 In the future, people **will** live longer.
3 I don't think Jerry **will** call you.
4 It will **be** cold tomorrow.
5 I **will have** a big house in the future.
6 He **won't** come to work tomorrow.

3

1 –	3 –	5 –	7 The	9 –
2 The	4 the	6 the	8 The	10 The

Vocabulary
4

1 per cent	3 square metres	5 kilometres
2 degrees	4 litres	6 kilograms

1 a   2 e   3 d   4 b   5 c   6 f

5

1 river	4 mountain	7 ocean	10 region
2 continent	5 sea	8 lake	
3 forest	6 desert	9 island	

6

1 explorer	4 travel	7 surface
2 rock	5 star	8 orbits
3 planet	6 astronomer	

Functions
7

1 First of all, we started our company in 1990.
2 Nowadays, more than 100 people work for our company.
3 Finally, we opened a new office in Peru.
4 In conclusion, I really think your work is important.
5 Thank you very much for listening.

Writing
8

1 Party June 10th.
2 Everyone welcome.
3 Dance music.
4 Entrance free!
5 More information at www.partytime.com

Photocopiable communicative activities

Unit 1 Communicative activity
Famous people party

First name: Albert
Surname: Einstein
Age: 55
Occupation: scientist
Country: Germany
Marital status: married
Family: wife

First name: Charlotte
Surname: Brontë
Age: 31
Occupation: writer
Country: England
Marital status: married
Family: husband, two sisters

First name: _____
Surname: _____
Age: _____
Occupation: _____
Country: _____
Marital status: _____
Family: _____

First name: Steve
Surname: McCurry
Age: 62
Occupation: photographer
Country: USA
Marital status: single
Family: father, mother

First name: Luciano
Surname: Pavarotti
Age: 49
Occupation: opera singer
Country: Italy
Marital status: married
Family: wife, four daughters

First name: _____
Surname: _____
Age: _____
Occupation: _____
Country: _____
Marital status: _____
Family: _____

First name: Anna
Surname: Pavlova
Age: 31
Occupation: ballet dancer
Country: Russia
Marital status: married
Family: husband

First name: Marie
Surname: Curie
Age: 34
Occupation: scientist
Country: Poland
Marital status: married
Family: husband, two daughters

First name: _____
Surname: _____
Age: _____
Occupation: _____
Country: _____
Marital status: _____
Family: _____

First name: Maria
Surname: Montessori
Age: 80
Occupation: teacher
Country: Italy
Marital status: married
Family: husband, son

First name: Thomas
Surname: Edison
Age: 74
Occupation: inventor
Country: USA
Marital status: married
Family: wife, two daughters, four sons

First name: _____
Surname: _____
Age: _____
Occupation: _____
Country: _____
Marital status: _____
Family: _____

First name: Christopher
Surname: Columbus
Age: 47
Occupation: explorer
Country: Spain
Marital status: married
Family: wife, two sons

First name: Gertrude
Surname: Elion
Age: 64
Occupation: scientist, Nobel Prize winner
Country: USA
Marital status: single
Family: three nephews, one niece

First name: _____
Surname: _____
Age: _____
Occupation: _____
Country: _____
Marital status: _____
Family: _____

Unit 2 Communicative activity

The two rooms

1 Make a plan of your room. Draw five things from the box in the room.

Sofa	bed	plant	armchair	television	mirror	desk
lamp	computer	picture	blinds	cupboard	rug	carpet

2 Answer your partner's questions about your room, *e.g. 'Is there a television?' 'No, there isn't.'*
'Is there a plant?' 'Yes, there is. It is next to the door.'

3 Ask your partner questions and draw the things in his / her room.

4 Compare your drawings. Are they the same?

My room

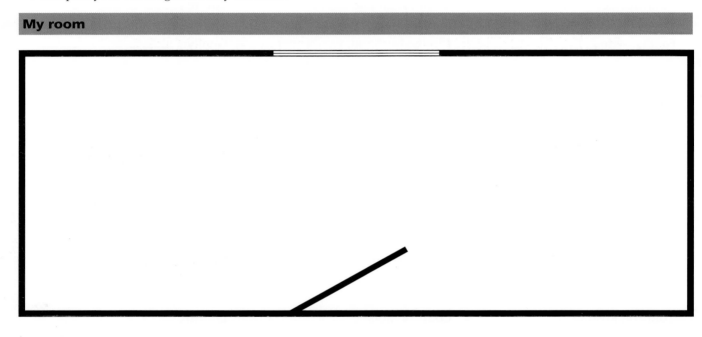

My partner's room

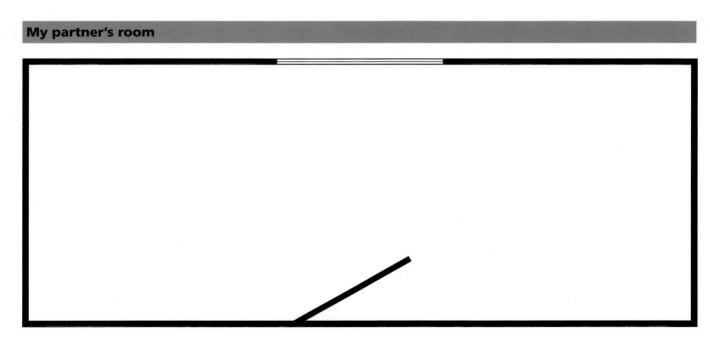

Unit 3 Communicative activity

Yes / No game

a doctor	a waiter
a photographer	a teacher
a film-maker	an archaeologist
a pilot	a biologist
a scientist	an explorer
a sailor	an accountant
a student	a writer
a farmer	a lecturer

A perfect job – questionnaire

❶ What is a good job for you?
Circle the options which are true for you.

Art	***	**	*
You like going to museums.	I love it.	I quite like it.	I don't like it.
You like learning new languages.	I love it.	I quite like it.	I don't like it.
You like singing and dancing.	I love it.	I quite like it.	I don't like it.
You can write a poem.	I can do it.	I can do it, but not very well.	I can't do it.

People	***	**	*
You like meeting new people.	I love it.	I quite like it.	I don't like it.
You like playing with children.	I love it.	I quite like it.	I don't like it.
You like helping people.	I love it.	I quite like it.	I don't like it.
You like going on holiday with your friends.	I love it.	I quite like it.	I don't like it.

Technology	***	**	*
You can repair the television.	I can do it.	I can do it, but not very well.	I can't do it.
You can repair a car.	I can do it.	I can do it, but not very well.	I can't do it.
You can use a computer.	I can do it.	I can do it, but not very well.	I can't do it.
You like reading technology magazines.	I love it.	I quite like it.	I don't like it.

Nature	***	**	*
You like growing plants at home.	I love it.	I quite like it.	I don't like it.
You like animals.	I love them.	I quite like them.	I don't like them.
You like visiting new places.	I love it.	I quite like it.	I don't like it.
You like reading *National Geographic* magazine.	I love it.	I quite like it.	I don't like it.

❷ Ask your partner. Is he / she an 'art', 'people', 'technology', or 'nature' person? Are you the same?
Check with the answers at the bottom of the page.

✂ -

ANSWERS:

More *** / ** Art answers: You can be a writer, journalist or a musician.
More *** / ** People answers: Good professions for you are a teacher, a doctor or a nurse.
More *** / ** Technology answers: You can be an accountant, an engineer, or an IT specialist.
More *** / ** Nature answers: Good professions for you are an explorer, a biologist or a vet.

Unit 5 Communicative activity

Food board game

START ↓	**9** Name something you can buy in a bottle (e.g. a bottle of water) →	**10** How much sugar do you have in your tea?	**FINISH**
1 Name two things you eat for breakfast	**8** How much coffee do you drink a day?	**11** Name two things you eat for lunch	**18** Name something you can buy in kilos (e.g. a kilo of sugar)
2 Name something you can buy in a bag (e.g. a bag of pasta)	**7** Name two orange types of food	**12** Name something you can buy in pieces (e.g. a piece of cheese)	**17** Name two things vegetarians don't eat
3 How much bread do you eat every day?	**6** Name two things you eat for dinner	**13** Name two things you can grow at home	**16** Name two red types of food
4 Name two white types of food	**5** How much salt do you put on your food? →	**14** Name two brown types of food	**15** How much fast food do you eat? →

Unit 6 Communicative activity

Amazing money facts

Student A

Choose the correct option for questions 2, 4, 6 and 8. Then read those sentences to your partner. Were you right? Correct your partner's answers.

1 In 1886, the face of **George Washington's wife** was on the 1$ note.

2 In the 1990s the US paper currency was **75%** _____ .
   A cotton   *B paper*   *C plastic*

3 **China** was the first country in the world which used paper money.

4 The USA started using the paper money in the _____ century.
   A seventeenth   *B eighteenth*   *C nineteenth*

5 For many centuries in Africa, people used **animals** as money.

6 Oliver Pollock invented the _____ sign in 1788.
   A dollar ($)   *B pound (£)*   *C euro (€)*

7 **Honduras** used the picture of a volcano on its money.

8 Madam C. J. Walker, the first woman who was a millionaire, lived in _____ .
   A the USA   *B England*   *C Australia*

✂ - ✂ - - - - - - - - - -

Student B

Choose the correct option for questions 1, 3, 5 and 7. Then read the sentences to your partner. Were you right? Correct your partner's answers.

1 In 1886, the face of _____ was on the $1 note.
   A George Washington   *B George Washington's wife*   *C George Washington's mother*

2 In the 1990s the US paper currency was 75% **cotton**.

3 _____ was the first country in the world which used paper money.
   A India   *B China*   *C Japan*

4 The USA started using the paper money in the **nineteenth** century.

5 For many centuries in Africa, people used _____ as money.
   A animals   *B stones*   *C food*

6 Oliver Pollock invented the **dollar ($)** sign in 1788.

7 _____ used the picture of a volcano on its money.
   A Italy   *B Brazil*   *C Honduras*

8 Madam C. J. Walker, the first woman who was a millionaire, lived **in the USA.**

Unit 7 Communicative activity
The flight of the *Vickers Vimy*

1 Read the text and try to remember the information. Answer your partner's questions.

> **The first nonstop Transatlantic flight**
>
> In March 1913 a British newspaper offered £10,000 to the first pilot to fly nonstop over the Atlantic.
>
> Pilots from all over the world entered the competition. Captain John Alcock and Arthur Whitten-Brown joined the race, too. They flew in a plane called *Vickers Vimy*. The journey started on the 14th June, 1919 in Canada and lasted 16 hours 12 minutes. The pilots had a lot of problems: they couldn't see anything because of the fog and heavy snow. Eventually, they arrived safely in Ireland and won £10,000!

2 Read the text then ask your partner for the missing information. Use the words in brackets to help you. Which answer is the same for both texts?

> **The first England to Australia flight**
>
> In March 1919 the Australian Government offered £10,000 to the first pilot to fly from England to Australia.
>
> The pilot Ross Smith and his brother Keith Smith started the dangerous and exciting journey in _____ (*When?*). They flew in a plane called _____ (*Name?*). The journey took _____ (*How long?*). The brothers had a lot of mechanical problems with the plane, because at that time _____ (*Why?*). The adventure finished in _____ (*When?*) in Australia.

- -

1 Read the text then ask your partner for the missing information. Use the words in brackets to help you.

> **The first nonstop transatlantic flight**
>
> In March 1913 a British newspaper offered £10,000 to the first pilot to fly nonstop over the Atlantic.
>
> Pilots from all over the world entered the competition. Captain John Alcock and Arthur Whitten-Brown joined the race, too. They flew in a plane called _____ (*Name?*). The journey started on the _____ (*When?*), 1919 in Canada and lasted _____ (*How long?*). The pilots had a lot of problems: they couldn't see anything _____ (*Why?*). Eventually, they arrived safely in _____ (*Where?*) and won £10,000!

2 Read the text and try to remember the information. Answer your partner's questions. Which answer is the same for both texts?

> **The first England to Australia flight**
>
> In March 1919 the Australian Government offered £10,000 to the first pilot to fly from England to Australia.
>
> The pilot Ross Smith and his brother Keith Smith started the dangerous and exciting journey in November 1919. They flew in a plane called *Vickers Vimy*. The journey took 28 days and 135 hours, 55 minutes. The brothers had a lot of mechanical problems with the plane, because at that time planes weren't very good. The adventure finished in February 1920 in Australia.

Unit 8 Communicative activity

You're teaching English

You're watching television	You're sleeping
You're opening a champagne bottle	You're taking a photo of a baby
You're talking on the phone to your boyfriend / girlfriend	You're reading a boring book
You're speaking Italian	You're cooking dinner
You're waiting for the bus	You're running a race
You're working on the computer	You're teaching your students English

Unit 9 Communicative activity

Plans for the weekend

Your name is **Alan**. Here are your plans for the weekend:
- see a film at the new cinema
- go shopping after the film

Your name is **Sarah**. Here are your plans for the weekend:
- see a film at the new cinema
- go shopping after the film

Your name is **Lily**. Here are your plans for the weekend:
- see a film on the TV at home
- go shopping after the film

Your name is **Mary**. Here are your plans for the weekend:
- see a film on the TV at home
- go shopping after the film

Your name is **James**. Here are your plans for the weekend:
- see a film at the new cinema
- go to the café after the film

Your name is **Andy**. Here are your plans for the weekend:
- see a film at the new cinema
- go to the café after the film

Your name is **Sophie**. Here are your plans for the weekend:
- go shopping
- go to the café after shopping

Your name is **Anna**. Here are your plans for the weekend:
- go shopping
- go to the café after shopping

Your name is **Vicky**. Here are your plans for the weekend:
- go to a theatre and see a play
- go to the café after the play

Your name is **John**. Here are your plans for the weekend:
- go to a theatre and see a play
- go to the café after the play

Your name is **Helen**. Here are your plans for the weekend:
- go to an art gallery and look at the paintings
- walk around the city

Your name is **Alex**. Here are your plans for the weekend:
- go to an art gallery and look at the paintings
- walk around the city

Your name is **Adam**. Here are your plans for the weekend:
- listen to live music at a rock club
- walk around the city

Your name is **Max**. Here are your plans for the weekend:
- listen to live music at a rock club
- walk around the city

Your name is **Emma**. Here are your plans for the weekend:
- see a film on the TV at home
- walk around the city

Your name is **Jack**. Here are your plans for the weekend:
- see a film on the TV at home
- walk around the city

Unit 10 Communicative activity

Find someone who …

Find someone who …

1 … has seen a 3D film. What was the name of the film?

2 … has met someone born on the same day. Who was it?

3 … has changed his / her name. Why?

4 … has slept in a tent. Where? When?

5 … has forgotten something very important. What?

6 … has sent someone a text message in the middle of the night. Who?

7 … has sung karaoke. Where?

8 … has lost a mobile phone. Where? When?

	Name	Extra information
1		
2		
3		
4		
5		
6		
7		
8		

Unit 11 Communicative activity

Life in Russia

1 In pairs, read the sentences about Russia. Do you think they are true or false?

		True	False
1	You don't have to get a visa to travel to Europe or America.		
2	Students usually have to wear a uniform at school.		
3	If you go out with a girl, you have to buy her flowers.		
4	Before you start travelling, you should sit down for a minute.		
5	You can buy a train ticket if you don't have a passport with you.		
6	At school, children have to stand up when the teacher enters the classroom.		
7	You can't go shopping at night.		
8	When a baby has his / her first tooth, you should give him / her a silver spoon as a present.		
9	You have to get a licence to keep a cat or a dog at home.		
10	You can get married at the age of 14.		
11	You can't smoke in cafés and restaurants.		
12	If somebody has a birthday, you should pull his / her ears.		

2 Check the answers with your teacher. Are any of these things the same in your country?

Unit 12 Communicative activity

How much do you remember? Do the quiz.

1 What's Louise Leakey's job? _____

2 How many people live in China? _____

3 Where do Mini cars come from? _____

4 Which opals are very expensive? _____

5 How many languages are there in the world? _____

6 Name the continent where the sun shines 24 hours a day in the summer. _____

7 How many people are there on Bazaruto Island? _____

8 How old is Borough Market in London? _____

9 Where is the Global Seed Vault? _____

10 How many countries have the face of Queen Elizabeth II on their money? _____

11 Whose faces can you see on a Mexican 500-peso note? _____

12 Who were the pilots who flew from England to South Africa for the first time? _____

13 To what country do wildebeests migrate every year? _____

14 Where is the Dinagyang Festival? _____

15 From what country did the tattoo culture come to Europe? _____

16 What did Aboriginal people in Australia paint on? _____

17 What can robot servants do? _____

18 What is the currency in Australia? _____

19 How many tourist come to Antarctica every year? _____

20 What is the temperature at the centre of the Earth? _____

Photocopiable communicative activities: Teacher's notes

Unit 1

AIM: To practise giving personal information and asking questions with *be*

MATERIALS: One photocopy for every five students, cut into ID cards

METHOD: Tell the students they are all famous people. Hand out one ID card and one blank ID card to each student in the class. If you have more than ten students, some students will have the same ID card, but that's OK. Ask students to walk round, and 'meet' one famous person. They then ask and answer questions to find out the information to complete the blank ID card. In feedback, ask students to tell the class what famous person they talked to and what they found out.

Unit 2

AIM: To practise *there is / are*, prepositions of place and the vocabulary of furniture

MATERIALS: One photocopy for each student

METHOD: Organise the class into pairs and hand out the worksheets. Tell the students they are going to make a plan of a room, (for example, a living-room or a bedroom). Tell the students not to look at each other's worksheets. They each draw five items from the box in their room. Then they ask *Is there a … ? / Are there … ?* questions to find out where the things in their partner's room are, and draw them on the other plan.

Students compare their drawings to check.

Unit 3

AIM: To practise asking and answering questions in the present simple

MATERIALS: One photocopy for each group

METHOD: Divide the class into groups of four or five. Make one photocopy of the worksheet for each group. Cut up the cards and give each group a set in a pile face down. One student takes a card. The rest of the group must ask *Do you … ?* questions to guess the job, e.g. *Do you work in a hospital?* until they guess the job correctly.

Unit 4

AIM: To practise present simple question forms, *can / can't*, *like + -ing*, and revision of the vocabulary of jobs

MATERIALS: One photocopy for each student in the class

METHOD: Hand out a photocopy of the quiz to each student. Tell them to read the questionnaire and circle the answers that are true for them. Then ask the students to interview their partner and find out if their answers are the same. Then they should read the answer key together and find out what their ideal job is.

Unit 5

AIM: To practise questions with *much / many, not much / not many, a lot, some / any*; general vocabulary from the unit

MATERIALS: One photocopy, a dice and two counters for each pair of students.

METHOD: Hand out a photocopy of the board game to each pair of students. Ask them to place their counters on the 'Start' square. They take turns to throw the dice, move the counter and answer the questions. If they answer correctly, they can throw the dice again. The student who reaches the 'Finish' section first is the winner.

SAMPLE ANSWERS

1 eggs, cereal, toast, bread   2 sweets, flour, potatoes, carrots   4 rice, sugar, eggs, salt   7 oranges, carrots, lentils   9 milk, juice, water, lemonade   11 salad, sandwich, pasta, chips, fruit   12 cheese, meat 13 tomatoes, salad, potatoes, carrots (this will depend where students live) 14 chocolate, nuts, lentils, bread   16 tomatoes, red peppers, strawberries 17 meat, chicken, fish   18 sugar, meat, potatoes, flour, etc.

Unit 6

AIM: To practise the past form of *be* and regular verbs

MATERIALS: One photocopy (cut into two) for each pair of students

METHOD: Organise the class into pairs. Hand out a worksheet to each pair. You may want to pre-teach the meaning of *cotton, $/£/€ signs, millionaire*. Student A has the answers to the questions 1, 3, 5 and 7, and Student B has the answers to the questions 2, 4, 6 and 8. Give the students some time to read the facts and to choose the option they think is correct. Then they read the completed sentences to their partner and check the answers (e.g. *In 1886 I think George Washington's face was on the $1 note. No, it wasn't. It was his wife's face*). If their partner is wrong, they must say the correct answer. Then they answer their partner's questions.

Unit 7

AIM: To practise questions using the past simple forms of regular and irregular verbs

MATERIALS: One photocopy for each pair of students (cut in half)

METHOD: Organise the class into pairs. Hand out the Student A half of the photocopy to one student in each pair. Give the other half to Student B. Tell them not to look at their partner's copy. Give students time to read both texts. Students must read the first text and just remember the information, then read the second text and think of the questions they need to ask to find out their missing information. Go round and help students with question forming. When students are ready, ask them to take turns to ask and answer questions with their partner to find the information. At the end, ask students to look at each other's texts to check their answers.

Answer: both planes were called *Vickers Vimy*, but they weren't the same plane.

Unit 8

AIM: To practise present continuous forms

MATERIALS: One photocopy for each group or for a small class, cut into cards

METHOD: Organise the class into groups of four or five. You may want to pre-teach *champagne*. Cut up the statements and hand out a set to each group in a pile face down. Each student in the group takes a card and thinks about how to mime the sentence on the card. When they are ready, one student mimes their sentence. The rest of the group must guess the sentence until they get it exactly right. Then it is another student's turn.

This could also be done as a whole-class activity.

Unit 9

AIM: To practise *going to* for plans

MATERIALS: One photocopy for each group or for the class, cut into one card for each student. If there are less than 16 students, you don't have to use all the cards, but make sure all the students find a friend to do things with at the weekend

METHOD: This is a whole-class activity. Hand out a different card to each student. Students must stand up, walk round and ask questions to find out what the other people in class are going to do at the weekend. The aim is to find someone who wants to do the same things.

Once students have spoken to all the other people in their group, they should decide who their perfect partner for the weekend is.

ANSWERS: Alan and Sarah, Lily and Mary, James and Andy, Sophie and Anna, Vicky and John, Helen and Alex, Adam and Max, Emma and Jack.

Unit 10

AIM: To practise present perfect for general life experiences, and past simple for giving extra information about the past

MATERIALS: One photocopy for each student in the class

METHOD: Hand out a photocopy of the worksheet to each student. Give the students time to think over the answers to the questions. Model the activity by asking one or two *Have you ever…?* questions and then asking follow-up questions. Then students must walk round and ask different people questions. When they find someone who says *Yes, I have* to a question, they must write the name in the table and add extra information by asking their partner questions.

Unit 11

AIM: To practise *can / can't, have to / don't have to, should / shouldn't*

MATERIALS: One photocopy for each group of four or five students

METHOD: Hand out a photocopy of the worksheet to each group. You may want to pre-teach some vocabulary like *silver spoon, to pull somebody's ears, the first tooth,* etc. Tell the students to read the information and decide in their group whether each sentence is true or false. Check the answers in class and ask the students if the things are the same in their country.

ANSWERS:			
1 F	4 T	7 F	10 T
2 F	5 F	8 T	11 F
3 T	6 T	9 F	12 T

Unit 12

AIM: To remember / revise information from the Student's Book in a quiz

MATERIALS: One photocopy for each student

METHOD: Divide the class into pairs to do the quiz. You could ask students to do it in one of two ways. You could ask them to do it without looking at the Student's Book – find out what they remember. Or you could do it as a research task – students look through the Student's Book in pairs to find the answers.

ANSWERS		
1	She's an explorer	11 Frida Kahlo and Diego Rivera
2	1.2 billion people	12 Van Ryneveld and Quintin Brand
3	England	13 Kenya
4	Red opals	14 in the Philippines
5	about 7,000	15 Polynesia
6	The Arctic	16 Rocks
7	0	17 Wash clothes, switch on the TV,
8	250 years	turn off the lights and change
9	on the island of	the music.
	Spitsbergen	18 Australian dollars.
10	over 30 countries	19 50,000
		20 about 7,500 °C

Workbook answer key

Unit 1

1a (pages 4 and 5)

1
1 First name
2 Surname
3 Age
4 Job
5 Country
6 Marital status
7 Address

2 Students' own answers.

3 1 h 2 f 3 e 4 b 5 d 6 c 7 a 8 g

5
1 What's
2 name's
3 Are
4 I'm
5 I'm not
6 are
7 is
8 Are
9 isn't

6 1 are 2 Are 3 'm 4 Is 5 is 6 isn't 7 aren't 8 'm

7
1 What's your name?
2 Are you from England?
3 How old are you?
4 Are you married or single?
5 Are you a student?
6 What is your address?

8 Students' own answers.

9
1 What's
2 is not
3 I'm
4 You're
5 I'm not
6 are not

1b (pages 6 and 7)

1 a 2 b 3 c 1

2 1 c 2 b 3 b 4 c 5 c

3
1 wife
2 boys
3 son
4 daughters
5 father
6 children

4
1 Charles / Ingma
2 George / Mason
3 Ranci
4 George
5 Joanne
6 Tom
7 Julie
8 Ranci

5 1 It 2 my 3 our 4 her 5 their 6 's 7 they 8 he

6 Students' own answers.

7
1 a They're b Their
2 a He's b His
3 a Are b Our
4 a You're b Your

1c (page 8)

1 1, 3, 4, 6, 8

2 1 28 2 1.6 3 27 4 60 5 English 6 60

3 1 c 2 d 3 a 4 b 5 e

4 Students' own answers.

5
1 They live **in** the USA.
2 55% of the population work **in** agriculture.
3 We live **in** Dubai.
4 Amanda and Nigel work **in** a shop.
5 49% of the people live **in** the countryside.

1d (page 9)

2
A: H J K
B: C D E G P T V
F: L M N S X Z
I: Y
O
Q: U W
R

4
Name: Doctor T Zull   Country: Australia
Name: Beata Polit   Country: Poland

5
1 I'm from
2 Nice to meet you
3 Nice to meet you too.
4 I'd like to introduce you
5 My name's
6 where are you from?
7 Nice talking to
8 See you later.

1e (page 10)

1 1 but 2 and 3 but 4 and 5 and 6 but

2 1 a 2 b 3 d 4 e 5 f 6 c

3 Example answer:
Hi! My name's Brendan and I'm 22. I'm single and I'm a student at university. I'm from Australia but I live in Italy. I speak English and Italian. I have two brothers but no sisters.

Wordbuilding / Learning skills (page 11)

1
1 in-law
2 grand
3 step
4 first
5 sur
6 middle
7 grapher
8 graph
9 sister
10 brother
11 father

3 Students' own answers.

4
1 mother
2 billion
3 East
4 agriculture
5 million
6 niece
7 Oman
8 explorers

Unit 2

2a (pages 12 and 13)

1
1 red, yellow
2 white, black
3 yellow, black
4 blue, yellow

2 Students' own answers.

3
1 hat
2 first-aid kit
3 torch
4 camera
5 gloves
6 map
7 mobile phone
8 compass
9 boots
10 shoes

4 1 hat 2 first-aid kit 3 map 4 shoes 5 boots

5
1 rucksack
2 maps
3 first-aid kit
4 torches
5 compass
6 gloves
7 hat
8 boots

6
1 mobile phones
2 people
3 boxes
4 torches
5 knives
6 cities
7 cameras
8 men
9 keys

7
/s/ boots, hats, maps
/z/ keys, knives, mobile phones
/ɪz/ boxes, cities, compasses

8 1 those, gloves 2 that, rucksack 3 these, keys 4 this, map

2b (pages 14 and 15)

1
1 nineteen
2 747
3 fifteen
4 five
5 1976
6 twenty-four
7 twenty-seven
8 seventy-six
9 two

2 1 T 2 F 3 F 4 T 5 T 6 F 7 F 8 T

3
1 take off
2 runway
3 hostel
4 on foot
5 cheap
6 cockpit
7 expensive
8 double

4 1 are 2 aren't 3 is 4 Is 5 isn't 6 are 7 is 8 is

5 1 on   3 the right   5 above
   2 next   4 left   6 under

6 1 chair   5 sofa
   2 rug   6 curtain
   3 blind   7 desk
   4 computer
   Mystery word: cupboards

2c (page 16)

1 1 b 2 c 3 a 4 d

2 1 global   5 furniture   9 Sweden
   2 300   6 beds, chairs, sofas 10 Poland
   3 36   7 cupboards   11 restaurants
   4 five million 8 desks   12 United Kingdom

3 1 Burberry is a British company.
   2 BMW is a German company.
   3 Gucci is an Italian company.
   4 Sony is a Japanese company.
   5 Petrobas is a Brazilian company.
   6 Inditex is a Spanish company.
   7 Alcatel-Lucent is a French company.
   8 Google is an American company. (*or* Google is a
    US company.)

4 1 France, Greece, Spain
   2 England, Poland, Sweden
   3 Brazil, Japan, Peru
   4 Canada, Germany, Italy

2d (page 17)

1 1 c 2 a 3 b

2 1 e 2 a 3 c 4 b 5 d

3 Students' own answers.

4 1 T-shirt   4 water   7 gloves
   2 one   5 one   8 ones
   3 black one   6 small one   9 large ones

5 1 This, that   3 This, that
   2 These, those 4 These, those

2e (page 18)

1 1 slow, fast   4 useful, useless
   2 expensive, cheap 5 modern, old
   3 small, large

2 1 new, green   4 old, Italian   7 nice, brown
   2 fast, Japanese 5 useful, French 8 useless, old
   3 small, white   6 strong, blue

3 Example answers:
   BUY NOW! I have a beautiful, old kitchen clock.
   Cheap at £5. Call 567 7456.
   FOR SALE! A pair of new, red and blue roller blades.
   Good for children. Email j_taylor@mfs.com
   SALE! Old, large English bookshelf. In good condition.
   Perfect for all your books! Call Jim on 657 4857.

Wordbuilding / Learning skills (page 19)

1 1 worker   4 Brazil   7 piano
   2 teacher   5 guitarist   8 Spanish
   3 saxophone   6 Vietnamese

2 1 ish 2 n 3 ist 4 r 5 an 6 ese 7 ian 8 er

5 1 possession   3 furniture   5 Mini
   2 climber   4 Dutch

Unit 3

3a (pages 20 and 21)

1 1 d 2 f 3 h 4 g 5 a 6 e 7 c 8 b

2 1 It's five o'clock.
   2 It's five minutes past seven.
   3 It's quarter past nine.
   4 It's twenty-five minutes past one.
   5 It's half past four.
   6 It's twenty-five minutes to four.
   7 It's quarter to nine.
   8 It's five minutes to eleven.

3 1 an airport   3 London
   2 Australia   4 a train station

4 Australia   a train station

   an airport   London

5 1 No   4 No   7 Don't know
   2 Yes   5 Yes   8 Don't know
   3 Don't know   6 Don't know

6 1 big   4 beautiful   7 intelligent / smart
   2 quiet   5 modern, new
   3 clean   6 crowded

7 1 small 2 dirty 3 ugly 4 uncrowded 5 old

8 1 go   4 work   7 meet
   2 don't have   5 study   8 don't live
   3 don't like   6 don't eat

9 1 What do you do?
   2 Where do you live?
   3 Do you go to work by car?
   4 What time do you eat lunch?
   5 Do you like shopping?

3b (pages 22 and 23)

1 a doctor   d sailor   g waiter
   b photographer e student   h accountant
   c pilot   f teacher

2 1 b 2 a 3 g 4 d 5 h 6 e 7 c 8 f

3 1 studio   4 boat   7 airport
   2 hospital   5 office building 8 classroom
   3 restaurant   6 university

4 1 T 2 F 3 F 4 T 5 T 6 F

5 1 with 2 for 3 for 4 with

6 1 comes   4 likes   7 doesn't work
   2 works   5 studies   8 sails
   3 doesn't spend 6 goes

7 1 Where does Brad come from?
   2 Where does he work?
   3 Does he spend a lot of time there?
   4 Does he like being under the water?
   5 What does he study?
   6 Does Gina go with him on expeditions?
   7 Does she work under the water?

8 /s/ likes, starts, works
   /z/ comes, goes, spends
   /ɪz/ dances, finishes, teaches

3c (page 24)

1 1 B   2 A   3 C

2 1 450   2 160   3 85   4 15   5 78   6 19   7 15   8 3

3 1 seven, five, two   3 six   5 twenty
    2 first   4 third   6 one hundredth

4 1 30   2 15th   3 66   4 3rd   5 80

3d (page 25)

1 1 tourist information centre   4 car park   7 hotel
    2 museum   5 library   8 aquarium
    3 park   6 theatre

2 1 bank
    2 theatre
    3 tourist information centre

3 1 B   2 C   3 A

4 1 near   4 Where   7 take   10 across
    2 straight 5 away   8 here
    3 turn   6 past   9 Go

3e (page 26)

1 1 Karachi   5 July   9 Haversham
    2 George   6 This   10 Grant
    3 French   7 I
    4 Monday   8 Morocco

2 1 c   2 b   3 a   4 e   5 d

3 Students' own answers.

Wordbuilding / Learning skills (page 27)

1 1 language   4 office   7 transport
    2 hotel   5 time   8 work
    3 park   6 centre

2 1 first   4 head   7 public
    2 friendly   5 closing   8 office
    3 wildlife   6 shopping

4 1 Norway   4 Atlanta   7 Australia
    2 Tokyo   5 China   8 Moscow
    3 Bogotá   6 Vanuatu

Unit 4

4a (pages 28 and 29)

1 1 play a musical instrument
    2 watch films
    3 meet friends
    4 play computer games
    5 do Tae Kwon Do
    6 play tennis
    7 go walking
    8 go to the gym

2 1 No   2 Yes   3 Yes   4 No   5 Yes

3 1 c   2 d   3 a   4 e   5 b

4 1 swimming   4 going   7 fishing
    2 singing   5 running   8 cycling
    3 living   6 watching

6 1 We like listening to music.
    2 Bob likes playing tennis.
    3 I love learning languages.
    4 They like watching football.
    5 Do you like going to the gym?
    6 My brother doesn't like dancing at nightclubs.
    7 The twins don't like doing homework.
    8 We like eating foreign food.

4b (pages 30 and 31)

1 1 D   2 B   3 C   4 A

2 1 A   2 B   3 A   4 A   5 A   6 C   7 B, C   8 A, C, D   9 C

3 1 never   3 sometimes   5 n't often
    2 always   4 usually   6 often

4 1 I often read a book before I go to bed.
    2 I always go to work at eight.
    3 I don't often meet my family.
    4 I sometimes go clothes shopping.
    5 I'm always busy.
    6 At work, I never take lunch breaks.

5a a 4   b 6   c 5   d 5   e 6   f 4

5b a John often travels abroad.
     b Shannon and Nicole are always busy.
     c He doesn't often have time.
     d How often does Shannon surf?
     e I read a newspaper every morning.
     f Michael is often tired.

4c (page 32)

1 1 b   2 c   3 a   4 d   5 h   6 e   7 f   8 g

2 1 h   2 g   3 a   4 c   5 b   6 e   7 f   8 d

3 2, 3, 5, 6

4 1 F   2 T   3 F   4 F   5 T   6 F   7 T   8 T

5 1 Can you   5 can
    2 can't   6 can't
    3 very well   7 well
    4 English well   8 How well can you

4d (page 33)

1 1 22
    2 Irish and Italian
    3 English, Italian and French
    4 Tennis and basketball
    5 Playing the guitar

2 1 d   2 g   3 f   4 b   5 c   6 h   7 e   8 a

4 1 a   2 b   3 a   4 a   5 b

5 1 speaking   3 playing   5 going
    2 doing   4 painting   6 watching

6 Students' own answers.

4e (page 34)

1 1 G   2 C   3 D   4 A   5 E   6 H   7 B   8 F

2 1 at work
    2 the cycling race
    3 Sandy's cousin
    4 Sandy
    5 Alex's place of work
    6 the cyclists

3 1 c   2 e   3 d   4 a   5 b   6 f

4 Example answer:
Hi Matt
I can help you. I'm good at fixing computers and printers. I can come to your office later today. Yes, I'm interested in coming to the restaurant. That sounds great. Where is it?

Wordbuilding / Learning skills (page 35)

1 1 go shopping
2 play chess
3 listen to (the) radio
4 do work
5 Read (the) article
6 meet clients
7 time (do you) spend
8 watch a DVD

2 Collocations in the text: go to work, spend all day, information shows, use computer, spend an hour a day, visit sites, play games, send emails, watch videos, do online shopping, search the Internet

3 1 Washington   4 polar bears   7 highlining
2 twins   5 Germany   8 gap year
3 harp   6 Arctic

Unit 5

5a (pages 36 and 37)

1 1 a   2 b   3 b   4 a   5 b

2 1 onions   5 eggs   9 lamb
2 peppers   6 milk   10 salt
3 lemons   7 rice
4 raisins   8 chicken

3 1 1   5 2   9 1   13 3
2 2   6 3   10 2   14 2
3 3   7 1   11 1
4 1   8 2   12 2

4 1 d   2 e   3 c   4 a   5 b

5 1 No (There isn't one good month because 'you can taste different types of cheese at every time of year'.)
2 Yes
3 Don't know
4 No
5 Yes
6 Don't know
7 Yes
8 Yes

6 1 C   2 U   3 U   4 C   5 U   6 C   7 C   8 C   9 U   10 C

7 1 some   2 an   3 a   4 any   5 any   6 a   7 an   8 some

5b (pages 38 and 39)

1 1 a lot of   5 a lot of
2 a lot of   6 a lot of / many
3 a lot of / many   7 a lot of
4 a lot of / much   8 a lot of / much

2 Students' own answers.

3 1 water   4 juice   7 salt
2 bread   5 eggs   8 chocolate
3 chicken   6 coffee

4 1 bag   4 tin   7 slices
2 bottle   5 cup   8 bottle
3 piece   6 kilo

5 1 d   2 b   3 e   4 c   5 f   6 a

6 1 sparkling   5 a bottle
2 a glass   6 a piece of chocolate
3 a kilo   7 a slice
4 yes, very hot   8 a tin

7 1 How much rice do you want?
2 How many apples do you want?
3 How much bread do you want?
4 How many eggs do you want?
5 How much pasta do you want?
6 How many packets of pasta do you want?
7 How much chocolate do you want?
8 How many bananas do you want?

8 1 g   2 a   3 e   4 b   5 d   6 f   7 c   8 h

5c (page 40)

1 1 a   2 c   3 b

2 1 a   2 c   3 b   4 a   5 c   6 b   7 c

3 1 b   2 a   3 d   4 e   5 c

5d (page 41)

1 1 starters   3 main course   5 desserts
2 soups   4 salads   6 drinks

2 Table 2
1 ~~glass~~ of ~~still~~ water. *bottle, sparkling*
~~Onion~~ soup *tomato*
Chicken kabsa
~~Large~~ green salad *small*
~~Cheesecake~~ no *dessert*
A cup of ~~tea~~ *coffee*

3 a Can I get you anything?
b Here is the menu.
c I'd like some water.
d I'll have a small green salad.
e Could I have the bill?
f I'd like a cup of coffee.
g That was delicious.
h Are you ready to order?

4 1 b   2 a   3 c   4 h   5 d   6 g   7 f   8 e

5 1 a   2 b   3 a   4 b

5e (page 42)

1 1 Mix   2 Chop   3 Pour   4 Put   5 Spread   6 Slice

2 1 shop, but you can also make
2 You need the following food: an egg, some
3 Put the flour
4 mix the egg and olive oil.
5 Next, you need a pasta machine.
6 Put the pasta
7 cut the pasta into long,

4 Example answer:
1 Put the eggs into a bowl.
2 Pour the milk into the bowl.
3 Mix the eggs and milk.
4 Pour the mixture into a frying pan and cook.
5 Put the eggs on a plate.

Wordbuilding / Learning skills (page 43)

1 1 chips   5 pavement   9 football
2 mobile phone   6 biscuit   10 full stop
3 bill   7 motorway
4 lift   8 petrol

2 1 d   2 c   3 f   4 b   5 g   6 j   7 a   8 i   9 h   10 e

3
1 petrol – gas
2 lift – elevator
3 mobile – cell
4 biscuit – cookie
5 football – soccer
6 motorway – freeway
7 bill – check
8 full stop – period

4 1 a 2 g 3 b 4 c 5 f 6 h 7 e 8 d

5 kabsa: Saudi Arabia / chicken (or fish), onion, salt, pepper, tomatoes, rice, nuts, raisins
pizza: Italy / flour, tomato, cheese, olive oil, salt
ceviche: Peru / fish, lemon juice, onions, salad
pierogi: Poland / potato, flour, mushrooms, butter, cheese

Unit 6

6a (pages 44 and 45)

1 1 earn 2 give 3 change 4 spend 5 Save

2 a 5 b 3 c 1 d 4 e 2

3 a 3 b 1 c 2

4 1 d 2 c 3 a 4 e 5 b

5
1 was
2 were
3 was
4 was
5 was
6 weren't
7 were
8 wasn't
9 was

6
1 Where were her parents from?
2 What was her father?
3 Was she interested in money?
4 How long were they on the Pacific Ocean?
5 Who was the blog popular with?

7 We stress the verb in negative sentences and questions.
2 He <u>wasn't</u> on the dollar.
3 <u>Was</u> he the President?
5 They <u>weren't</u> Spanish.
6 <u>Were</u> they artists?

8
1 in my early twenties
2 in your mid thirties
3 in her late forties
4 in our early sixties
5 in his late fifties
6 in their mid twenties

6b (pages 46 and 47)

1
1 From a TV show.
2 Yes.
3 Banking and saving money.
4 His friend.

2 1 b 2 d 3 a 4 c

3
1 a interesting b interested
2 a excited b exciting
3 a boring b bored

4 Students' own answers.

5
1 lived
2 worked
3 discovered
4 phoned
5 studied
6 paid
7 received
8 died

6
1 /t/
2 /d/
3 /ɪd/
4 /ɪd/
5 /t/
6 /ɪd/
7 /d/
8 /ɪd/
9 /d/
10 /d/
11 /t/
12 /d/

7 In 2001 I lived in France. I studied French at university. After university I wanted to live in France so I returned in 2003. I worked in a currency exchange office in Paris. I liked the job and I travelled all over the country at weekends. Last year I started a job in a bank and I married a French woman.

8
1 went
2 had
3 was
4 arrived
5 died
6 discovered
7 pulled
8 gave

6c (page 48)

1 b

2 1 c 2 a 3 a 4 c 5 b 6 a 7 c 8 a

3
1 notes
2 coins
3 cheque
4 debit card
5 credit card
6 bank transfer

6d (page 49)

1
1 a buy b sell
2 a give b take
3 a spend b save
4 a lend b borrow

2 1 No 2 Yes 3 No 4 Yes

3 1 d 2 e 3 a 4 h 5 b 6 g 7 c 8 f

4 1 ☺ 2 ☹ 3 ☺ 4 ☹

5 Students' own answers.

6e (page 50)

1
1 Hi
2 Thanks
3 Love
4 Thank you for
5 See you
6 Best regards
7 Dear Mrs
8 Thank you very much
9 I look forward to
10 Yours sincerely

2 Example answers:
1 Hi!
Thanks for the money! Here's a cheque.
It was very useful!
See you soon
Love

2 Dear Barbara
Thank you for my time in Cologne. I was pleased with our work and I enjoyed our meal at the restaurant. See you again next year.
Best regards

3 Dear Mr Smith
Thank you very much for your interest in our holidays.
Please find enclosed the brochure for our holidays.
I look forward to hearing from you in the future.
Yours sincerely

Wordbuilding / Learning skills (page 51)

1
1 basketball
2 credit card
3 Tourist information
4 mobile phone
5 armchair
6 full stop
7 roller blades
8 post office

3
1 George Washington: USA / First President of the USA
2 Frida Kahlo and Diego Rivera: Mexico / Artists
3 Arthur Honegger: Switzerland / Composer
4 Ichiyo Higuchi: Japan / Writer
5 Howard Carter: England / Archaeologist

Unit 7

7a (pages 52 and 53)

1 1 fly 2 drive 3 cycle 4 take 5 sail 6 travel

2a Land: bicycle, car, drive, train, walk, wheels
Sea: boat, sail, ship
Air: aeroplane, fly, hot air balloon, wings

3
1 didn't survive
2 didn't stop
3 didn't return
4 didn't travel
5 didn't enter

4 1 A air B sea C somewhere else (space)
   2 A aeroplane B ship C satellite

5 1 A 2 A 3 B 4 A 5 B 6 A 7 A

6 1 What did Orteig offer in 1919?
   2 When did Charles Lindbergh fly from New York to Paris?
   3 How long did the journey take?
   4 When did five ships leave Spain?
   5 Where did Magellan die?
   6 At night, what did people look for in the sky?
   7 How many times did it travel round Earth?
   8 When did it enter Earth's atmosphere?

7b (pages 54 and 55)

1 1 d 2 b 3 a 4 c

2
1 6 million	4 200,000	7 1,500
2 3.5	5 1,000	
3 15,000	6 13,000	

3 and 4
   1 are <u>longer</u> than any other bird
   2 are <u>more dangerous</u> and difficult
   3 is <u>colder</u> than other parts of the world
   4 for <u>longer</u> than two hours

5
1 shorter	4 busier	7 wetter
2 easier	5 cheaper	8 nicer
3 bigger	6 sadder	

6
1 cheaper	4 faster	7 better
2 hotter	5 safer	8 worse
3 more expensive	6 older	

7 and 9
   1 My <u>brother</u> is <u>shorter</u> than <u>me</u>.
   2 <u>Walking</u> is <u>slower</u> than <u>cycling</u>.
   3 I think <u>rock</u> climbing is more <u>difficult</u> than <u>surfing</u>.
   4 <u>Giraffes</u> are <u>taller</u> than <u>elephants</u>.
   5 <u>Camping</u> is <u>cheaper</u> than <u>staying</u> in a <u>hotel</u>.
   6 <u>Canada</u> is <u>bigger</u> than <u>Iceland</u>.
   7 A <u>taxi</u> is more <u>expensive</u> than a <u>public</u> <u>bus</u>.
   8 <u>Cities</u> are more <u>crowded</u> than <u>towns</u>.

7c (page 56)

1 a 2 b 1 c 3

2 1 F 2 T 3 F 4 F 5 T 6 T 7 F 8 T

3
1 shortest	4 slowest	7 saddest
2 easiest	5 cheapest	8 nicest
3 biggest	6 fastest	

4
1 highest	4 shortest	7 easiest
2 best	5 most populated	8 busiest
3 largest	6 furthest	

7d (page 57)

1
1 journey	3 trip	5 trip
2 travel	4 travel	6 journey

2 1 a 2 d 3 e 4 b 5 c

3 1 a 2 b 3 b 4 c 5 a

7e (page 58)

1 1 a blog b website
   2 a writer b blogger
   3 a online b homepage
   4 a upload b download
   5 a comment b post

2 1 The bus was cancelled so we waited for the next one.
   2 The flight was cancelled because the weather was terrible.
   3 The food was hot and spicy so we drank a litre of water with our meal.
   4 The meeting was long and boring because the managing director spoke for two hours!
   5 The restaurant didn't take credit cards so I paid with cash.
   6 The hotel restaurant was closed so we went into the centre of town for a meal.

3 Example answer:
I took a train across the country. We went past mountains and there was snow. Suddenly we stopped. The train couldn't move because there was snow on the line. It was night. We spent hours on the train and it was very cold. Fortunately, a man on the train had a guitar and he played songs. Everyone sang to the music. In the morning it was sunny and finally the train started moving again.

Wordbuilding / Learning skills (page 59)

1 1 The journey was very/really good.
   2 The food was very/really good.
   3 The meetings weren't very interesting.
   4 The party was really great!
   5 The weather was very/really bad.
   6 It wasn't very sunny.
   7 The meal was nice.
   8 The hotel was really amazing!

2 1 c 2 a 3 b

4 1 They sailed to America in the *Mayflower* in the 17th century.
   2 The *Mayflower II* sailed to America in 1957.
   3 The *Silver Queen* took 44 days to fly from to Cape Town.
   4 The saiga travels 35 kilometres per day.
   5 The tree frog migrates 30 metres.
   6 The loggerhead turtle travels 14,000 kilometres in fifteen years.
   7 *Voyager* took off in 1977.
   8 Jupiter is 349,000 kilometres from Earth.

Unit 8

8a (pages 60 and 61)

1
1 boring	3 crowded	5 fun
2 noisy	4 colourful	

2 1 F 2 F 3 T 4 T 5 F 6 F 7 T 8 F

3
1 eyebrow	3 nose	5 lips	7 chin
2 eye	4 ear	6 cheek	

4 1 beautiful 2 short 3 curly 4 dark

5 1 have got 2 're 3 has got 4 has got 5 's

6
1 lips	4 mask	7 blonde
2 eyebrow	5 cheeks	8 handsome
3 ugly	6 straight	

8b (pages 62 and 63)

1 1 b 2 e 3 a 4 c 5 d

2
1 No.	6 It's very warm.
2 England.	7 Red and black.
3 The United States.	8 Long, black hair.
4 A reservation.	9 Selling things.
5 Red, yellow and purple.	10 Her dress and her hat.

3 1 We like buying new clothes.
2 Your new dress is like mine.
3 These shoes are like my old ones. / My shoes are like these old ones.
4 I don't like my uniform.
5 This hat is like a cowboy hat.
6 Jason likes wearing jeans.

4 1 Sentences 1, 4, 6   2 Sentences 2, 3, 5

5 1 isn't wearing, 's wearing
2 's buying, isn't selling
3 isn't making, 's designing
4 isn't playing, 's reading

6 1 What's he wearing?
2 Is Trisha buying or selling clothes?
3 What is Georgio designing?
4 Is he playing a computer game?

7 1 comes   5 Do (you) know
2 're staying   6 'm walking
3 take   7 Are (you) learning
4 are (you) standing   8 Do (you) like

8 1 hat   4 jumper   7 skirt
2 dress   5 shirt   8 socks
3 shoes / boots 6 belt
Mystery word: trousers

8c (page 64)

1 1 deer ✓   5 lion ✓   9 Arctic fox ✓
2 squirrel   6 butterfly ✓   10 giraffe
3 zebra ✓   7 chameleon ✓
4 elephant   8 polar bear

2 1 Yes   4 Don't know   7 No
2 No   5 Yes   8 Don't know
3 No   6 Yes

3 1 foot   4 back   7 knee
2 hand   5 leg   8 arm
3 neck   6 shoulder

8d (page 65)

1 1 A family.
2 Dinner.
3 The boy.
4 Serious (and perhaps they are hungry).
5 Because of the women's hats and clothes.

2 1 This photo
2 On the right
3 in the middle
4 in front of her
5 The family looks
6 They are wearing
7 I think
8 The photo is interesting

4 1 t 2 w 3 d 4 b 5 h 6 k 7 e 8 n

8e (page 66)

1 1 UR   6 Weds   11 l8   16 atm
2 4u   7 @   12 sry   17 :-)
3 CU   8 RU   13 thx   18 w/e
4 2day   9 GR8   14 <3
5 b4   10 pls   15 4get

2 1 pls come on weds
2 RU :-) 2day?
3 Sry I'm l8
4 R we meeting @ w/e?
5 I <3 the film
6 I have GR8 news!
7 Call me b4 U leave
8 CU l8er

3 Example answer:
A: Sry I'm l8 :-(
B: Where RU?
A: On the train atm. Where RU?
B: I'm w8ing 4U @ the cinema
A: Can we meet l8er?
B: What time?
A: @ 2?
B: 2 is ok. I'll w8 in the café
A: OK. CU there.
B: tks

Wordbuilding / Learning skills (page 67)

1 1 Put on   3 eat out   5 turn off   7 Take off
2 get up   4 Look at   6 Go back   8 look up

3 T: put on, look at, turn off, take off, look up
I: get up, eat out, go back

4 1 In the Philippines.
2 'Capgrossos' or large masks.
3 In Papua New Guinea.
4 In ice.
5 Tattoos.
6 Chris Rainier.
7 Reinier Gerritsen.
8 Emoticons.

Unit 9

9a (pages 68 and 69)

1 1 actor   3 screen   5 front row   7 back row
2 actress   4 audience   6 aisle   8 seat

2 1 romantic comedy   3 documentary   5 Science fiction
2 horror   4 animation   6 comedy

3 1 d 2 b 3 c 4 a

4 1 a 2 b 3 a 4 c 5 a 6 b 7 c 8 c

5 1 d 2 b 3 e 4 c 5 f 6 a

6 1 'm going to watch   4 's going to meet
2 're going to play   5 're going to have
3 's going to buy   6 're going to make

7b 1 /tə/   3 /tuː/   5 /tuː/   7 /tuː/
2 /tə/   4 /tə/   6 /tə/   8 /tə/

9b (pages 70 and 71)

1 1–3 actor, audience, musical
4–7 actor, audience, film, screen,
8–9 artist, painting
10–12 audience, music, musicians
13–14 novel, writer

2 ●●: artist, novel, painting, theatre, writer
●●●●: actresses, cinema, gallery, musical
●●●●: director, musician

3 1 e 2 c 3 d 4 h 5 a 6 g 7 b 8 f

4 1 I'm going to borrow this book to read about film-making.
2 I'm going to download this song to listen to it.
3 I'm going to book tickets to see a play.
4 I'm going to buy this film to watch it later.
5 I'm going to evening classes to learn French.
6 I'm going to drama school to study acting.

5 1 to make his next film
2 to live there for two years
3 to play their new songs
4 to watch a TV documentary
5 to show the artist's most famous paintings
6 to book tickets

9c (page 72)

1 1 butterflies   4 kangaroos   7 Rock
2 trees   5 mountains   8 sea
3 fruit   6 leaves

2 The book: 1   The play: 2   The film: 3

3 1 T   2 F   3 T   4 T   5 F   6 T   7 F   8 T

9d (page 73)

1 1 To a meeting.   4 He's working late.
2 They are free.   5 At seven.
3 Tomorrow night.   6 Outside Max's work.

2 1 Do you want   5 I'm sorry
2 would you like to   6 Let's meet
3 I'd love   7 That's
4 Are you   8 See you

3 1 ☺   2 ☹   3 ☺   4 ☹

4 Students' own answers.

5 1 're meeting   5 's talking
2 'm wearing   6 'm not taking
3 're going   7 's working
4 are you going   8 aren't playing

6 1 F   2 P   3 F   4 P   5 P   6 F   7 F   8 P

9e (page 74)

1 1 loud   3 well   5 beautiful
2 worried   4 very old   6 delicious

2 1 sounds   3 feels / felt   5 smells
2 tastes   4 look

3 Example answers:
1 The Alhambra is a new Middle Eastern café in the centre of town. Its sandwiches taste delicious. There's a nice mix of old and new furniture and the staff are very friendly.

2 *War Horse* is a play at the theatre about a horse called Joey in the war. The horse looks amazing on stage and also it's a really interesting story. My only negative comment is the music. It sounds very loud.

3 *Digital Hero II* is a new computer game. The graphics on the screen look modern but I felt a bit bored at times. I think that's because it isn't very different to *Digital Hero I*.

Wordbuilding / Learning skills (page 75)

1 1 student   4 painter   7 director
2 musician   5 explorer   8 manager
3 writer   6 artist

2 1 watching   4 at   7 interesting
2 listen   5 much   8 handsome
3 on   6 play

3 a 4   c 7   e 8   g 3
b 6   d 1   f 2   h 5

Unit 10

10a (pages 76 and 77)

1 1 technology   4 biology   7 neuroscience
2 astronomy   5 physics
3 zoology   6 chemistry

2 1 physics   3 technology   5 neuroscience
2 astronomy   4 zoology

3 1 a download   b CD
2 a library   b search engine
3 a map   b sat nav
4 a podcast   b radio
5 a text   b send

4 1 c   2 a   3 b

5 1 Have you ever used   7 has
2 've used   8 has left
3 have you ever made   9 have pressed
4 haven't   10 Have you switched
5 've never seen   11 haven't
6 've done

6 Students' own answers.

7 a 4   b 5   c 3   d 5   e 3   f 5   g 3   h 4

8 a I've printed the photos.
b She hasn't sent a letter.
c They've booked tickets.
d Have you ever learned Spanish?
e No, I haven't.
f Has he sent the email?
g Yes, he has.
h It hasn't worked today.

10b (pages 78 and 79)

1 1 b   2 d   3 a   4 c

2 1 Reason 1: as a historic city with lots of interesting places to visit. Reason 2: for difficult roads.
2 Because visitors become lost in the old streets.
3 In 1865.   4 Two years.   5 No.   6 No.
7 The hippocampus. It's the part that stores memories.
8 It's bigger than in the brains of other people.

3 1 a   2 c   3 a   4 c   5 b

4 1 buy   5 put   9 read
2 bought   6 sent   10 win
3 paid   7 forget
4 put   8 made

5 1 read   5 put / read
2 won   6 paid
3 buy / win   7 forgotten
4 send

6 1 Have, taken, took
2 Have, studied, studied
3 Have, taught, taught
4 Have, learned, learned
5 Have, written, wrote

10c (page 80)

1 1 iPod   4 knife   7 fire
2 vacuum cleaner   5 electricity   8 Internet
3 wheel   6 sticky tape

2 a 3   b 1   c 6   d 7   e 2   f 5   g 4   h 8

3 First question: c
Second question: a
Third question: b

4 1 Ten points.
2 In 1901.
3 They are short and long.
4 In the first century.
5 North and south.
6 Blue team.
7 Fourteen.
8 Twelve.

10d (page 81)

1 1 a 2 c 3 a 4 b 5 b
2 1 g 2 b 3 d 4 e 5 a 6 h 7 c 8 f
3 1 three 2 Insel 3 A 4 afternoon 5 seven

10e (page 82)

1 1 at   5 www dot   9 underscore
2 dot com   6 double slash   10 dot co dot uk
3 slash   7 colon
4 dash   8 dot org

2 1 h_schmitt@hotmail.co.de
2 www.concordia.com
3 www.instolisten.org/dailypod-2

3 1 Call Stacey back.
2 Send everyone a letter.
3 Take Mr D'Souza to the station.
4 Book a table for two.
5 Buy more paper.
6 Print these photographs, please.
7 Email the designs to g_rich@gmail.com.
8 Telephone the hotel.

4 1 Name of caller: Lisa Farrell
Message for: Dr Nakao
Message: Meet her in the hotel reception at 2pm.
2 Name of caller: Richard Nowitz
Message for: Dan Moore
Message: Email the designs before 12 tomorrow.
His email is r_nowitz@nowitz.com
Urgent ✓
3 Name of caller: Max Lloyd
Message for: Christine
Message: Friend of George. He's interested in renting the
room. Call him on 0990 768 2238 or email him:
m36.lloyd@hotmail.co.uk

Wordbuilding / Learning skills (page 83)

1 1 send   4 Search   7 call
2 Study   5 show   8 stop working
3 memorise   6 find

2 1 a forget b remember
2 a take b leave
3 a teach b learn
4 a receive b send

4 Example answers:
a biology, technology, zoology
b email, text, letter
c email, search engine, satellite navigation
d public telephone, postcard, sticky tape

Unit 11

11a (pages 84 and 85)

1 1 camping 2 sightseeing 3 backpacking 4 hiking
2 1 return ticket   5 tour guide
2 sightseeing   6 souvenirs
3 check in, carry on 7 book
4 rent
3 1 Yes   4 No   7 Yes
2 Yes   5 Don't know   8 No
3 Don't know   6 Yes
4 1 b 2 e 3 f 4 c 5 d 6 a
5 1 should   3 should   5 shouldn't
2 shouldn't   4 should   6 should
6 1 You should book a hotel room.
2 He shouldn't work late.
3 Should we buy a ticket here?
4 She should check in her bag.
5 You shouldn't rent a car.
6 What should we eat?
7 Hi!
I've booked my tickets and I'm arriving on the 21st! Before I
arrive at your house, I'm going to travel round the country.
<u>Should I rent a car or go by public transport</u>, do you think?
Also I'm going to spend some time in the capital. <u>What
should I see there? And should I book my hotel in advance?</u>
Can you give me any advice? Oh! And what's the weather
like? Is it cold? <u>Should I bring lots of clothes?</u>
See you soon!
Mike ☺
8 Example answer:
Dear Mike
I'm really happy that you are coming to my country. Here is
my advice:
When you travel round the country, you should go by public
transport because it's cheaper than a car and there are lots of
buses and trains.
In my capital city, you should see the parliament buildings
and the old castle.
For hotels, I think you should book the hotel online.
It's very easy.
At the moment the weather is very cold, so you should bring
a warm coat!
See you soon!

11b (pages 86 and 87)

1 1 e 2 b 3 a 4 f 5 d 6 c
2 1 A motorbike.
2 No.
3 Asia.
4 A coat and a jumper.
5 England.
6 People drive on the left (or 'the wrong side') and the signs
were difficult to understand.
7 Everyone.
8 The US embassy in your country.
9 A phrase book.
10 In smaller towns.
11 Before.
12 For 'big things' like a hotel or a meal in a restaurant.
3 Across: 1 climate 3 visa 5 zones 6 licence 7 cultural
Down: 1 currency 2 hand 4 illegal

4 1 a 2 c 3 b 4 c 5 c 6 a 7 b 8 a

5 1 flight DL3345 have to go to
2 You cannot carry, in your bag.
3 in business class do not have to wait in
4 with children can get on the plane

6 1 /hæftə/   3 /hæftə/   5 /hæftə/
2 /hæftə/   4 /haef tuː/   6 /haef tuː/

11c (page 88)

1 They talk about Greece and South Korea.

2 1 Do   4 Do   7 Do
2 Do   5 Don't   8 Do
3 Don't   6 Don't

3 1 thing   4 thing   7 thing
2 where   5 body   8 body
3 body   6 where

4 1 anybody   4 Everything   7 Somebody
2 something   5 everybody   8 anything
3 nowhere   6 somewhere

11d (page 89)

1 1 F
2 T
3 T
4 F
5 T
6 T
7 F (Marie thinks it's expensive.)
8 F

2 1 Can I make a suggestion?
2 You should go to Morocco.
3 You could travel on your own.
4 Why don't you go with a tour?
5 How about going on a package holiday?

3 a 5 b 4 c 2 d 3

5 1 bus /ʌ/   4 but /ʌ/   7 cruise /uː/
2 book /ʊ/   5 should /ʊ/   8 could /ʊ/
3 you /uː/   6 food /uː/

11e (page 90)

1a 1 Did   4 How   7 What
2 Was   5 Would   8 Why
3 How many   6 Were

1b a 3 b 1 c 4 d 2 e 5 f 8 g 6 h 7

Wordbuilding / Learning skills (page 91)

1 1 manager   5 backpacker   9 design
2 photograph / photo   6 visit   10 designer
3 photographer   7 visitor
4 study   8 cook

2 1 manage   5 visitor
2 photograph / photo   6 cooker
3 student   7 designer
4 backpack

3 photograph (3) / photo (2) photographer (4)
backpack (2) backpacker (3)
visit (2) visitor (3)
study (2) student (2)
cook (1) cooker (2)
design (2) designer (3)

4 1 b 2 a 3 f 4 c 5 d 6 e

Unit 12

12a (pages 92 and 93)

1 1 Arctic Circle   5 Antarctic Circle
2 North Pole   6 South Pole
3 Northern hemisphere 7 Southern hemisphere
4 Equator

2 1 c 2 b 3 e 4 a 5 f 6 d

3 1 14,000,000km²   4 30%
2 0°C   5 130m
3 2.5 l   6 419,455kg

4 1 e 2 a 3 d 4 b

5 1 a 2 b 3 c 4 b 5 c 6 a 7 c 8 a

6 1 cars will   4 the summer won't
2 houses will   5 the winter will
3 children won't   6 people won't

7 1 'll 2 'll 3 will 4 'll 5 will 6 will 7 'll 8 'll

12b (pages 94 and 95)

1 1 island   4 mountain   7 River
2 Ocean   5 Lake   8 Desert
3 forest   6 Sea

2 1 the   5 Ø   9 the   13 the
2 the   6 the   10 Ø   14 the
3 Ø   7 Ø   11 the   15 the
4 Ø   8 Ø   12 Ø

3 2 Which ocean is the Madagascar in?
4 Where is the Lake Vostok?
6 Where is the Mount Ararat?

5 1 b 2 d 3 a 4 c 5 e

6 1 old 2 high 3 tall 4 well 5 long 6 fast 7 far

7 1 43   5 ten minutes
2 39km   6 1,342km/h
3 100m   7 31km
4 really well

12c (page 96)

1 1 star   5 surface
2 planets   6 rock
3 orbit   7 travel
4 Astronomers

2 1 c 2 a 3 d 4 b

3 1 Astronomers   4 humans   7 star
2 orbits   5 discovery   8 planets
3 Earth   6 exoplanets   9 universe

12d (page 97)

1 1 Jamaica.
2 The first Friday.
3 50,000
4 Everyone from schoolchildren to business people.
5 In local parks and communities.
6 In the gardens of a home for old people.
7 Have the same day.

2 1 c 2 g 3 b 4 a 5 f 6 d 7 e

3 1 Today, I'd like to talk about an important day.
2 First of all, my country's national day is on 4th July.
3 Since then, people have always celebrated this day.
4 Nowadays, everyone has a day off.
5 Next, families have a big meal together.
6 In conclusion, I really think it's important.

12e (page 98)

1a Possible answers:

1 Everyone ~~is~~ invited ~~to our~~ New Year's Party!
2 ~~The~~ Annual Party ~~is~~ at ~~the~~ Town Hall on 1st May.
3 ~~There is a~~ huge sale at ~~the~~ Big Bed Shop ~~all~~ this week.
4 ~~You can~~ eat delicious sandwiches at Jill's Café.
5 Visit ~~the website~~ www.greenfest.org for details.
6 The entrance to ~~the~~ disco ~~is~~ free.
7 ~~Listen to~~ live music and ~~look at~~ local art at ~~the~~ Mayberry Arts Festival.
8 ~~You are~~ welcome to ~~our~~ Midsummer Party at nine.

b Possible answer:

You are invited to <u>plant a tree on 7th October</u> for <u>National Tree Planting Day</u>. We will give you <u>free seeds to plant in the local park</u>. There will be <u>lots of people</u> there and <u>lots of entertainment</u>, so <u>bring the whole family</u>. We'll have <u>hot and cold food</u>, and <u>local shops</u> will sell <u>environmentally friendly products.</u> We'll also have <u>presentations</u> about <u>how to help the environment</u> and <u>information about gardening</u>. The event is in <u>Tenant Park</u>, and it starts at <u>two o'clock</u> and it <u>finishes</u> at <u>five o'clock</u>. The <u>entrance is five euros for adults</u> and <u>free for children under 16</u>. You can <u>telephone</u> us on <u>088 678 4955 for more information</u>.

Wordbuilding / Learning skills (page 99)

1 1 depth 2 height 3 weight 4 length 5 width

2 1 a long b length
2 a height b high
3 a weight b weigh
4 a deep b depth
5 a wide b width

3 Adjectives: long, high, deep, wide
Verb: weigh* (note the adjective for weigh/weight is 'heavy')

6 1 914 trillion litres – the Earth's rainfall every day
2 47 metres – the depth of the Black Hole of Andros
3 2009 – the year James Cameron made the film *Avatar*
4 18 trillion – distance in kilometres between the Earth and Gliese 581g
5 20 million – the number of people at the first Earth Day in 1970

IELTS practice test

Listening

1 C   I saw a notice about a photography club
2 B   I'm going back to pick up a book I ordered.
3 Tuesday   On Tuesday evening there's a storytelling workshop
4 £1.50   and that's only £1.50
5 Internet   on Thursday at two p.m there's an Internet club
6 Thursday   on Thursday evening there's a film club
7 £8.50   look at the price – £8.50 a week
8 7.45   That's at seven forty-five too
9 Website   on Saturday mornings there's a course in website design
10 £2.75   It's cheaper too – only £2.75
11 A   your interview is actually on Monday
12 A   When you arrive at the college, go to the main reception
13 B   Howard Green … will be interviewing you
14 B / F   we do need to check your identity.
15 F / B   a photograph … if you could bring one with you, that would be useful
16 photocopying   There is some photocopying to do
17 (tele)phone calls   and there will be telephone calls to deal with
18 10 / ten   ten hours a week
19 £8.00   The basic rate of pay is £8.00 per hour.
20 22 days   Twenty-two days a year
21 C   most of the world's rabbits … live in North America
22 B   but ten to twelve years is more normal
23 one hour   it's going to take one hour every day
24 clean   It is necessary to clean the place where they live
25 health   you need to check their basic health every single day
26 £50   having microchips fitted will cost another £50
27 £250   A good rabbit house costs £250 to buy
28 Equipment   Then you need to buy equipment to go inside the house
29 £12   one for food costs £12
30 month   £10 per month
31 C   what is important is to spend a fixed period of time each day
32 B   a relaxed type of activity
33 A   you don't have to give up the football training
34 B   The local park is fine and jogging on grass is much better for your feet.
35 eight weeks   the programme lasts for eight weeks
36 cyclists   the type that you see cyclists wearing
37 socks   You should buy … special socks.
38 cotton   don't wear clothes made out of cotton as they will make you feel too hot
39 drink   this probably means that you need something to drink …
40 cold   If … you've caught a cold, then you should stop training until you feel better.

Reading

1 C   six days a week
2 C   £5.50 per hour
3 E   weekly bus ticket to the city centre provided
4 B   free meals when on duty
5 B   uniform provided
6 A   supermarket cashier
7 C   ability to speak French or Spanish an advantage
8 F   temporary contract (six weeks)
9 D   possibility of extra hours next month
10 C   you have to work in a team
11 TRUE   carried out a survey … as part of their course
12 TRUE   city residents … a sample of local inhabitants
13 FALSE   asked them all the same questions
14 NOT GIVEN
15 FALSE   About 12% of the people they asked
16 TRUE   In second place in the list was swimming … and in third place came keep-fit exercises
17 FALSE   a few very keen walkers who go for long walks in the countryside
18 TRUE   walking holidays are the most popular of all
19 FALSE   There were an equal number of men and women going on walking holidays
20 FALSE   Boating holidays … are the ones where you find the largest number of single people
21 viii   Cycling holidays are much greener than holidays by car, train or plane
22 ix   a company which makes all the arrangements in advance
23 v   It's up to you what distance you want to cover every day
24 i   It isn't necessary to be very strong to ride a bike, but you should be in good health.
25 ii   a range of options when it comes to how long to stay away and how to make sure you have a bed for the night
26 iv   Holiday companies sometimes arrange for your suitcases to be sent on … This means that you only need to carry a few things
27 iii   How much your holiday costs will depend on which type you choose.
28 Scotland   Cycling in Scotland, for instance, where there are lots of hills, will give you a good physical work-out. But if that sounds too much like hard work
29 centre-based   where you return to the same hotel every evening and can have a good meal and a shower
30 March   March is the typical month for the birds to arrive.
31 July   back again … normally in July
32 C   The young cuckoos are born in England.
33 C   all spent the winter in the Congo region of central Africa
34 A   Lyster flew across France, Spain and Morocco before crossing the Sahara desert
35 B   Lyster flew back to England via Algeria … Chris also crossed the Algerian desert
36 C   They put a tiny satellite tag on each bird's back to see where they went when they left England.
37 B   The three other birds did not return to England and the scientists think they died on their return journey.
38 C   the five tagged birds all travelled about 10,000 miles that summer
39 C   Algeria were countries that the other three birds flew over … Chris/Lyster flew back … via Algeria
40 A   Lyster flew across Spain … flew back via Algeria … but this time didn't fly over Spain

How to mark the Writing Test

Task 1

There are four criteria for marking the Part One tasks, which are equally weighted.

Task achievement

This is an assessment of how well the student has fulfilled the task.

A successful task will:
- include at least the minimum number of words
- have a text structure appropriate to a letter
- be relevant to the context established in the input material
- achieve the writer's intended purpose
- cover the functions indicated in the bullet points

Coherence and cohesion

This is an assessment of how clear and fluent the writing is.

A successful task will:
- be appropriately organised
- successfully link information and ideas
- contain logical sequencing
- make effective use of cohesive devices

Lexical resource

This is an assessment of the use of vocabulary.

A successful task will:
- include a range of relevant vocabulary
- use vocabulary accurately
- use vocabulary in an appropriate way

Grammatical resource

This is an assessment of the use of grammar.

A successful task will:
- use an appropriate range of grammatical forms at sentence level
- use grammatical forms accurately

Task 2

There are four criteria for marking the Part Two tasks, which are equally weighted.

Task response

This is an assessment of how well the student has responded to the task.

A successful task will:
- make clear the writer's position on the issues raised in a question or statement
- develop arguments to support that position
- support the arguments with evidence and examples
- include at least the minimum number of words

Coherence and cohesion

This is an assessment of how clear and fluent the writing is.

A successful task will:
- be appropriately organised
- successfully link information and ideas
- contain logical sequencing
- make effective use of cohesive devices

Lexical resource

This is an assessment of the use of vocabulary.

A successful task will:
- include a range of relevant vocabulary
- use vocabulary accurately
- use vocabulary in an appropriate way

Grammatical resource

This is an assessment of the use of grammar.

A successful task will:
- use an appropriate range of grammatical forms at sentence level
- use grammatical forms accurately

How to mark the Speaking Test

The speaking test is an assessment of how effectively students can communicate in English.

There are four criteria for marking the Speaking Test, whichare equally weighted.

Fluency and coherence

This is the ability to:
- talk at a consistently normal speed
- link ideas and language together in logical sequences
- use the language features which create coherent, connected speech

Lexical resource

This is the ability to:
- use a range of relevant vocabulary
- use words appropriately to convey meaning
- use paraphrase strategies when required

Grammatical range and accuracy

This is the ability to:
- use a range of grammatical forms appropriately
- use grammatical forms accurately

Pronunciation

This is the ability to:
- use a range of phonological features to convey meaning
- produce intelligible individual sounds
- use stress, rhythm and intonation effectively

IELTS practice test 🎧 [2.42]

PRESENTER: IELTS practice test. In this test, you'll hear a number of different recordings and you'll have to answer questions on what you hear. There will be time for you to read the instructions and questions, and you will have a chance to check your work. The recording will be played once only. The test is in four sections.

Now turn to Section 1 on page 100 of your book. You will hear a student called Ian telling his friend about the public library. First you have time to look at questions 1 and 2. You will see that there is also an example which has been done for you.

Now we shall begin. You should answer the questions as you listen because you will not hear the recording a second time. Listen carefully and answer questions 1 and 2.

WOMAN: Hi Ian. I was looking for you. Where have you been?

IAN: I went to the public library in the town centre. There's a book I need for my science project. They haven't got it at the college library, so I went to see if they had it in the public library instead. It's much bigger than the college library and I soon found what I was looking for. But they've got a really good sports section and so I decided to have a look round. I found a really good book on the history of cricket.

WOMAN: Gosh. I never thought of going in there. What else have they got?

IAN: Well, not just books actually. There's online access, of course, but also newspapers and magazines you can read, and a noticeboard with lots of information about local events. Actually, I saw a notice about a photography club that meets there every week – sounds interesting. There's a room there where they have lectures and meetings and stuff.

WOMAN: Right. I didn't know that. I'll have to go in one day.

IAN: Come with me tomorrow if you like. I'm going back to pick up a book I ordered. If they haven't got the one you want, they can get it from another library in 48 hours. So, I ordered one I need to read for my course.

WOMAN: Wow. That's brilliant! So, are you going to join the photography club?

IAN: I haven't decided yet. I want to ask how much it costs. So, are you going to come tomorrow?

WOMAN: Yeah, why not!

PRESENTER: Before you listen to the rest of the conversation, you have some time to read questions 3 to 10. Now listen carefully and answer questions 3 to 10.

IAN: Oh look, here's a leaflet I picked up about events at the library. You see the photography club is on Mondays, at seven thirty in the evening.

WOMAN: Oh, right. And look, it tells you how much you have to pay – £2.50 a week.

IAN: That's not much, is it?

WOMAN: No, in fact all the events are quite cheap. Look. On Tuesday evening there's a storytelling workshop at seven o'clock, and that's only £1.50.

IAN: Oh, I wouldn't be interested in that.

WOMAN: No, but I am. My friend Jane's really into storytelling. I must tell her. And look, on Thursday at two p.m. there's an Internet club, and that's only £1.50.

IAN: But everyone knows how to use the Internet. Who would go to that?

WOMAN: Well, it's in the afternoon, so it's probably for old people.

IAN: Yeah, you're right. Look, on Thursday evening there's a film club. It starts at quarter to eight. That sounds more like our sort of thing.

WOMAN: But look at the price – £8.50 a week. The college film club's only £5.00 and I expect they have the same films.

IAN: Yeah, you're right.

WOMAN: But look, on Friday, they have a poetry workshop. That's at seven forty-five too, and only £3.00. I think I'd like to go to that.

IAN: OK. And on Saturday mornings there's a course in website design. That sounds more interesting than the Internet one, and it only costs £4.75 a week.

WOMAN: But look, it starts at ten fifteen in the morning. You never get up before lunchtime on Saturdays! Look, there's map reading in the afternoon. That would be better for you. It's cheaper too – only £2.75 – and you'll be awake by then because it doesn't start till a quarter to three.

IAN: Very funny. I can get up early if I need to.

WOMAN: Really?

PRESENTER: Now turn to Section 2 on page 101 of your book. You will hear a woman called Hilary talking on the phone about a job interview she is going to have. First you have some time to look at questions 11 to 15. Now listen carefully and answer questions 11 to 15.

MAN: Hello. Southdown College, personnel department. Jon speaking.

HILARY: Oh, hello. My name's Hilary Brown. I've applied for a job in the accommodation office at the college.

MAN: Ah yes, and we've invited you for interview, haven't we? On Tuesday, I think.

HILARY: That's right. Only in your voicemail message you said it would be on Monday.

MAN: Ah, yes. Here it is. Yes, some people are coming on Tuesday and Wednesday, but your interview is actually on Monday at ten o'clock in the morning.

HILARY: Oh good. I was actually ringing to ask where I should come to. How do I find the personnel department? Is it in the main building?

MAN: Well, the personnel department is in another building actually, but we're not holding the interviews here. When you arrive at the college, go to the main reception and ask for room 341. They will give you directions.